Surrounded by Bad Bosses

Also by Thomas Erikson

Surrounded by Idiots
Surrounded by Psychopaths

....

Surrounded by Bad Bosses (and Lazy Employees)

How to Stop Struggling, Start Succeeding, and Deal with Idiots at Work

Thomas Erikson

ST. MARTIN'S
ESSENTIALS
NEW YORK

First published in the United States by St. Martin's Essentials,
an imprint of St. Martin's Publishing Group

SURROUNDED BY BAD BOSSES (AND LAZY EMPLOYEES). Copyright © 2021 by Thomas Erikson. Translation © 2021 Rod Bradbury. All rights reserved. Printed in the United States of America. For information, address St. Martin's Publishing Group, 120 Broadway, New York, NY 10271.

www.stmartins.com

Library of Congress Cataloging-in-Publication Data is available upon request.

ISBN 978-1-250-76390-7 (trade paperback)
ISBN 978-1-250-76391-4 (ebook)

Our books may be purchased in bulk for promotional, educational, or business use. Please contact your local bookseller or the Macmillan Corporate and Premium Sales Department at 1-800-221-7945, extension 5442, or by email at MacmillanSpecialMarkets@macmillan.com.

Originally published in Sweden by Forum.

First U.S. Edition: 2021

10 9 8 7 6 5 4 3 2 1

Contents

Author's Note — xi
Introduction — 1

PART 1—SURROUNDED BY BAD BOSSES

1. Really Bad Leadership—and Its Appalling Consequences — 11
2. Why You Should Choose Your Boss, Instead of Your Employer — 21
3. Leadership Is a Process of Communication — 29
4. How to Understand and Predict Your Boss's Behavior — 44
5. The Most Common Color Combinations and How to Recognize Them — 53
6. Why You Sometimes Feel Stressed at Work — 63
7. Why You Definitely Want a Red Boss — 79

8. Why You Should Hope for a Yellow Boss 91
9. Why a Green Boss Is the Best Option 100
10. Why a Blue Boss Is the Ultimate Solution 109
11. Why We Do What We Do: What the Colors Don't Show 119
12. The Author's Profile and What You Can Learn from It 131
13. Distinguishing Between Colors and Driving Forces 140
14. The Difference Between Your Personality and Your Behavior 150
15. How to Adapt Effectively to Your Boss's Color 155
16. The Missing Piece of the Puzzle: When Colors and Driving Forces Aren't Enough 165
17. Surrounded by Superfluous Bosses 180

PART 2—SURROUNDED BY LAZY EMPLOYEES

18. Why It's So Hard for Your Staff to Get the Job Done 189
19. How to Read Your Staff's Colors 203
20. Whip or Carrot—How to Motivate Your Staff 212
21. Leader—or Specialist? Your Job as a Boss 225
22. If You're an Efficient Red Boss 238
23. If You're an Inspiring Yellow Boss 253
24. If You're a Caring Green Boss 267

25. If You're an Analytic and Objective Blue Boss	279
26. The Best Way to Put a Team Together	291
27. Helping Your Team Become Active Participants	299
28. When Everyone Agrees but Still Doesn't Do Anything . . .	316
29. Where the Real Slackers Come From	326
30. Feedback . . . the Hardest Part	342
31. Why "Why" Is the Most Important Question	358
Final Words: People Quit to Leave Their Boss, Not Their Job	368
Resources	*377*
Index	*379*
About the Author	*387*

Author's Note

This book is based on thirty years of experience—first as a manager, then training other managers in leadership, and finally becoming a manager again. Much of what you will read is my interpretation of the various theories and models that have been developed to deal with the complicated and sometimes difficult-to-understand process called leadership.

You probably won't agree with everything you read, that would be impossible, but the more open your mind, the easier it will be for you to absorb what I'm hoping to convey. There are many other theories and methods that I don't discuss for building functional dialog in the workplace. And doubtless more ideas will be developed in the coming years; few subjects are as discussed as leadership. In this book, I've focused on the methods that I've successfully used myself. To make this book as helpful as possible, I've tried to be as concrete as I could. Feel free to read the book with a notebook next to you and a pen in hand. Or why not make your notes directly in the book?

Everything you will read is based on the techniques and tools I've found are crucial to making interactions between employees and their managers as smooth and efficient as possible. In my experience, it's always better to have some kind of leadership plan instead of no plan at all. You're about to take part in mine.

Finally, think of this book as an introduction to the subject of leadership. In three hundred pages, I don't have time to do more than scratch the surface. But if you want to know more, I recommend going to the resources section at the back of the book. That's exactly what I did when I first immersed myself in what has become the great interest of my life.

Enjoy reading.

—Thomas Erikson

Introduction

Why You Should Read This Book

Let's get straight to the point: the world is full of bad bosses. Team leaders, group leaders, departmental managers, unit managers, deputy managing directors, managing directors, and the bosses of managing directors. Sometimes the boss is a chairman of the board in a *Fortune* 500 company, and sometimes the same chairman is at the head of a local sports team. At every level, in all types of organizations, there are bosses who have ended up in the wrong place and cause problems for themselves, who cause problems for their staff, who are incompetent, and who are naïve. There are bosses who are far too nice, and there are ones that are just plain mean. Some can't manage to learn the names of their staff, and some just sneak away from their own responsibility. Some of them are so incompetent that the company would have been better off without them.

These are the superfluous bosses. The ones that aren't really needed and that the rest of us would manage better without. Who don't contribute anything at all, except for headaches and stress.

It used to be that the boss's responsibilities were simple: to lead and say who should do what. If you managed that, then you were doing your job. A good friend of mine often quotes his own father when it comes to leadership: *Never become the boss, because you'll end up doing everything yourself.*

Why is it so hard to define a boss's role? Is it really that difficult? Perhaps it's the simplest thing in the world? If you just sit down and give it a shot.

And the bosses who function brilliantly in their roles—what do they understand that others don't? Is there actually a secret?

This book is divided into two parts. The first, Surrounded by Bad Bosses, describes how hard it is to do your job when you have a bad boss. Here we will look at examples of poor leadership and what you, as an employee, can actually do about it.

This section isn't designed for the reader who is already a competent boss and actually knows what they're doing. But if you are a boss and you think there's still a lot you can learn about how to best manage your employees, you might find this section valuable. The second part of the book is Surrounded by Lazy Employees. Because there are some workers who aren't exactly in the running for employee of the month. Everybody has different strengths and weaknesses. Read on to find out how you can you help your staff discover their potential and find their genuine driving forces.

But for those of you who really wonder why on earth your boss behaves like that—just keep on reading. You'll learn the reasons why some bosses function well—and others don't function at all.

Surrounded By Idiots?

A few years ago, I wrote a book called *Surrounded by Idiots*. It's about differences in communication styles, and why certain people can be so difficult to understand. I introduced William Moulton Marston's DISC system which, over time and with further development by others, evolved into a simple model based on four colors: Red, Yellow, Green, and Blue. The point was to show how you can better understand people who don't function or communicate like you do. Of course, the model doesn't answer all the questions when it comes to how we function day to day, but it does give us a good starting point for discussions and ways to institute change. A person is rarely just one color, but most often has elements of two or even three.

Here are a few things to know about the DISC model:

- The DISC model cannot explain everything about an individual's behavior.
- There are other models that seek to explain behavior, but I use this one as a starting point because it is pedagogically simple to grasp.
- There are more pieces of the puzzle than "the colors" to map various behavior patterns.
- The DISC model builds upon thorough psychological studies, is used throughout the world, and has been translated into fifty different languages.
- Historically, there have been similar models in different cultures, such as the system of the four humors created by Hippocrates, who lived in ancient times, around 2,500 years ago.

- Approximately 80 percent of all people have a combination of two colors that dominate their behavior. Around 5 percent have only one color that dominates behavior. The rest are dominated by three colors.
- Entirely Green behavior, or Green in combination with another color, is the most common. The least common is entirely Red behavior, or Red in combination with one other color.
- There can be differences in behavior between the sexes, but I do not deal with the gender perspective in this book.
- The DISC model cannot be used to analyze ADHD, Austism spectrum disorder, borderline personality disorder, or other diagnoses.
- There are always exceptions to what I outline in this book. People are complex—even Red people can be humble and Yellow people can listen attentively. There are Green people who can handle conflict because they have learned how to do it, and many Blues understand when it's time to stop double checking that the documents are correct.
- Everything that I talk about is connected to personal insight and awareness. Problems arise when personal insight is limited.
- My own colors are Red and Blue with a bit of Yellow. No Green to mention. Sorry.

In *Surrounded by Idiots*, I didn't focus on the different roles we have in the workplace. And I've received many questions about whether it's possible to take the whole thing one step further. And of course, it is.

If we take an experienced individual who is very results-oriented and make them solve a problem alongside a person who values security and calmness above all else, problems are going to arise if they don't both learn to meet each other somewhere in between. But if we layer in the complication that the first person is the boss of the second, then a new problem appears, right? Or what if the second person happens to be the boss of the first? That would really make the situation fascinating. When we bring leadership into the equation, the idiot epithet is not far away.

I do realize that you would never call your boss an idiot—at least not to their face—but you are aware of the fact that there are workplaces with problems directly related to incompetent bosses. We need to understand our different personal qualities while also finding a way to take into account the fact that, in work scenarios, one of us has power over the other.

If you have a friend who is a bastard, you can always just walk away. If your boss makes unreasonable demands on you, it immediately becomes more complicated, and the value of having a working dialogue to help those situations is so much greater. That's what I'll be giving you in this book.

But if You Put Your "Boss Hat" on, It Must Mean Something, Right?

And yet . . . my personal belief is that bosses are held to a higher level of responsibility. They should deal with the issue and find solutions. But naturally, the boss can be stressed for one reason or another. The boss might be in a sticky situation with *their* own boss, but they are still responsible for their staff. You can't hide behind your own stress or blame the fact that there wasn't enough time. As the boss, you have a responsibility to your staff, to watch out for them and at least *try* to give them what they need—preferably before they ask for it themselves.

Nor do I think that a boss should be able to blame ignorance of the parameters of their job or of what it means to be boss. Anybody can work out that it entails more than just sitting at your desk.

During my twenty years as a consultant focusing on leadership issues, I have, of course, met many bosses who are skilled in the art of leadership. Some have a natural inclination for it, others have learned it the hard way. Their staff admire and love them and would put up with quite a lot for their sake. These are the stars that others want to follow.

But I have also met an endless number of bosses who have been practically useless. Some of them haven't grasped what the job requires. Some of them would like to learn, while others aren't even interested in that. Which—in my opinion—makes them even less suitable. Some of them are just superfluous. They're in the way. The organization doesn't really need them.

The reasons that many bosses are ineffective, do, of course, vary, but there are nevertheless certain patterns. And it's a good idea to learn to recognize these patterns.

To Have Responsibility but No Authority

I've been there myself as an employee—situations where I've had lots of responsibility but no authority. The expectations from management have been more or less impossible to fulfill. I've received criticism and grumbling when something has gone wrong, but never praise when something has gone particularly well. I'm not one of those people who demand compliments and movie tickets just because I've done my job. But if I've done something above and beyond, then it's nice if somebody (read: the boss) notices it. Often all it takes is an appreciative thumbs-up in passing.

Sometimes, the demands have been absurd. More or less unsolvable tasks have been placed on my shoulders. But the expectation that I fix the situation remains. Sometimes I've succeeded, and other times I've ended up in the ditch.

You know what it's like. You can't succeed in everything. Sometimes it ends up one hell of a mess.

It is frustrating to only be at the receiving end of a problem, without being able to make decisions and influence how the job should be done in the first place. And it's even more frustrating when nobody listens to your proposals and ideas. Sometimes my boss has listened politely, nodded, and said *I hear what you're saying*. This is often followed by a *but* . . . You know what that means, right? What they actually mean is: *I hear that you are saying words but I couldn't care less about your idea*. Your boss has already decided. So why did they even ask you?

Or your boss does actually listen, and says: *do what you want, but it'll be your responsibility if it all goes wrong*.

Well, thanks a lot for that vote of confidence.

I've never been able to keep quiet. As a young man I thought authority figures were a pain. This sometimes led me down troublesome paths. Now and then, even in later life, I've questioned certain structures and routines. Systems are often totally illogical; one might hear *that's simply how it is*. Or *that's how we do things here*. My favorite is *we've always done it like that*, as if that was a genuine argument.

I know what it means not to be able to influence your situation as an ordinary employee.

Obviously, there are exceptions. I've also had bosses who have been good listeners and been open to the thoughts and ideas of members of their staff. Some of them have even had the decency to admit whose idea it was in the first place.

I, probably just like you, have often wondered how my boss thinks and functions. Because I really don't know what they're doing. So why not take a look at some of the reasons behind their behavior?

Let's dive into the strange world of being a boss.

Ready to jump into the deep end? OK, let's go.

PART I

Surrounded by Bad Bosses

{ 1 }

Really Bad Leadership—and Its Appalling Consequences

Good leadership is dependent upon the boss and the staff understanding the symbiosis they are working in and both parties realizing that they are dependent upon each other to get the system to work.

Being a boss can look irritatingly simple. All you have to do is run around to a lot of meetings and look very important. Talk a lot on the phone and play golf on Friday afternoons. Yeah, anyone could manage to do that sort of pretend-job. If things go well, the boss takes all the credit; if it all goes wrong, then he or she always has somebody else to blame.

Okay, that's a bit of an exaggeration. The job involves a bit more than that. But as most people who have had a bad boss know: it can be done wrong.

Every one of us, at some time or another, has had an incompetent boss and wondered why he or she doesn't do their job better. Some bosses don't actually exercise any leadership at all, which makes them unnecessary. And that raises the question: a boss who doesn't actually lead—what's the point?

There are quite a lot of bosses who shouldn't even have been given keys to the office.

I am pretty sure you will recognize a couple of these types:

- The boss who never says anything with the slightest trace of a positive attitude
- The boss who does nothing but complain and grumble about everything you do
- The boss who blames you for mistakes he has made himself
- The boss who takes the credit for what you have done
- The boss who doesn't have a clue what you do every day
- The boss who never gets back to you as promised
- The boss who has sudden outbursts of anger for no reason
- The boss who expects you to be able to read his thoughts
- The boss who makes a spectacle of everyone's mistakes for clients
- The boss whose instructions are so confused that it's a hopeless task to understand what he or she wants
- The boss who is simply a scatterbrain and has so little structure that they can never find their papers
- The boss who is a control freak and interferes in absolutely everything you do
- The boss who checks everything in detail down to three decimal places
- The boss who never hands over any responsibility to anyone

- The boss who insists on making all the decisions herself
- The boss who always finds himself somewhere else
- The boss who never gives any direct orders but hopes you will get the message anyway
- The boss who doesn't care if some of the staff don't do a proper job
- The boss who is so afraid of conflict that just about anything goes in the workplace
- The boss who demands obedience simply because she is the boss
- The boss who makes such an effort to make it look like he is listening, that he doesn't hear a word you say

Bosses have often learned their leadership style from their own managers. They've been influenced by what others do, and often times they are trying to do their best. One can congratulate some of them for having managed to stay afloat despite the lack of a proper plan or any kind of management training.

Of course, most people don't take on a managerial position with the intention of doing a bad job. The majority of bosses probably try to do a decent job. But sometimes things go crazy in a way that's quite unfathomable.

My leadership techniques were influenced by really bad bosses. I would get angry simply being in the same room as some of them. This frustration led me to study their attitudes and then do exactly the opposite. A fairly well thought-through strategy, to my mind.

For example, I had a boss who always sat in his office with the door closed. That bothered me, and it bothered my colleagues. I promised myself that I would always be accessible if I got a managerial position and an office of my own. And when I did get that office, I made sure the door was always wide open.

Another boss that I had repeatedly made mistakes in his work. Anybody can make a mistake, but how do you behave when it happens? You accept that you've done something wrong and you move on. You don't say it's not your fault, and above all, you don't criticize your staff or blame them when you've made a mess of things. I saw this several times and promised myself I would never do the same. If I treated one of my staff badly, then I would simply have to apologize. Nowadays that's what I do, and sometimes I have to gnash my teeth a while before I manage it. But I think it's part of being a good role model—to take responsibility for your own mistakes no matter what.

But being a boss can be confusing. Believe me, I know. And when the symbiosis between the boss and their team is broken, it can create a deeply toxic atmosphere for a very long time.

The Salesman Who Was Too Good for His Own Good

Am I sitting here now, blowing my own horn? Do I think I have all the answers? Am I the best boss in the world?

Certainly not.

It's easy to be arrogant in such contexts. You know how the story usually goes, right? The author of the management book tells a complicated story about some disastrous episode or other, which ends with him or her saving the situation through their incredible ability and brilliant talent. Of course, it's never as simple as that.

My first management position, the first time I was a boss, was when I was twenty-four years old. I was a good salesman, so I knew how to "sell" a brilliant image of myself. When you're young, you're filled with self-confidence, and I was no exception. I had rehearsed my strengths and competences for days before the interview. *Choose me*, I said. And they did. They liked the fact that I seemed to be clever and enthusiastic, and they appreciated my "winning style." *That guy can do great things for us!*

They ought to have known better.

I stormed in to my new workplace full of energy, full of self-confidence, feeling like I could save the world. And I had colossal goals. Nobody could deny that I *meant well* at the time. I think that my team of thirteen people felt that too. They certainly must have noticed that here was somebody with energy. So far, so good.

And what did I do with all this energy?

Yes, well . . .

You know, this is twenty-five years ago, but it's still difficult to talk about it. Some time ago, I almost bumped into a woman from my old team. I saw her when I was about to cross the street, and I instinctively ducked behind a pillar. I am not proud to admit it, but I was still ashamed of what a poor support I was for her at that time.

I couldn't look her in the eye, even though half a lifetime had passed since then.

Motivation and Self-Confidence Aren't Everything

I had a full tank of gas, but I didn't know how to arrange my days. No structure, no planning; I had no idea what "follow-up" meant, and I had lost my common sense somewhere en route—it was all one big mess. I simply ran around most of the time and grabbed and pulled at anything that impeded my "progress." I was familiar with the business after a few years in the branch, so I could deal with some clients. Perfect—that's what I would do! So I dealt with some clients. Which was okay, except for the fact that it wasn't the reason why I was there.

At this new office, there were also lots of mysterious rules that I wasn't aware of. The unwritten laws could have filled a book.

I remember one of the questions that my team came to me with the first week: *What should we do with the lunch schedule?* I had no idea what they were on about. *Eat when you're hungry!* But that didn't work, because we couldn't just drop everything during lunch. (This was at a branch office of a big bank in the days when the public still used their valuable time to visit such places.) Now, in retrospect, I imagine that the team could have figured this out without my involvement. But my reaction was: *fix it*.

That was my stock response to questions that I didn't have any answer to.

Fix it.

A customer is standing by the counter, shouting. *Fix it*.

The cash in the till doesn't tally. *Fix it*.

Ulla has a day off and Marja is ill—we haven't got anybody who can cover us over lunch. *Fix it.*

One member of my team was so stressed at work that she had a stomachache virtually every day.

On one occasion, she showed me her calendar and it was a catastrophe. Her schedule was crazy. She had customers lining up to see her from eight in the morning to five in the afternoon. She'd scheduled meetings during her lunch break and didn't even have time to go to the bathroom. It couldn't go on like that. But I remember that I simply stared at the woman's disastrous calendar and said something like "Oh wow!"

Later, I understood that she was asking for help, but it pains me to remember my initial reaction: *fix it*. I didn't have answers. I had no idea what was needed. I didn't even know how the situation had come about.

We'll simply have to work harder.

That's not the advice that somebody who can hardly breathe wants to hear.

But that was often my response. And this was in the early 1990s. Such admonishments were popular in those days: *Don't present problems—present solutions.* And I went all in for that. Sure, there's something in it. Sometimes you shouldn't just look for problems, but it also depends on how you deliver that cocky advice.

My timing was rarely successful.

Sure. Sometimes members of my team came up with solutions and wanted to know what I thought. And I didn't have an opinion. I also didn't know what was best.

I often just said in a mumble: "Fix it."

And I remember how my team members stared at me.

My focus was somewhere else. I had just gotten married. We were expecting our first child. To be honest, my thoughts were always elsewhere. Sure, I realized that I had problems, but I was young and I thought I was really smart. I gradually grew out of that.

In the end, I was sent to take a management course. There, I got to learn all sorts of things about what it was like to be a boss. I was impressed by the course leader, but I don't really know what I learned from it all. Now I can hardly remember what the course consisted of, to be completely honest.

I very rarely went to my own boss to ask for help. That would have been a dreadful defeat, so I kept silent the whole time. Besides, she wasn't there very often, which was a brilliant excuse for me. I had no one to turn to!

In the end, everything collapsed like a house of cards. My team might not have started a mutiny, but they did complain about me. They thought that I didn't understand their situation. I think that they almost liked me as a person, but they weren't satisfied with how I ran the office.

I don't blame them. Because they were right.

The Final Fiasco

Nothing got better as time passed. On the contrary, it was like going deeper into a pitch-black tunnel. I couldn't sleep at night because for the first time in my professional life it actually looked as if I was going to fail in my work. I was on my way towards my first true failure and I wasn't ready at all. Nobody had prepared me for the fact that everything could collapse. After almost a year in my position, I realized that the game was over.

In the end, I went to the boss of my boss and asked to be removed from the job. I remember that he stared at me. I don't suppose he'd ever heard a request like that before. When I left that office, I didn't get a going-away present from the staff. They hadn't even managed/wanted/been able to motivate themselves to collect for it. My personal insight was sufficiently sharp for me to get the message. I'm glad that I didn't have to hear the conversation they must have had on the subject.

I remember that I gave the staff a potted plant and said that they had taught me a lot more than I had taught them. Nobody disagreed with that. There was some mumbling, and one of the members of my former team muttered that things were at least getting a bit better at the end.

It was horrible.

What I Learned from It All

It is damn hard to be a boss. It isn't simply a matter of energy. People didn't become world champion employees just because I was in the room. Yes, I know how it sounds, but I must remind you that I was twenty-four years old and ready to save the world.

But I also learned that even bosses need to ask for help. That it's not a sign of weakness if you don't know what you should do.

But above all, what I started to understand—and what I have developed since then—was that leadership is an art. It's a job, a task among many others. And you simply have to learn the job from the basics up, because you affect other people when you do it.

The boss has a greater effect than other colleagues on the atmosphere of a company. The boss has more authority. And with that follows greater responsibility.

But remember: that doesn't mean that I *can't* demand responsibility from my staff members. They have a responsibility for themselves and their work, but mine is to keep the whole thing going. If I'm not ready to fill those shoes, then maybe I ought try a fascinating career in telemarketing instead.

{ 2 }

Why You Should Choose Your Boss, Instead of Your Employer

You can go to school or college and train for just about anything: there are courses for welders, nurses, economists, plumbers, engineers, dentists, agronomists, cooks, hairdressers, and a million other professions. But not for bosses.

There are no courses in high school and nothing meaningful in college and university programs and courses. Leadership is mentioned in lots of places, but no practical skills are taught. Any instruction only goes as far as theories, and these are often taught by people who have never been the boss of a single soul.

It's really fairly natural that there are thus quite a lot of consultants who—like me—try to educate people on these competences, these skills needed for leadership. Some of us are good at what we do; others seem to know just as little as the people in the organization they are working for. There are many pitfalls, even for an experienced leadership coach.

A Modern Version of the Emperor's New Clothes

Let me explain what usually happens.

An organization starts a project to give their bosses leadership training, and everyone involved is extremely positive. This is going to lead to great things. They bring in an inventive consultant who tells the people that make the decisions that "we will sort this out!" The consultant shows lots of PowerPoint images with an extremely complicated description of the process. Arrows and graphs and God knows what else.

Then the consultant goes around and interviews individuals at every imaginable level within the organization. Asks smart questions and finds out how everything works or doesn't work. Then he goes to the person who ordered the report—in the best case, the managing director is involved in this, but not always—and explains that there are serious shortcomings in the firm. But he happens to know how the management structure *ought* to work. And then he presents an ambitious program that will correct the most serious problems.

No sooner said than done. Plans are made and a pilot project is arranged with the senior management group, who say that "this is really good stuff. We'll go ahead with it." Of course, they are all very busy and stressed as usual, but they feel that the question of leadership is going to be easier to handle in the future, because soon they'll have a consultant who can be blamed for the general incompetence.

Then all the bosses are put through whatever development program has been chosen. This can go on for well over a year.

Afterwards, the whole caboodle is evaluated. The consultant has, of course, feathered his bed and made him- or herself popular with all the participants. He or she makes sure that they get a good rating in the feedback evaluation from all the middle managers so that they'll report back to the top management and praise what a brilliant consultant they've brought in.

Then it's *thank you* and *goodbye* and *good luck in the future* when you use these (most certainly) fantastic tools in your everyday work. Everybody solemnly and earnestly promises to implement all this newly acquired wisdom.

Soon, unfortunately, some sort of crisis takes place and people totally lose their focus. The organization reacts instinctively. Everybody goes back to doing things the way they've always been done.

All that's been achieved is that some money and a great deal of time have been wasted. Time is what costs the most. You can always earn more money, but you can never get back all the time that these bosses spent sitting and listening to their coach.

What happened? Why did it all fizzle out?

Simple. There was nobody really in charge of the issue.

When There Isn't a Problem, You Don't Need a Solution

What they missed from the very beginning was the need to consider why they have bosses in the organization in the first place. The question that the managing director—and you can swap "managing director" with the title of your own highest boss if that's helpful—ought to ask is why he or she has any middle managers at all.

What do they *actually* contribute? Why doesn't the top boss simply use a remote control to steer all the staff from the comfort of her desk?

The problem often lies in the fact that we don't know why a boss has gotten that job and what exactly it should comprise. We need somebody who's responsible, in case everything ends up a mess. But what else?

What are the bosses there for? Why does the organization have them? Do we have any particular goal in all this? When we've ascertained what it is, then we can teach them any skills they're lacking to meet that goal.

Think about it for a moment: if you don't know where you are going—how can you know what you need to get there?

When the Boss Is All Wrong

I assume that you've sometimes wondered: *How hard can it be? I could easily manage that myself.* And sure. Perhaps it *ought* to be easy to be a boss and to understand what your staff need to do their job, but how often have you (if you are *not* the boss) thought about what it actually means to be a boss?

What are the demands that the boss is trying to juggle? And what effect do these demands have on the results the boss achieves? How much do you actually know about the everyday life of a boss?

Most management roles contain at least two parts. The

Leader	**Specialist**
Achieves results through others	Achieves results themselves

manager/boss needs to be a leader and give his staff what they need. By that, I mean instruct, educate, explain, and show how the work should be done. But also to support, to coach, and to pep; to plan the group's work, to give feedback, to motivate, to lead group meetings, as well as lots of other things designed to make things easier for their staff.

The other part of the job is to be a specialist. The specialist part is what fills the rest of the day. It's when the manager solves problems himself, takes care of customers, plans activities that aren't part of leading his staff but are about the job itself.

Managers are often involved in various types of projects and take part in the management group's work, but much of that doesn't include things that affect their staff's ability to do a good job.

The challenge lies in making the right priorities timewise. And a lot of managers simply give priority to the wrong part of their managerial role. They try to do everything themselves, but that doesn't work. They work more as if they were specialists rather than leaders.

As a consequence, they tend to get stuck in problems connected to purely specialist functions, things that in many cases you (as a member of their staff) could have dealt with yourself. Instead of letting you solve your own problems, your boss interferes. It's not guaranteed that the outcome will be better because of this interference, but what can you do? He's your manager. The boss is the boss.

During my years as a consultant, I've seen many hair-raising examples of bosses who behaved like specialists 99 percent of the time. They sit at their desk swamped with commitments that aren't the slightest bit connected with management and leadership. Because of this, they don't have time to lead anybody at all. And bear in mind that they might have a staff of fifty people or more.

Have you had a boss like that? She or he doesn't have time for anything at all but is always in a colossal hurry. It's often your boss's boss who makes demands this way. Instead of asking how things are going with management, they ask for Group A's results.

And just like the rest of us—managers want to deliver whatever is being asked for. Bosses are, after all, ordinary people, don't forget.

That Sounds Awful! We're in the 21st Century Now!

Since the top management in the company is often more interested in business successes than in the staff, the question of efficient leadership is—quite simply—not given priority. You'll have to think about whether you can find motivation and knowledge somewhere else. Perhaps you don't need to be dependent on your boss? Perhaps you can find ways to get the information and guidance you need yourself? Wouldn't it be liberating to have the solution in your own hands!

Why You Should Read This Book

The fact that you've even picked up this book at all indicates that you want more knowledge, you suspect that there are many challenges to effective management, and you might be curious about human behavior in a general sense. Or you simply might read books about management and leadership because you have the ambition to become the boss yourself.

You'll find it useful to keep an open mind. You need a bit of imagination to be able to understand other people. If you always base your understanding on what you yourself are like and what you think is right or wrong, then you will continue to misunderstand others.

If, on the other hand, you know that you're reading this book in hopes of finding some *quick fixes*, then I advise you to put the book back on the shelf. Save your money. When it comes to people, there are rarely any simple solutions.

"But I'm Not a Boss. Do I Need to Learn Anything About Leadership?"

If you are one of many employees at a large company and have opinions about how the organization is led, this might very well open your eyes to management struggles you might not have been aware of.

I have no intention at all of making excuses for poor managerial behavior, but with certain insights about the challenges of leadership, perhaps you might be more willing to make allowances when your boss makes everyday mistakes. And perhaps, after having read the book, you might be able to give your own boss a better sense of what you yourself need from management. My real ambition is that you'll be able to go to your boss and explain what resources or support you need to do an even better job.

After all, this is about *your* ability to do your work.

{3}

Leadership Is a Process of Communication

The ability to communicate effectively with their staff is the most important skill a boss can have. The ability to reach them, regardless of what the message is. And some bosses—let's be honest—aren't much good at that. Praise, criticism, instructions, or support—if communication doesn't work, then nothing works.

If you knew how many clichés there are on the theme of management and being a boss, you would fall off your chair, but let's stick to the core essentials.

To be a *boss* is comparatively simple. It's a function, a title. A little square in the organizational hierarchy. Somebody has been appointed manager. Congratulations. That role leads to certain mandates and powers; certain areas of responsibility and concrete work tasks. That somebody is now in charge of decisions, responsible for the budget, and even manning the organization. That somebody is also responsible for setting goals and achieving results.

It's a role, a task, a job—but it is not a behavior.

To be a *leader* is considerably harder. It requires that the person who accepted the appointment can handle people in an effective manner. Leadership is a communication process, nothing else. To get there, you need to know how you communicate. How you lead people forward. How you create motivation and commitment. Leadership is more of what you do than who you are. You act in a way that creates commitment, faith, trust. You can't achieve any of this by virtue of your title. But by acting professionally, you can actually work miracles.

So, Boss or Leader?

Boss is what you are. Leader is what you do.

Or as a woman said to me many years ago: "The boss is the person I *must* follow, and the leader is the person I *want* to follow." The best scenario would be if the boss and the leader were one and the same person. And sometimes they are.

So what is your boss like? Is he or she just a boss, or do you also notice distinct leadership qualities? Are we talking about a sufficiently effective communicator? Is your boss completely serious about their task?

I'll try to keep the high-flown phrases to an absolute minimum here. A person who wants to be regarded as a really good leader needs to be a bit of an expert at communication. You can only truly influence your staff if you know how to reach each and every one of them.

And from that it follows: anybody who accepts a role as boss needs to understand other people. The very second he or she steps into their new office is the last time they can simply base everything on themselves. From now on, that person is not who is important here.

Bad bosses, such as those that you and I have come across over the years, have been bad at communicating. They haven't listened, they've talked too much about themselves; sometimes they've behaved badly and sometimes they've been decidedly despotic. And in most cases they've based everything on their own worldview, a worldview that has been ridiculously one-sided. And everybody except them has seen that's what they're doing.

To be respected in their leadership role, they need to learn how *you* function. They need to know who *you* are and how they can reach *you* in particular, and do that in the most efficient and elegant manner.

I use William Moulton Marston's writings and theories as a starting point to describe this type of communication. There are other methods too, but this model covers what you need to know.

There are many things that affect how a person functions—many, many things—and in this book I am going to deal with two of them: a person's driving forces and a person's development level. Don't send me any emails complaining that I've simplified everything. I already know that. But we have to start somewhere. And I've chosen to start here. Before long, you're going to better understand something that may have left you endlessly baffled: your boss.

Communication Is Key!

I don't know whether you've read my book *Surrounded by Idiots*, but if you have, then you'll soon be getting a little review course on the basic behavior patterns of the "colors." In the unlikely event that you should think you know everything about these "color behaviors," I'd nevertheless recommend that you have a look at the following pages. I'm going to describe things that weren't included in any of the earlier books. In this instance, we're assuming that the dialogue takes place between you and your boss.

Task-Oriented vs. Relationship-Oriented

So, how different can people really be? Let's see if we can try to understand this together. To start with, we have task-oriented and relationship-oriented people. It's neither more right nor more wrong to be one or the other, but they each have a different focus.

Task-Oriented: More Interested in Questions About Tasks and Issues than in Relationships

To be task-oriented means to focus on what needs to be done. Instead of doing much thinking about who should be in the work group, you look at what actually needs to be done and

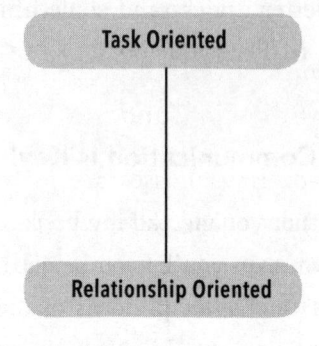

Task Oriented

|
|

Relationship Oriented

then you get on with it. You're not necessarily uninterested in other people, but you do put the job first. Sure, you can talk about football and vacations, but you can do that after the job is done. Over lunch, for example.

Advantages with Task-Oriented Behavior

Task-oriented individuals don't need a lot of support to get the job done. They don't get bogged down easily in emotional issues; they don't lose focus in the same way that relationship-oriented people can, and it's simpler for them to steam ahead.

Disadvantages with Task-Oriented Behavior

Since an awful lot of tasks require cooperation, a task-oriented boss can neglect to consider the opinions and attitudes of the other members of the team. There is a risk that the boss just goes ahead instead of listening to input from others. Since the majority of the population are actually relationship-oriented, conflicts can sometimes arise because task-oriented people can be regarded as insensitive and harsh.

Relationship-Oriented: More Interested in Relationships than in Concrete Tasks and Issues

The relationship-oriented bosses are more focused on the people at the workplace, and the interactions between them, than in the task. This doesn't, of course, mean that they aren't interested in getting the job done, but relationships are important for them. To work well in a team, they need to know their colleagues, know who they are, and understand them at least to some degree. It's only then that the job will get done well.

Advantages with Relationship-Oriented Behavior

These bosses are decidedly more natural when it comes to listening to the opinions and ideas of the other members of their team. It's no effort for them to remember to look around and reflect on what others might think. They are also more likely to be able to sway their colleagues and to think through different ideas before they start on a project.

Disadvantages with Relationship-Oriented Behavior

They might have a tendency to listen more to people they like than to the people who really have the knowledge. If a member of their team doesn't perform well, the relationship-oriented boss immediately feels uncomfortable. Because now they need to give negative feedback, which these bosses are not at all keen on doing. They would prefer to maintain a positive atmosphere in the group, and are only too happy to avoid potential conflict. This can mean that the job will suffer.

That's one dimension of the DISC system. It's straightforward and quite simple to deal with. The other pair of opposites is a little more complex.

Extroverted vs. Introverted Behavior

The challenge lies within this next dimension: extroverted versus introverted behavior. Now it gets really interesting. Things can go quite wrong between these two.

Extroverted: More Outgoing than Introspective

Being extroverted means you are susceptible to impressions that come from outside yourself. This makes some individuals action-oriented in a different way than the introverts. Extroverted people proceed fairly quickly from thought to action and devote less time to reflection. They are quite often result-oriented, and they like it when things are moving along.

Their energy is directed outwards, towards other people and the entire world around them. Diversity of thought is a good thing, and they gain strength from the outer world. This makes them surround themselves with people. Energy comes from activity and from thinking up new ideas all the time. To plop an extrovert down on a sofa so that they can "rest" a while just creates more stress. Being alone is boring and energy-draining. They like to discuss with others, and they would rather express themselves in speech than in writing. Experiences are important to them, otherwise they won't stay engaged.

This is the personality type that came up with the idea of open office floorplans. They wanted to create dynamism,

| Introverted | — | Extroverted |

quick decisions, and communication across boundaries. They get energy from the pulse of people around them. But then the open office landscapes were filled with introverted people.

The Advantage with Extroverted Behavior

Extrovert bosses rarely waste their time overanalyzing data and details and paying too much attention to those around them. They have strong egos and quickly decide what they think about an issue. This makes them natural decision-makers, and they're happy to take risks. They're usually unafraid and dare to make a place for themselves among larger groups of people. Since they are influenced by impressions from outside themselves, they also get lots of new ideas.

The Flip Side of Extrovert Behavior

Sometimes the quickness in, say, decision-making, causes problems. It can be rapid but wrong, but since these bosses are dynamic, they can stand up for their ideas even when others have clearly shown that those ideas simply aren't viable. Since their egos are so strong, they sometimes take up too much space and forget to listen to what others think. Their own ideas tend to be the only acceptable ones.

Introverted: More Introspective than Outgoing

Then we have the introverts, those who are active in their own inner world. There is a lot more going on under the surface than others might realize. They have more of a "wait-

and-see" attitude. They think twice before they do anything and can spend a lot of time collecting information when a major decision is being made. The path to a decision is just as important—if not more important—than the decision itself. The introverts get energy from being able to withdraw and be inside their own heads. They need that solitude; forcing them out onto the dance floor or dragging them off to endless parties for mingling will only create exhaustion.

They direct their energy inwards, towards their own inner world and what is going on there, so they need quite a lot of peace and quiet to be able to concentrate. They are often circumspect, and the ideas they come up with are not about inspiration but about reflection. They've been sitting there thinking and finally come up with something. And they do indeed want and appreciate reflection. The written word is worth more than something that is spoken—both when they're giving and receiving information. So while they might not take part in a discussion, they will, however, email you afterwards with their thoughts.

These are the people who have a problem with open office layouts. All those endless interruptions and sometimes noisy environments mean that they have to "re-start" every thought all day long. They can't think clearly in those kinds of conditions. A study showed that for a really introverted person, working in an open floorplan is like working slightly drunk. They simply lose their sharpness.

The Advantage with Introverted Behavior

Introverted bosses aren't likely to be careless about anything. They like to be thorough, which means that their answers to particular questions are often well-thought-out. It's not a problem for them to wait and see and to allow others to do their work unimpeded. On the contrary, they are often seen as humble, and rarely do they express a demand without a good reason for doing so.

The Flip Side of Introverted Behavior

It's obvious that introverted bosses sometimes wait and see too long. They will quite often sit quietly at a meeting without really sharing their view. Staff, particularly extroverted ones, can interpret this silence as approval. This can be a serious mistake. Silence is not the same thing as approval in this case. It can just as easily mean that the boss doesn't feel comfortable expressing their own view. Or that they simply haven't finished thinking it through.

Here are the basics in Marston's model. As you can see, we have a couple of decisive differences.

But what about the colors, where do they come in?

We have four different basic behavior patterns from the two dimensions task/relationship and introvert/extrovert. To

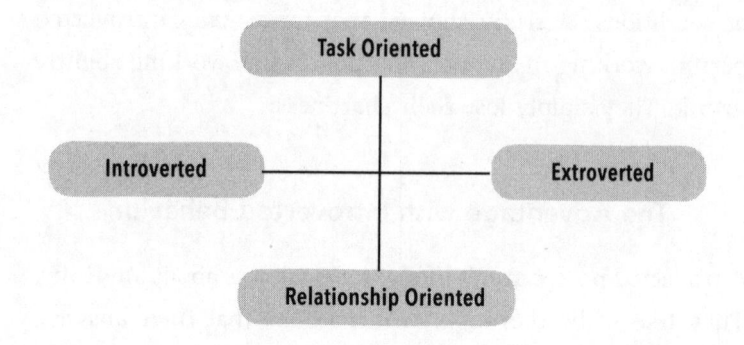

```
          Task Oriented
                |
Introverted ————+———— Extroverted
                |
       Relationship Oriented
```

explain the four basic behaviors, we use Lücher's psychological colors. And that is where Red, Yellow, Green, and Blue behavior comes from.

Red is the color of fire, yellow is the color of air, green stands for the earth, and blue for the sea.

Okay, so what does all that mean?

This is what each of the colors stand for:

The Reds, task-oriented and extroverted, are governed by a drive to deal with problems and difficult challenges. The tougher the demands, the better they perform. If something goes a bit too smoothly, they almost become suspicious. What's the catch? Why is it so easy? It should be hard, it should be difficult. You have to put some effort into it. Perhaps it should be a bit painful. Pain makes you tough. They like speed, action, and a bit of oomph!

While Red is about *doing*, **Yellow, relationship-oriented**

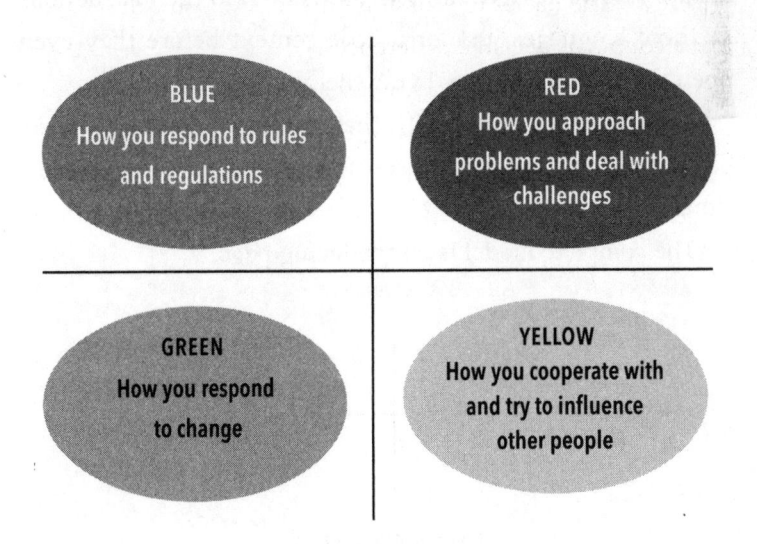

BLUE
How you respond to rules and regulations

RED
How you approach problems and deal with challenges

GREEN
How you respond to change

YELLOW
How you cooperate with and try to influence other people

and extroverted, is about *interacting*. These are the people who always have to convince everyone else to think and feel the same way they do. They can't leave the room until everyone agrees. And they see sunshine even where the rain is pouring down! Yellows also like it when things move quickly.

Green, relationship-oriented and introverted, is about a love of stability. A lot of Green means there is little interest in changing things. Even if the change is entirely necessary, it will be regarded with suspicion. These are people who say things like *it was better before; you know what you have, but not what you get* and *the grass isn't always greener on the other side*. New ideas are dismissed with an *everything is working just fine as it is, thank you*.

Finally, **Blue, task-oriented and introverted**, is about appreciating rules and regulations. They go by the book and always know the right thing to do. They read the instructions in three languages just for a little context before they even open the package of new IKEA shelves.

These four attitudes, with their orientation towards tasks or relationhips and differences in introversion and extroversion, respectively, lead to unique behaviors.

The complete model is on the facing page.

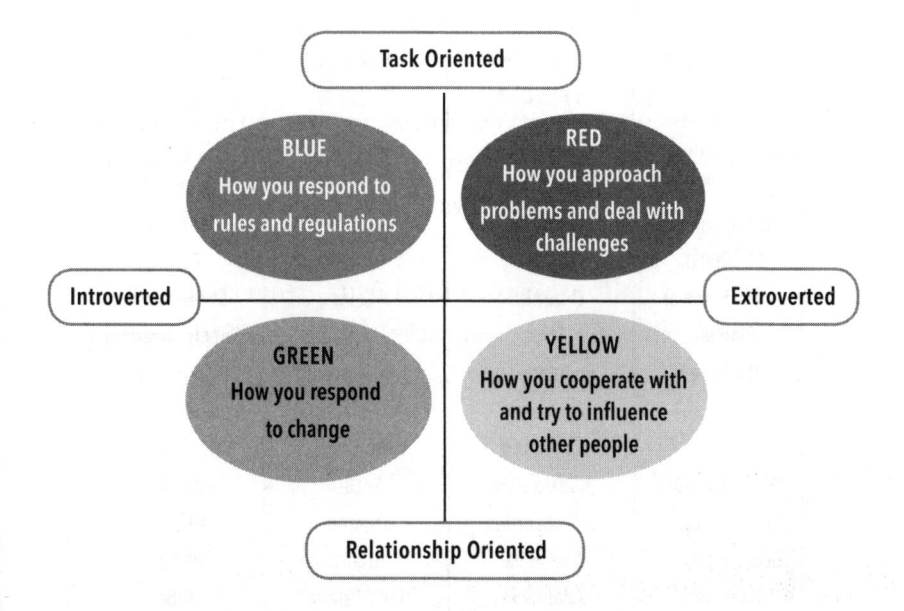

```
              Task Oriented
    ┌─────────────┬─────────────┐
    │    BLUE     │     RED     │
    │ How you     │ How you     │
    │ respond to  │ approach    │
    │ rules and   │ problems    │
    │ regulations │ and deal    │
    │             │ with        │
    │             │ challenges  │
Introverted ─────┼───────── Extroverted
    │   GREEN     │   YELLOW    │
    │ How you     │ How you     │
    │ respond     │ cooperate   │
    │ to change   │ with and    │
    │             │ try to      │
    │             │ influence   │
    │             │ other people│
    └─────────────┴─────────────┘
          Relationship Oriented
```

What Concrete Behaviors Result from This?

If we look at the impact of these characteristics, we begin to see clear differences in every possible respect. On page 42, you can see a number of specific qualities that are connected with a particular color. It goes without saying that there are exceptions. There are always exceptions. People are complicated, and it can be hard to understand them. But every quality or characteristic is specific to the color concerned. (On page 43 is an everyday example of what it can look like.)

DOMINANT RED	INSPIRING YELLOW	STABLE GREEN	COMPLIANT BLUE
Energetic	Talkative	Patient	Thorough
Ambitious	Enthusiastic	Relaxed	Systematic
Strong-willed	Persuasive	Restrained	Distanced
Go-ahead	Creative	Reliable	Correct
Problem-solver	Optimistic	Calm	Conventional
Pioneer	Social	Loyal	Seems uncertain
Decisive	Spontaneous	Unassuming	Objective
Innovative	Expressive	Understanding	Structured
Impatient	Charming	Thorough	Investigative
Wants control	Joie de vivre	Secure	Perfectionist
Convincing	Self-absorbed	Discreet	Needs time
Goal-oriented	Sensitive	Supportive	Reflective
Powerful	Adaptable	Good listener	Methodical
Results-oriented	Stimulating	Helpful	Seeks facts
Takes initiative	Encouraging	A doer	Discerning
Fast paced	Communicative	Stamina	Examines
Aware of time	Flexible	Wait and see	Follows rules
Intensive	Open	Considerate	Logical
Opinionated	Relation-oriented	Hides feelings	Questioning
Direct	Imaginative	Thoughtful	Conscientious
Independent	Easy-going	Friendly	Circumspect
			Reserved

Going up?

Blue Silently calculates the total weight of everyone in the elevator and compares that with the "maximum permitted load" sign. Might even change elevators if the math doesn't check out.	**Red** Goes straight into the elevator and presses the button (repeatedly).
Green Actually uses the "Open the door" button so that everyone has time to enter.	**Yellow** Sees the elevator journey as a marvelous opportunity to chat with the people they haven't seen for a long time. Can even hold the door open a while to continue a conversation with somebody who is not taking the elevator…

Above is an everyday example of what each color can look like. But the different colors also affect an individual specifically in their work and in their leadership. As you read further in this book, you will find examples of what these characteristics and behaviors look like in everyday life from the perspective of both bosses and employees. I will focus entirely on work life, since this book is about the relationship between you and your boss.

{ 4 }

How to Understand and Predict Your Boss's Behavior

If you look at how people function in general, there are noticeable patterns. You already know that we're governed by emotions. Some people like to question that—and quite often they're Blues—but they too are governed by emotions. It just looks a bit different.

Red bosses have the shortest tempers by far. They can lose their cool in a fraction of a second. Because they're so impatient, they react quicker when others slow them down or try to delay this and that. Fury is lurking just below the surface, and the rest of us must expect a little outburst at almost any time. Even if the Red has learned to restrain themselves and not show their anger, those around them will still see (and feel) the irritation. Some Reds don't see any point in hiding their annoyance. They let their anger be known, and it can sometimes be quite a storm. This makes many people avoid them and keep silent around them, which can mean that the Red bosses end up out of the loop and cut off from key information.

Yellow bosses are, basically, extremely optimistic. They

see things from the bright side, and find it hard to deal with bad news in a calm, levelheaded way. Most of all, they want to remain positive all the time, and so they like to avoid bad news. They trust most people, and they spread this positive energy and feeling wherever they go. But this also means that they can become short-tempered with anyone who threatens those positive vibes. The Yellows might take longer than the Reds to lose their temper, but they can easily end up just as angry once they finally do. Luckily the outburst often exhausts them, and anyway they'll soon have forgotten what it was even about. Life goes on. This can lead to a situation where staff members don't feel able to go to their boss about problems. They'd just be waved aside anyway.

Green bosses are extremely slow to get angry—perhaps *too* slow, in fact. They often tend to completely hide their feelings, which means that people around them don't know what they're thinking. Greens don't want to trouble others with their worries, so they keep quiet and sometimes turn their strong emotions inwards. They don't show anything on the outside, and it takes a long time before their true feelings are visible in their behavior. If you ask a Green person how things are, the answer will probably be positive. This doesn't, however, tell you anything about the real state of things. A problematic consequence of this is that they are far too tolerant. For example, they are unlikely to correct employees who underperform, which can infuriate the members who actually do perform.

Finally, we have the Blue boss. A lot of people interpret this person as not having any feelings, which of course isn't correct. The more Blue an individual shows in their behavior, the more they are going to follow the rule book for fear of being revealed as incompetent. Because the facial expressions and body language of the Blues are often controlled, it's easy to miss what they really feel when confronted with a challenge. But others often experience this as a widespread need of control, as if there is only one acceptable way of carrying out a task.

Yin and Yang

Every color has its self-evident strengths, but also its typical weaknesses. We need to look at both parts.

To make it really interesting, we shall look at it on the basis of the colors of your boss. Perhaps you still don't have a clue where your boss would end up in a communication profile.

Let's see if the following pages can help with the analysis. Here, knowledge means power, and the more you understand about the colors, the easier you'll be able to interpret your boss and their behavior. Your boss's profile might have a profound influence on your career.

The Alpha Behavior of the Red, Result-Oriented Bosses

As I've already mentioned, Red bosses bring energy and a go-getter attitude, but also value structure and order. They like to organize work. They appreciate action and are very quick to take command. They do this without making a big fuss—it simply happens.

They don't put up with any nonsense, and they lead by controlling workflow and their staff's time and focus. Their goals will always be clear and concise, and nobody will be in doubt about the objective. We're moving forward, and we're doing so quickly. They prefer that the rest of us maintain a high standard, since they value results above all else.

And Are There Disadvantages?

Well . . . if you've had a Red boss, you might have noticed that sometimes it feels like your creativity has diminished. Perhaps you aren't as motivated to put forward your own proposals and ideas when the reception hasn't been particularly enthusiastic. Or to put it bluntly: it's not nice to be shot down every time you suggest something. Red bosses can sometimes create increased uniformity among their staff. Everyone around them simply adapts to the boss, and some even become defensive in response. All told, the dynamics within the group may suffer if the boss is too dominant. Your motivation and enthusiasm for the job can become dangerously low if the boss is too controlling.

The Cheery Style of the Yellow, Inspirational Bosses!

Yellow bosses add a whole lot of inspiration and energy. Whoopee! They often create the most enjoyable working atmosphere, and they appreciate a good mood and positive news. Through their charisma and enthusiasm, they tend to encourage their team to come up with ideas. Yellow leadership is often extremely inclusive—everybody should be on board! The focus is directed towards encouraging great achievements and creating comprehensive visions of the future.

Sounds Really Great, Right?

Uhmm. The problem can be that oftentimes you won't know what's actually going on. The Yellow boss loves to talk about the latest and greatest idea, and they are always changing their goals and concepts. Since new ideas are always popping up, you and your colleagues are going to have certain challenges (read: *major problems*) when it comes to keeping up with the constant changes of direction. Sometimes this means employees just give up. What's the point of embracing a new routine or a new project, when it's going to be forgotten in three weeks?

In the Safe Arms of the Green, Supportive Bosses

The focus of the Green boss lies on you and all your fellow workers. You'll always be seen by the Green boss. He or she will make an effort to unite absolutely everyone with mutual values and goals, or perhaps a shared vision of some sort. It's important that everybody finds their right place within the organization. The Green boss supports every single person all the time and likes to solve problems by involving everyone and through general consensus. They often enjoy the confidence and support of others since it's so easy for them to cooperate with other people.

This Does Sound Really Cozy!

Oh, sure. But Green bosses can be somewhat vague when they delegate. Their method of managing is partly based on the expectation that you'll intuitively know what they really want. They're not always comfortable giving clear orders, and can thus express themselves extremely vaguely. They don't necessarily get straight to the point. They hope that you will understand that this is going to be a bit of a tough ride. Since they are people-oriented, they can sometimes prioritize their own relationships rather than seeing to it that the job actually gets done. If conflicts do arise, your Green boss might check out completely. Conflict is unpleasant, and not something they want to know about. You might need to check under the rug now and again. Who knows what's been swept under there?

The Blue, Observant Boss—A Stickler for Details

If you like analyzing and getting to the bottom of everything that comes your way, then you're going to understand your Blue boss. These are the detail-oriented people who lead by analyzing and dissecting problems. They're experts at problem-solving as long as the question interests them. One way of solving problems is to create rather exhaustive solutions and thus reach results. They're good judges of competence, and they value professional skill. Knowing all the right people is not going to impress them if you can't do the job.

Orderliness. That's What I Like!

Depending upon your own profile, you might consider your boss somewhat reserved. Perhaps even distant. You might not get to know them. If your relationship with your boss is important to you, you might be disappointed since they rarely share anything about themselves. Blue bosses can also become entangled in their own work-related problems or tasks and completely forget to actually manage their staff. They are often skillful specialists who can be slightly awkward in leadership roles.

So How Does This Information Help You During an Ordinary Work Week?

We react differently to different behaviors. Depending on what color you are, you're going to be more or less affected by your boss's behavior. If you're Red, then you won't react to the somewhat dominating style of the Red boss. If you are Yellow, then it might not bother you if your Yellow boss starts every sentence with "I." If you're predominantly Green, then you might think it's nice that your boss never pushes too hard. And if you're Blue, you'll appreciate the way your Blue boss keeps one hand on the emergency brake and one foot hovering over the brake pedal. But it all depends on the situation.

Sometimes, a Red boss can stay quiet and listen attentively. It depends on whether you've reached them or not.

The Yellow boss can—in their better moments—refrain from talking about themselves and actually let you into the conversation.

The Green boss can tire of too much vagueness and put their foot down quite decisively. When this happens, everyone tends to notice.

And the Blue boss can—if there's enough evidence to show it's necessary—open up and become slightly personal. Who knows, you might even get to hear about their neighborhood and whether they have kids.

There are no rules without exceptions. People are complex beings. Even if the major traits of a particular behavior are present, you probably shouldn't bet everything on knowing what your boss is going to do next. But with the right approach, everything becomes so much simpler.

Does Personal Insight Play a Part?

I've probably been asked this question a thousand times over the last twenty years: *Bosses are typically Red, aren't they?* I don't have any exact figures, but the frequency of Red behavior seems to increase the higher up you go in an organization. Does this mean that Reds are better bosses? Perhaps, but not necessarily. What we do know is that they are often tougher than other people and that they don't back down if things get rough. And that can help them on their way to the top.

But the most important thing I've learned during my years as a management-development consultant is that a person's personal insight is often the deciding factor as to whether or not they'll be a successful boss. The style of communication isn't what's important; rather, what distinguishes a successful boss from a less successful one is being aware of that style of communication, whatever it may be. The more a boss learns about themselves, the better they are at leading others.

There aren't any shortcuts here.

There have been studies looking at every facet of this. Bosses with a high degree of personal insight are skillful communicators, they achieve better results, and they win the confidence of their staff. They are considerably more effective in leadership, and they actually find it easier to progress in their career. They are more self-confident, and their relationships—at work and outside work, too—function better. An interesting side effect—they lie less than the other bosses.

So why not choose your boss, instead of your employer?

{ 5 }

The Most Common Color Combinations and How to Recognize Them

People are rarely one single color. You've probably already worked that out. And here we have some statistics to back that up. It's important to remind yourself that even though there are only four fundamental elements, these can be combined in lots of ways.

Approximately 5 percent of the population exhibits behavior that is dominated by a single color. And that 5 percent is for any color at all—Red, Yellow, Green, or Blue. These people are thus fairly uncommon, but they do exist. They're easier to recognize than some of the other combinations because their behavior is easily discernable. I'm not claiming that profiles with only one color are better; all I'm saying is that they are easier to identify. This applies to their strengths as well as their weaknesses.

The more common situation, however, is for a person to have two colors dominating their behavior. This could be a combination of Red and Yellow, or Blue and Green, or in fact any combination at all. Without getting too technical—this is easy to see with the help of a profile analysis—as much as 80 percent of analyzed behaviors are a combination of just two colors. This gives a somewhat more balanced picture of this individual. A Green-Blue person is indeed still introverted, but is neither extremely fussy nor extremely afraid of conflict. You could describe it as a sort of hybrid behavior that doesn't stick out as much. This applies to both the positive and the negative aspects.

Finally, we have those who have three dominating colors in their profiles. These can be any combination at all.

Red-Yellow Motivators: Creative and Flexible

The Red-Yellow combination is innovative, creative, enthusiastic, and flexible. They like ideas and quickly and easily see possibilities. They like to think up new projects. However, implementation of those projects might be a little haphazard. But if they're interested in their work, they can stick with it for a long time.

Within the group, the Red-Yellows introduce themselves boldly. They need affirmation and approval if they are going to really shine. But they spread energy and motivation around them.

They can become the engine of the group.

They adapt effortlessly to new tasks.

They know how to persuade and get others on board.

They have charm and usually rely on their own ability.

They are accustomed to multitasking, but leave many things unfinished in their wake.

FOCUSED ON THE MISSION
Determines norms

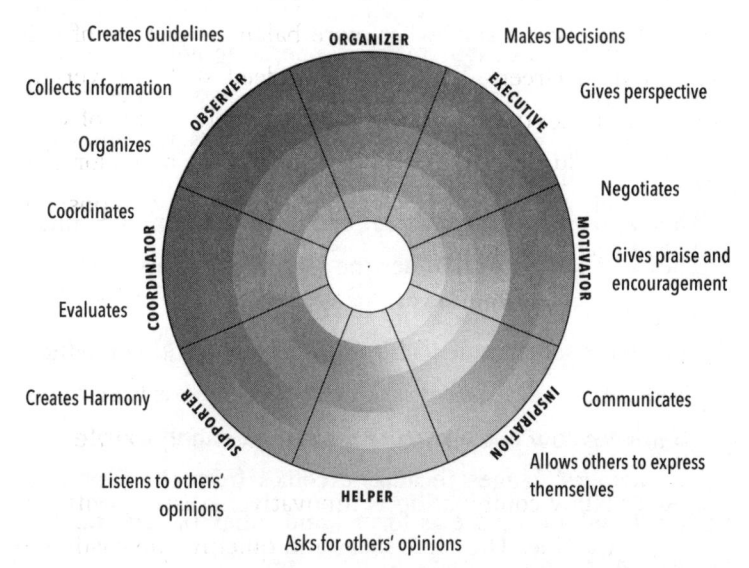

- Creates Guidelines
- Collects Information
- Organizes
- Coordinates
- Evaluates
- Creates Harmony
- Listens to others' opinions
- Asks for others' opinions

- Makes Decisions
- Gives perspective
- Negotiates
- Gives praise and encouragement
- Communicates
- Allows others to express themselves

ORGANIZER, EXECUTIVE, MOTIVATOR, INSPIRATION, HELPER, SUPPORTER, COORDINATOR, OBSERVER

FOCUSED ON THE PROCESS

They find it hardest to deal with the Green-Blue coordinators, who are far too systematic and orderly for their taste.

Yellow-Green Helpers: Open and Understanding

The Yellow-Green combination is relationship-oriented. They display openness, enjoy participation, and are often very understanding of others. They want to be liked and can be protective of others. They want to feel valuable, and their self-esteem is often based on what others think about them. They can and will adapt themselves, sometimes beyond what they're really comfortable with, in order to fit in. When they contribute, they want something in return—some attention at the very least.

Within the group they often completely ignore their own interests which, of course, makes cooperating with them very easy. These helpers can become a bit too indispensable for the others, who will start relying on them also in other—perhaps personal—matters.

They appreciate tasks where relationships are important.

They are happy to shoulder the role of helper and advisor.

They are extremely loyal to their group.

They have some tendencies to feel inferior to others, which can lead them to seek out people with power. This is an obvious challenge in a managerial situation, for example.

The helpers' biggest headache comes from the Blue-Red organizers who they see as formal and inflexible and far too focused on the job.

Green-Blue Coordinators: Systematic and Organized

People with this combination are reflective and often question things around them. They process large quantities of data and evaluate them clearly and competently. Although they are extremely talented within their field, they tend to underestimate their competence. Sometimes they need somebody else to bring them to the fore.

They are loyal and extremely dutiful.

It's no problem for them to stay in the same job for many years. On the contrary, they often prefer it.

Within the group, they shoulder the coordinating role.

At the beginning of a project, their combination of good listening and sense of organization is extremely valuable. They also make sure that tasks are properly finished. If they feel threatened, however, they can surprise themselves and those around them by strongly defending themselves.

They help as long as it seems logical.

They might find it difficult to understand the needs of others and are sometimes suspicious of the motives of others.

They never act impulsively and are not distracted by what's happening around them.

The Green-Blues have little patience for their opposites, the Red-Yellow motivators, whom they see as completely frivolous but, thank God, fairly easy to fool.

Blue-Red Organizers: Rational and Disciplined

This combination is hardworking, extremely rational, and independent. They usually weigh the pros and cons and balance speed and caution as best they can. They always want to improve themselves and avoid any kind of mistake. All discussions they have are logical, and they will keep the debate alive until an issue has been settled.

They can be regarded as arrogant, skeptical, and pedantic.

They place great demands on their bosses, who need to be honest and upright and always provide clear guidelines.

As long as the rule book is followed and their responsibilities are clear, they feel comfortable.

Within the group, the organizers feel surprisingly contented if everyone stands for the same thing. Their strength lies in their ability to organize. Unfortunately, they can be hobbled by their own internal critic, who is forever harping on about everything they ought to have done differently and better . . .

They don't like to be told what they should do or how they should do it.

They can irritate others by refusing to give in.

They can concentrate well and remain realistic.

Yellow-Green helpers are nightmares for the Blue-Reds because they perceive helpers as being far too emotional for the common good.

Now, That Was a Lot to Keep Track of . . .

When we look at the combinations, things get more complicated.

It isn't only the four basic behavior patterns you need to consider; how they relate to each other is just as important. The above are four common combinations, but they're not the only ones.

A Green-Blue boss with more Green than Blue behaves one way. A Green-Blue boss with more Blue than Green has a lot in common with the first, but isn't exactly the same. And if I were to describe the profiles with three colors, we'd really have to start paying attention. The more factors that are included, the harder it is to see the nuances.

If we believe the statistics, though, your boss is probably one of these combinations of two colors. And since four out of five people are one of these combinations, you can assume that the answer lies within reach.

But, you may ask yourself, what about Red-Green profiles? Or Blue-Yellow? Well, we've got other challenges there, of course. Purely Red-Green (i.e., with just as much of each color in one individual) profiles are—for some reason—uncommon. The Blue-Yellow combination is actually more common. Nobody knows why. They have a combination of analysis and inspiration, and they demand a considerable portion of personal insight from the person concerned.

The reason that I—despite what the statistics tell us—mainly discuss the four basic colors separately is that I want to be clear about the characteristics of each of them. And what type of behavior they can result in. I trust that you will be able to put together the pieces of the puzzle when you find yourself standing in front of another person.

Some people I meet maintain that you can't measure a person's behavior. And that it's even wrong to do so since it's so complicated. And sure, you can pull your hat down over your eyes if you don't want to see reality. But, as I described earlier, you can train your ability to identify a person's type by paying attention to the tiny signals.

Imagine a recipe for an ordinary cake. It contains milk, flour, sugar, eggs, and baking powder. Depending on how much you use of each ingredient, you'll end up with a delicious cake or something a little off. But if you want to understand how to properly make the cake, you need to know what milk is, and it's helpful if you know what baking powder is actually capable of.

Most of the people you meet—with the occasional refreshing exception—have learned to smile and nod and look as if they enjoy your company. And that, of course, is a part of a person's behavioral adaptation, their socialization. You pretend. The best way to see an individual's color, however, is to observe them when they think nobody is watching. Try to find the person in a situation where he or she has no reason to adapt.

The best advice I can give you is to be bright and alert when you meet new people. Don't just stare into space when you meet people or stand there with your mind elsewhere. If you're mingling at a party, pay attention to what people say. Stop hoping to bump into someone more interesting. Be present. Be there. Listen, reflect, and try to judge what sort of person you have in front of you. You'll learn lots by having your antennae out.

Now and then, I meet people who say that they don't want to do any of that. They refuse to divide people up into some system. They say it's wrong to analyze and pigeonhole people. Instead, they prefer to rely on what one might call their "gut feeling."

You can do that too. In fact, it's probably what most of us do!

Einstein's Definition of Madness

The main reason behind our lack of awareness of others is, I believe, convenience. A lot of people simply can't be bothered to learn what makes other people tick. It's far too arduous to really digest these insights. And in the worst case, you might realize you need to change your own behavior. It's a hell of an effort! So the easiest way out is to say that you follow your "gut feeling."

Whose feelings? Your own, of course. You commit the cardinal error of using yourself as the starting point. That is *not* the definition of social competence.

Let's say that you need some electric work done in your house. You don't know very much about wiring, but you need to install a couple of new outlets. You go to an electrician who shows you how to do it. Now you run some new wiring and install them successfully. This newly acquired skill might not make you an electrician, but it does mean that you now know a bit more about electrical installations. If you want to move some outlets from one wall to another, you'll need to learn some more, so you go back to your specialist, who shows you what to do. And you move the outlet—now you know a bit more about how electricity works. It still doesn't make you an electrician, but you've greatly increased your understanding of how electrical work is done.

You can think about knowledge of the colors in the same way. You can't learn everything in one go, but if you are interested in the subject, you are going to get better at communication. Now I'm being a bit impudent, of course, but following your "gut feeling" is too simple. Anybody can do that. And that's exactly what creates so many conflicts around us. Far too few of us make the effort to think twice.

The more you observe, and the more you practice recognizing the different colors of the people around you, the better you will become at "reading" the nuances. Think of it like learning a new language. The more you practice, the better you're going to get. But don't forget that there are lots of "dialects" in this language!

Now back to the subheading: what does Einstein have to

do with all this? Well . . . Einstein said that if you repeat the same thing time after time and expect a different result, then you're actually crazy. So forget your "gut feeling," and start becoming more observant. Particularly of your boss!

So What Can You Learn from How Your Boss Behaves?

That bosses function just like everybody else. They have positive and negative sides. We might understand their personality right away, or it might take some time to figure out what makes them tick. Even though your boss is ultimately responsible for ensuring that communication happens smoothly, you can also help things along.

Sometimes you feel as if the boss has stepped on your toes. They were stupid and said something too abrupt or even too harsh. But perhaps we're talking about a Red boss who didn't allow themselves the necessary time to soften their wording to get the message across more gently. Of course, that doesn't excuse the impolite conduct, but if you understand the intention behind a particular behavior, you may find it less upsetting.

A tip: observe your immediate boss very closely during the coming week. How does he or she go about things, communicate, talk, and give instructions and feedback? Make a (secret) note of what you observe and try to draw some conclusions from what you have seen. Many of the patterns you discover can most likely be explained by what color(s) the boss has in their profile.

Now you've got a good foundation to build on.

{ 6 }

Why You Sometimes Feel Stressed at Work

What does it mean that the majority of the people we meet have two colors? Some behaviors become more balanced. The Red boss with Yellow in their profile becomes a little "softer" in their approach and not quite such a pain for those around them; if Red is combined with a bit of Blue, they become more likely to stop and consider the details.

When combined with Red, the Yellow boss becomes slightly more concrete, but together with Green they become calmer and more intuitive.

The Green boss in combination with Yellow becomes more open and finds it easier to absorb new ideas, and in combination with Blue will become more introverted.

The analytical Blue becomes softer and more accepting when paired with Green, but in combination with Red slightly harder and in more of a hurry.

After my lectures I often get questions and reactions from the public.

The Reds are completely inhuman, aren't they?

The Yellows are awful, they never shut up!
Green people just seem so horrrribly lazy . . .
Those frozen Blue types almost scare me!

That type of comment says more about the person expressing it than about the actual behavior in question. It would be a good idea for all of them to be more observant.

Unfortunately, when we judge and appraise someone's behavior, we are often comparing it to our own. It's probably impossible to completely avoid using yourself as a basic measure. But with knowledge and insight we can become better at understanding the thoughts of others.

No behavior profile is more right or wrong than another. When you see a behavior that you don't understand, remember this:

Just because you're right, it doesn't necessarily follow that your boss is wrong.

But when communication fails, stress is ready to pounce.

When You Feel Inadequate

The most common stress factor at work is probably the feeling of inadequacy. If you completed ninety-seven work tasks during a tough week and still have three left on your desk—which do you think about in the car on your way home on Friday evening?

Do you congratulate yourself for having managed ninety-seven things, or do you agonize about the three you didn't deal with? If you're like most people, then you'll know the answer: the three that didn't get done will be whirling around in your head all the way home. Those tasks will be on your mind all weekend. In the worst-case scenario, you're going to spend forty-eight hours NOT doing them. There's probably a reason why those particular tasks were left until last. But stress is often the feeling of having too much to do and too little time to do it. There simply isn't enough time.

However, it's not always about not having enough time. Sometimes you're just bad at prioritizing, or you're a muddler who never finishes anything. Sometimes, the demands you make on yourself are completely unreasonable.

If you're really unlucky, your boss will be sending you constant emails on Saturday and Sunday (with the excuse that nobody asked you to open your email during the weekend). This doesn't make it any easier—these digital tools have undoubtedly tripped us up. It has become too easy to reach us. The French were the first to forbid bosses to send emails outside of office hours. Let's see if more countries follow that example.

If you're under a lot of pressure and feel burdened by high expectations, you can feel stressed even if you're not really short of time. The pressure, the demands, and the expectations create stress and can make you feel sad, be powerless to act, have difficulty sleeping, or feel aches and pains in your body. And sometimes you do actually need to talk with your boss.

Different People React Differently to Stress

That heading is logical. But have you thought about exactly *how* differently people react under stress? It can sometimes be linked to our colors. Different colors can experience the same event in different ways, and the same person can experience similar events differently on different occasions. It partly depends on the day and how you are feeling. If you've had plenty of rest and are feeling good, then you'll consider a tough work week with a long to-do list a stimulating challenge. But if you're tired and feeling low, you might experience the same week as simply miserable.

How does your communication style—your *color*—influence your stress? The short answer is that it doesn't really say very much about your stress threshold. I've met all sorts of people who have suffered occupational burnout. But your communication profile does say something about what stresses you out and how you will probably react to stress.

Do you know what stresses you? Are you aware of how you tend to react when the pressure gets to be too much? Most of us aren't aware of our behavior patterns under stress. When things get crazy, we tend to focus on how to get things done, not on how we're broadcasting that stress to others.

The Most Stressful Thing Is . . . Your Boss

In the previous chapter we talked about your boss's colors, but you should also take a look at your own. They can provide clues as to why you experience stress. And besides, if you can understand where the stress comes from, then you can always discuss it with your boss. If you understand what your primary stress factors are, you can make sure you don't fall into that trap unnecessarily. You can communicate earlier when something is going to become a problem. If you have a good boss, they'll help you. If you have an incompetent boss, that person might very well be what causes your stress. There are studies that show that your boss has an extremely large influence on your general well-being. And it's my personal conviction that bad leadership is the reason behind many cases of burnout.

If we look at leadership, we can see interesting patterns. It's evident that your immediate boss affects you on an everyday basis. If they do their job well, it will motivate you; if they do it badly, it can smother your motivation.

Badly executed leadership can have serious effects on the well-being of staff, or what is called the "psychosocial environment in the workplace." If the boss is exceptionally incompetent, this can trigger physical stress reactions.

Red Stress: Close to the boiling point

If you are primarily Red, these can be things that make you stressed:

- Not being involved in the decision-making process
- Not being challenged sufficiently
- Not achieving any results
- Time-wasting and general inefficiency
- Routine work
- Not being in control
- Being asked to lower your voice

The problem Reds have with stress is that it leads to "less than charming" (read: *rather brusque*) behavior. You blame others.

Since the Red person is often surrounded by a whole crowd of idiots, it's easy for them to point the finger at scapegoats.

And they tend to be very outspoken when they want to dump a load of crap on somebody because something went wrong. Red people have high standards for themselves, and they expect a lot from their boss. They can be very demanding and vocal under pressure.

If you are Red, then you are probably afraid of being used. Since you're aware of your diligence, you may find it irritating if somebody tries to persuade you to do lots of extra work. Why don't they ask someone else?

This is actually a bit complicated. Being Red, you also lose energy if you aren't challenged. You get bored. Without fail, passivity follows, and you don't focus on what you need to do. You can get stuck in a situation that's hard to break out of.

Routine work is a struggle. After all, you want to keep moving forward, and you don't want to have to busy yourself with everyday nonsense that's tiresome and doesn't lead anywhere. I don't know if that applies to you, but a lot of Reds are pretty hopeless when it comes to details, and they probably know it. Somebody else ought to deal with the dull routine work, since you Reds think you have a better view of the big picture.

If you feel that you lack the mandate to act independently, problems can arise. Not being able to take part in decision-making is something that most Reds find very difficult. Partly because you think you have better ideas and partly because you think that you simply ought to be in charge of this project.

Wanting to have control over others might seem to be a less-than-flattering trait, but that too lies within the scope of Red behavior. The Red's need to be in control can be comprehensive. This isn't about controlling details and facts, because they can be rather careless about that. They want to control the people around them. What those people do, what they *don't* do; *how* they do it or don't do it. Without that control, the Red can become frustrated. A lack of results is also very difficult for Reds. And everyday inefficiency is just as bad. When it comes to communication, the worst thing I can do is to tell the Red to cool it or to lower their voice. That will make them angry.

Or if I tell the Red speed demon to calm down, ease up on the stress, to do . . . nothing for a while. Incredibly stressful! There's nothing more frustrating for a Red than inactivity; while others want to relax during the weekend to recharge, the Red will zoom through their free time and return to work full of energy on Monday after all they've done.

A skillful leader understands this. And realizes what it can lead to. A bad leader becomes irritated and goes head-on against the Red's nature, trying to dampen it and totally wasting the potential energy that's there.

Stress ought to be kept at manageable levels; as a Red you are, of course, going to make it quite clear to those around you if things have got out of hand. And others are going to get a taste of your bad mood. Not only your boss.

But there's a remedy for this. You can liberate a little of that stress and de-escalate the situation.

Apart from simply pulling yourself together, you might need to take a quick break, go home, and do something physical. A stint down at the gym, or going for a run. That usually helps, and when you come back the stress has blown away.

Physical activity is superb for a Red person. Think about whether it would work for you.

Yellow Stress: Up in the stratosphere

If you are primarily Yellow, these stress factors will feel more familiar to you:

- Being invisible or ignored
- Feeling that your boss has no confidence in you
- Boring and run-of-the-mill work tasks
- Being isolated from the group
- Statements like *You need to start taking things more seriously*
- Haggling over small things
- Public criticism

Many Yellows are transformed into grumpy small children when they become stressed. Not you, of course, but other Yellows can be really irritating when something goes wrong. Some of them can stay angry for a long time once they get stressed, so you need to keep your eyes as open as you can. In the worst cases, they'll assert themselves even more than usual. Their egos mean that they can't refrain from puffing themselves up to compensate for the fact that they're feeling down. Perhaps you have a colleague like that!

Yellow people have an underlying fear of being socially rejected or of not being liked. Since they are relationship-oriented people, it's important to be "one of the gang." Being socially accepted is a determining factor for whether the Yellow will feel comfortable at their workplace. Being ignored or bypassed is frustrating. When that happens, the Yellows can start acting in a less flexible manner. They want to feel important. Not having somebody to talk to can really stress a Yellow individual. The Yellows want to have someone to tell their stories to. They are always seeking connection.

This means that many Yellows actively look for increased attention. This could be through ordinary conversations, but also via telephone, text, or Facebook. If nobody sees them, they'll be convinced that they're of no importance in the world. Then there's a risk that they'll compensate by looking for more attention—using up all the oxygen in the room, talking as they inhale, and taking up all the space during meetings and in their relationships. A really wound-up Yellow person will put themselves in the center of just about every situation and involve everybody in their problems.

Even ordinary skepticism and pessimism is dreadfully dull. The Yellows want to have fun, hear good news, and generally have a nice time. If somebody digs their feet in and uses (what the Yellow sees as) negative terms, then everything can grind to a halt for the Yellow. Humor and fun and games are important ingredients. If laughing at your workplace is viewed as "not being serious," then you're going to feel extremely restricted.

Just like with the Reds, the Yellows can experience routine, focused, and supervised work schedules as decidedly negative. They see these structures as limitations, and in most cases consider them to be bad news. You Yellows are free souls who need a bit of space to "spread your wings." After all, built-in spontaneity is the Yellow's real strength. If your surroundings smother you, you might start exhibiting an extremely bad attitude towards everyone around you.

Even though as a Yellow you aren't necessarily afraid of

conflict, or at any rate not like a Green is, you won't welcome incessant confrontations. That creates imbalances and it damages relations. Thoughts like "nobody likes me" can easily take root, and this will of course have a negative influence on efficiency.

For a boss, it can be quite a challenge to deal with a really stressed Yellow person. If you've got a good boss, then they'll know that Yellows assert themselves and talk too much under stress. Optimism that turns into an unrealistic perspective isn't always what the organization needs. But smart bosses also know that it's useless to ask Yellows to be quiet. It would be like cutting off your oxygen supply. The trick is to get the best from this happy volcano of ideas. And that demands commitment.

Sometimes you need to take command of your own stress. Change the pattern. Make sure you do something that's fun. Anything at all. Arrange an activity at work, an after-work get-together perhaps—anything that will distract you from what's boring and stressful. Make sure you socialize, relax, laugh, fool around. The more you're together with others, the happier you'll be. Then you'll be able to do your job so much better.

Green Stress: Deep down in the abyss

The Greens function differently from all the other types when it comes to stress. And you might find some of the things on this list stressful if you're Green:

- A general feeling of insecurity
- Loose ends at work

- Too many people too close by
- Constant and inexplicable changes
- Conflict—of course
- Being forced to be the center of attention
- All forms of criticism—especially public criticism

All of these make you Greens feel really awful. Some more than others. The challenge is that this stress might not show on the outside. Green people are delighted to hide their feelings. When you're stressed, you are prudent, your body language is formal and stiff, and you can even display a total lack of feeling. You are cold and unresponsive even towards people you usually care quite a lot about. You don't like this at all, but now we're talking stress.

Stress makes Green people more insecure than usual, and you're afraid of making mistakes. This could be at work, but also at home. And you also often blame yourself for the situation and can end up in a total deadlock. *I'm so stupid!*

A lot of Greens get bogged down in stubbornness or pigheadedness and frustrate people around them by refusing to change anything. Even when they see that a situation is no longer workable, they can refuse to act. This can seem really strange, but Green stubbornness takes over and stops them from doing anything.

Green people are afraid of losing their stability and security. Knowing what the status quo is and being able to move within it is—in theory—an absolute necessity. Green people rarely appreciate change—and they particularly dislike rapid ones. In fact, everything that happens unexpectedly is extremely stressful. Does that ring a bell?

The greatest cause of stress, however, is probably conflict. If you're Green, you will sense potential conflict just about everywhere. Every little setback, however small, can lead to conflict. Even a ten-second squabble about which sort of coffee is the best can be enough to get you to start re-evaluating your relationship with the other person. A wrong look from somebody or an unguarded comment can seriously alter your opinion of them.

Everybody should agree about everything all the time. But since that's an impossible utopia, you Greens want to be in a team where everyone at least agrees to sweep tricky issues under the rug. If there's a person in the group who incessantly raises difficult questions and problems, the other Greens will start to freeze that person out. After all, who wants to work with a troublemaker?

When people feel less secure, they lose energy. When the boss rearranges the team, everything gets completely muddled. And ending up in the "wrong" team (i.e., with people that you for one reason or another don't appreciate) will undoubtedly stir up feelings. Under the surface, that is; as usual, it won't be visible on the outside.

How does your boss deal with this? Does your boss see your natural loyalty, or only your passive opposition? Really smart bosses have a natural feel for how all this can be handled. They know that they need to listen to you Greens, otherwise you're going to be reticent and get caught in obstinacy and sulkiness.

And that is rarely good news.

But the good news is that you can assist here too. You can ask your boss to make fewer demands of you, at least temporarily. Get yourself a bit of "dead time" such as gardening, sleep, or some other type of relaxation. This could mean planning a really calm weekend without too many activities or finding a good book by your favorite author that will take you two days to read. You don't really want to do anything at all. And that's fine as long as it doesn't threaten your entire everyday life. At least until the stress has eased up. And then you'll be your old self again.

Blue Stress: Close to absolute zero (−459.67°F)

You thought the Blue folks were imperturbable, didn't you? With their (in some cases) stone faces like Easter Island statues, there's nothing that can get them off balance, right? But there is. And if you're mainly Blue, the following stressors will seem relevant:

- Having your competence questioned, even though you really are an expert
- Spontaneous (i.e., not well-thought-through) decisions made by your boss
- All types of risky behavior and long shots
- Constant, unplanned interruptions among your colleagues
- Stupid mistakes made by others
- Being called a "stickler for details" when you're just explaining how the regulations work
- Emotional people who talk about personal things

So what's involved when you, as a Blue, become stressed? The simplest way to describe this is to say that you become even more Blue. You can become exaggeratedly pessimistic. Oh yes. The world can be enveloped in total darkness, and you might even struggle with depression. Indifference is common, and you might find that nothing holds your interest any more. Armageddon is upon you. We are lost.

You can be unbearably finicky. You slam on the emergency brake, because now there's no time to make irritating mistakes. The people around you can handle some criticism. You are going to point out every single tiny mistake you notice. Others will likely think you are an insufferable know-it-all.

Blue people hate criticism of their work. Since you are extremely conscientious when it comes to quality, you will have serious problems if somebody hints that what you've done isn't up to the standard. Or that you're wrong about a particular issue. A whole array of interesting defense mechanisms will pop up. If you're fairly Blue, general irrationality and emotional outcomes are not for you. That sort of thing is hard to deal with and leads to stress. Quite often you simply don't know what's happening. Rational thinking does not explain sloppy sentimentality.

You can go along with logical and well-thought-through arguments, but if unplanned changes pop up out of nowhere and disturb the agenda, they won't be welcomed one little bit. You won't be able to concentrate anymore and won't want to have any part of it.

Risks are something distasteful to be handled with appropriate suspicion. Even if it's possible to work out the benefits of a new approach, you see it as a risk. And that creates stress since you are no longer in control of the situation, which is in itself a risk.

In fact, the same applies to all forms of unpredictability. This shouldn't be confused with the Green's unwillingness to change; it's more about the need to be in control. To avoid not knowing, being uninformed. It always feels better to be in the know, in control. You simply want to be sufficiently well prepared. If management's new proposal had been included in the annual report, that might have been okay.

Another thing that can be extremely frustrating for Blues is people who break the rules and ignore regulations. Since you would personally never even dream of doing that, this can often lead to serious clashes. Rule-breakers are looked upon with disapproval, and you can spend more time trying to control what other people do than you spend carrying out your own job.

If your boss is observant, then they'll understand how you function in such contexts. They will understand that when you are under stress, you can slide over from a negative attitude to open pessimism.

Bad bosses just stand there and nag at the Blue person to hurry up. To think positively. To accept the situation and get on with it. Ugh! Not good leadership. Let's hope that your boss is better than that.

What you actually need is total seclusion to have time and space to think. Since you want to analyze the situation and understand how things are connected, you need time to do just that. Ask for some extra space, and then you'll get back to your usual (fairly fussy) self in the end. But if you fall too deep down into the blackness of despair, you might need to ask for more direct help. Book a meeting with your boss and work through your list of possible measures to deal with the problem.

What Happens Now?

Did you discover what your stress factors are based on the combination of your colors? Did you gain any insights?

My recommendation to you is: accept that you, just like anyone else, can suffer stress. It isn't your fault. It's simply a consequence of the world we happen to live in. But it can be valuable to know what triggers your particular stress reaction. Because then you can predict and understand it better, which makes for a considerably better balance in life.

The worst thing that can happen is that you live with one or more stress factors for a long time, without doing anything about them. That's what leads to occupational burnout.

Do you see a pattern in your work and stress that you could discuss with your boss? Because the best thing you could do is to talk about it. Good bosses see these signals early on; bad bosses don't. You will always be expected to carry out your job and take responsibility for your work, but you can also ask for reasonable conditions to allow you to do that.

Your boss is no doubt a really excellent person, albeit not a mind reader. They might not know what causes you stress, but if you yourself know, then there's at least something to talk about. Make sure you book that meeting now.

{ 7 }

Why You Definitely Want a Red Boss

How to Get Your Boss to Really Listen

There's something wrong with that heading.

Yes, what did we say earlier in the book? Who is responsible for ensuring that communication works well? My opinion is that the boss has a greater responsibility, but that doesn't mean that you don't have any responsibility at all. You have a lot of influence on how communication happens. The idea that *it's completely the boss's job to ensure that everything works; that's what they get paid for. It's their job and not mine* is far too simplistic.

When you say that it's not your responsibility to ensure good communication, you're turning yourself into a powerless victim. You'll be caught in a negative situation. You decrease your ability to influence your situation. Bit by bit, any hope of change withers away.

If you hand over all the responsibility to your boss, you'll always be able to blame the lack of results on them. But you must also realize who is hurt most by this in the long run. If your boss doesn't understand you, you can choose to call them an idiot. Or you can try to get a grip on the situation yourself. Sure, the boss ought to understand better. It would be ideal if the boss had the right tools to handle every situation all the time. But if that isn't the case—what can *you* do about it?

If you, for example, really want to change your workplace, you're going to be obliged to work with the only element you are in complete control of—yourself.

"But It's My Right!"

A few years ago, a new law came into practice in Sweden that obliged drivers to stop at pedestrian crossings. Pedestrians had the right of way. It was probably a good law. But if you ask the traffic safety authorities today about crossing the street, they recommend (and this is rather frightening) that you don't use pedestrian crossings when you cross the street! The reason is that more accidents take place there. In fact, the accident statistics show that the number of accidents on pedestrian crossings has increased since the law came into power. However crazy that sounds, it's true.

My own interpretation, which has some support in the official studies too, is this: pedestrians have handed over responsibility for their own safety to drivers. They step right out into the street at the marked pedestrian crossing and assume that the drivers will stop because the law says they must.

You get my point? If it's in your own interest, then get involved and take responsibility for improving things. Everybody—not least you yourself—gains from that in the long run. Having said that, the question is: how do you "reach" your boss, depending on their color?

You Want a Red Boss Most of All

According to statistics, the proportion of Red people increases the higher up you go in an organization. So are Reds better bosses? Unfortunately, it isn't quite so simple, but the Red behavior does indeed include some qualities that make it suitable for certain positions.

Red bosses are good at being objective since they are task-oriented. This means that they think rationally and can set feelings aside, for example, when they make decisions. And sometimes you need someone who keeps a cool head, right? While a lot of people can dilly-dally for weeks, Red bosses will always decide something.

They're also good bosses because they always make things happen. They never sit still; their greatest strength lies in their desire to move forward. An organization that needs somebody who stands up for new ideas and keeps up a head of steam will find it very useful to have a Red boss. Nobody is going to die of boredom, at any rate.

Their clarity also makes the Reds good bosses. It's often said that the boss should not be vague. In general, people hate it when they don't know what the boss thinks. That rarely happens with a Red boss. They say what they think and make it clear what direction you're going. Perhaps they could use a few more words sometimes, but there will be no shortage of clear and distinct instructions.

Nor does the Red boss suffer from a bit of opposition. It's

only a minor problem if there isn't total agreement; it's a pity if there are some people who don't appreciate their direct style, but they can live with it. Opposition and even conflict can actually fuel them with more energy.

To put it bluntly: the Red bosses can tolerate a punch to the nose better than the other colors. And even if they take quite a beating, they'll soon bounce back. If the boss is on the side of her team—which of course we hope they are—that's a real asset. The Red boss will be a strong protector against anything that threatens the team. The Red boss is always ready for battle.

So How Do You Get Through to These Alpha Personalities?

This is a good time to remind you of what I wrote a couple of pages ago: you too have a responsibility to ensure that you have a working communication with your boss. When you've read this section, I will remind you again.

The answer to the question in the heading is simple. Act a bit Red yourself.

Stick strictly to the point

Red people don't have much time, and Red *bosses* have even less time. They are also lacking something spelled p-a-t-i-e-n-c-e. And what's the consequence? Overlong expositions that aren't terribly interesting make the Red boss lose their concentration faster than you can say supersonic. You don't need a megaphone to be heard. But, like my wife says when I babble on too long: "so many words."

The boss is busy, with a calendar that is crammed full and overflowing, and everything that steals time away from those things needs to be extremely important to warrant their attention and time.

When you think you've shortened your message or presentation to what is absolutely necessary—shorten it a bit more. Even if you're contemplating giving some background on why, for example, a particular project has failed—don't start there. Start with the actual point.

The project has failed.

Now you've got the attention you want. Red bosses know when you don't go straight to the point. They realize that there is trouble coming. Start with the final point. It could be: *I want us to choose alternative C. I need a new computer. I don't feel comfortable in my job. I need some time off.*

You get the idea. Say it like it is, and say it directly.

Be professional

Try to look like you know what you're doing. Stick to the subject and the agenda. If you've set aside thirty minutes to go through A, B, and C—do that. But avoid everything else. Things will go quicker, and quick meetings are good meetings. Your boss will want to know if there's a problem, and if there's a solution. If there aren't any problems, you don't need a solution, right?

Red bosses don't go for empty talk. Once a subject has been dealt with, they simply move on to the next task. And can you get much more effective than that? Look at what needs to be done, do it, and then close the case. Simple.

That is professional. If your boss sees that you behave in the same way, then you'll gain a reputation as someone who gets the job done. And most bosses like that, regardless of their color.

Prepare yourself *before*, not *during* the meeting

You can't simply stroll in and start saying whatever comes into your mind about any old thing. Sure, it can be entertaining to hear a little anecdote from last summer. But your Red boss is not going to appreciate it. Red people in general, and Red bosses in particular, will be irritated if you waste their time.

So prepare yourself thoroughly. Get everything ready in advance and make sure all your papers are in order. If you are working digitally, open all the documents on your computer and make sure they are arranged so that you know exactly where they are. You might be asked questions—probably not about details, but even so—and if a document is missing that will automatically lead to problems. If you are forced to search for a piece of information, your boss will waste seconds of their time.

A Red boss might pick up their cell phone and start reading an email, sending a text, or even making a phone call—or simply leave the room while you fumble with all your badly organized documents. That is bad news.

So be sure you are very well prepared. Even if 95 percent of your material is never going to be used, you will come off as a person who knows what they're doing.

Focus on results and targets

While you are concise and stick to the agenda, it's also not a bad idea to actually focus on the content of the above heading. You've already realized that your boss is task-oriented. From now on, you aren't going to ask too much about the people on the team and what they experience or feel.

But your boss isn't really interested in the entire project—they're mainly concerned with the end product, i.e., the result. To start with, you'll set a goal, and that can be an ambitious goal. You don't need to inflate the possibilities of the new product or the new workflow to stratospheric proportions. That's more of a Yellow behavior, and Yellow bosses like it, but your Red boss does still believe in impossible goals ("impossible" = just takes a bit longer). So be prepared with a target in mind.

If you're talking with your boss about a course you want to take and you need his approval—talk about how the goal of the course will help you be a more effective worker. Do you need a new computer or a new cell phone or better software or sharper knives? Then explain that the goal is to be able to do your job better and quicker in the future.

But then we also have the question of the results. How did it go last time? Did we earn anything from proposal X? Did we gain from bringing in person Y to help? How do we improve the result? How do we become more profitable?

Not all Red bosses chase pennies. But the ones that do really go for it. And the result can be measured in different ways. It can also be about increasing the staff's comfort and well-being by X percent. Or by getting at least 3 points higher average value in future customer-satisfaction surveys. Or reducing waste. It can be about anything at all, but a Red boss wants to see results of some sort. Otherwise there's no point in making an effort, is there?

Don't take everything personally—for real

I don't know how many times I've had to explain that Red bosses are not actually angry—they just sound like they are. They tell it like it is, they don't sugarcoat, and they look you straight in the eye in a way that doesn't always feel comfortable. I have to admit that it's not always charming behavior.

Nobody wants a grumpy boss. But you need to look at the intention behind certain comments. If your Red boss sounds critical, it's because they don't try to soften the message, but you can at least count on honesty. Personally, I respect people with the ability to look at you straight and say something wasn't okay. There are far too many Swedes who simply clench their fists in their pockets. Sometimes we need to know the truth, even if it might be unpleasant to hear it.

Strong opinions, delivered loud and clear. Well, if you ask your boss how you're doing, you are going to hear it.

You could have done a bit better, if you'd done what I said.

Ouch! It was no fun to hear that. I would rather have heard that I'm a real asset to the team!

But look at what the words actually mean. It might very well be true that I *could* have gone further with the project if I'd done what the boss had said. At the back of our minds we know that is sometimes true. But—and this is important—sometimes the boss gets it wrong too. The method that they suggested wouldn't have worked. In that case, the only thing you need do is explain that you couldn't follow their suggestion because of factor X.

Nothing weird about that.

A lot of people make the mistake of never contradicting their Red boss. That is rarely a strategy that works. If you don't contradict them, they will interpret this as agreement. And your boss will think you are fully dedicated to doing a job you have never said "yes" to.

Conclusion: if you don't want to know what your boss actually thinks about you—don't ask. There is, of course, a risk that you'll find out anyway.

Was That All?

No, in fact it's not. It's not only about what you can do to get through to your Red boss; there are also a couple of things you actually ought to avoid—mainly for your own sake. So here are a few more tips.

These are things you should keep away from:

Don't waste time on nonsense

Red bosses don't appreciate it when somebody steals their time to talk about things that have nothing to do with the matter at hand. Anything that is not on the agenda is irritating to listen to. And the reaction will be immediate. If you stray from the subject, you will be met with a wrinkled brow and a sour look.

It's easy to fall into the trap. All you have to do is start the meeting by asking: "Did you see the game yesterday?"

No, your Red boss didn't see the game. He was reading

emails until nine at night. You should have been doing that too. Why weren't you working? And even if your boss did see the game, he didn't come to the meeting to talk about it. That's a lunchtime subject. Don't bring it up while you're working.

Making yourself understood

Your boss asks you: "Are you coming to the conference this fall?"

What are your alternatives in that situation? You can answer yes. Quite a good answer. It means you realized that it's important. You could also answer no. Not an answer that will be as welcome, but it's understandable at any rate.

But a lot of us are rather challenged when it comes to responding in a clear manner. A possible answer would be to express your thoughts on the subject out loud.

The conference? Oh yeah, that. You mean the one this fall? Okay, am I going to be there? Well, you know, conferences can be nice. It's on a Saturday, right? Oh dear, Saturdays are free time. I'll have to think about it. Maybe?

What does this mean? Your verbal diarrhea is extremely irritating. It's a bit like a "perhaps," but what is your boss going to do with such an answer? "Perhaps" is totally worthless. Better to say *no thank you* straight away (if that alternative is even there). If you whirl around too long, your boss might cross you off the list. Now you can't go at all.

All forms of buddy talk

You should build relationships at your workplace, of course. Absolutely. But not with the wrong people. There are some bosses who want to be friends with their staff, but they're not usually Red bosses. Sure, some of them might know somebody in the group from before, and then perhaps they might hang out in their free time. But don't count on becoming friends with your boss if you haven't grown up together.

I saw you at IKEA last Sunday!

No, no, no. You're simply wasting your time. He didn't see you anyway.

Anything that can be interpreted as flattery or obvious sucking-up will have the absolute opposite effect. If your boss sees you as a suck-up then you'll suddenly have more problems than you need.

The boss is not there to be pals with you. If you're asked about your summer vacation—fine. But make sure you do actually have that sort of relationship first. What your boss did last Christmas, or whether they're booking a summer cottage, or how things are going for their children in school, or where their partner works—that's private. Respect it.

Be clear about this: Red bosses are not stupid. They've learned the game. They smile and nod like everybody else when people socialize during working hours. But they don't like it. They want to get back to work. Remember that.

Pretend that you can find things in the chaos

It's not efficient if you can't find your papers or you show that there's no organization to what you do. If you find it hard to get organized—ask for help. Your Red boss isn't necessarily a control freak, but they'll appreciate it if you keep your papers in order.

Perhaps you're one of those people with a desk that looks like a bomb has exploded over it. You might try to convince yourself and everybody else that there's some order in the chaos and that you can find everything you want.

Your Red boss won't buy that. They'll think you are disorganized. Stop doing that, thank you.

Note, however—this is not about how things look. If you want to work on top of a garbage dump—go ahead. It's about you stealing time from more important things if you are not organized. The problem with being disorganized is that it takes longer to get things done. And since things are always a rush with a Red boss, it's best for you to know where you have everything and to be well prepared for the meeting that we spoke about earlier.

See that as a point in your best interests.

Hugging . . .

Well. We've begun to adopt an international culture even up here in cold Scandinavia.

Often it's extremely pleasant. Even we Swedes—cold and rather formal—have even learned that it isn't dangerous to touch each other.

Your Red boss would have a few reservations about that. You can of course do what you want, sure, give your boss a big hug when you've had a good day, do it! But bear in mind that might not be what your boss wants from a person they consider to be a strictly professional associate.

{ 8 }

Why You Should Hope for a Yellow Boss

There are quite a lot of Yellow bosses too. It's not hard to work out why. Leadership is a process of communication, and the Yellows are the smartest communicators. They're good at winning people over to their side. Skilled communicators who can make the most depressing news sound like a fantastic success. Who wouldn't want to follow such a person?

It's often claimed that *what* you say doesn't matter very much and that *how* you say something is what really matters. Various studies show slightly different results, but the actual meaning of the message is thought to have a less than 10 percent effect on the recipient; how you present it, about 30 percent; and the rest is related to what you look like as you do it.

Body language, that's what this is about.

And Yellow bosses really have the knack for sharing a message in such a way that you simply must listen. Their positive attitude, mood, and the lighthearted way they explain complicated processes means they are skillful at winning our confidence. Leadership is largely based on confidence and if we add to that the fact that the Yellow boss makes us feel good too . . . well, of course we're on board!

They are good salesmen too. They get ideas and are brilliant at convincing others that you just have to go ahead. And besides—Yellow behavior is based on inspiration. And who doesn't want to be inspired? There's something about the spark they have. The joy of doing things well. I've seen Yellow bosses conjure up inexplicable energy in people I've hardly ever seen get up out of their chair.

And another thing. They often want to be at the center of everything. They love being in the limelight. And you absolutely must have fun at work. Only a Yellow person could have come up with that phrase. Yellow bosses instinctively know that happy people do a better job than grumpy, dissatisfied ones. So they're always busy trying to maintain a good atmosphere in the workplace. They simply make us feel better.

So How Do We Get This Natural Entertainer to Stay Focused in the Meeting?

Gaining the attention of your Yellow boss isn't really that difficult. The challenge is keeping their attention. These people are decidedly extroverted. The effect is obvious: even if you're in the middle of a conversation with your Yellow boss, they will always be tuned in to the world around them. Their cell phone is just one moment away. But there are ways of retaining the focus of your Yellow boss. Here are a few tips:

Be warm and lovely

Okay, your Yellow boss is relationship-oriented to a maximum degree. Which means that even though they're your boss, relationships are just as important—if not more important—as ever. This person reacts to a bad atmosphere or aggressive attitude the same way a canary in a mine shaft reacts to invisible carbon monoxide. Even if your Yellow boss has taken a management course and learned that you should distinguish between what a person is like and the job they do, they'll definitely be influenced by what sort of relationship you have.

When you've stopped your Yellow boss in the hallway, it's smart to smile a lot. Show that you have friendly intentions. Unlike a Red boss, your Yellow boss needs to be liked. They do realize that it's impossible for everyone to like them all the time. The Yellows aren't stupid, but if you're happy, you'll have a good relationship with them. I don't mean that you have to keep your opinions about what isn't working to yourself, but be careful how you express them.

Make sure you emphasize your mutual interests. That will help your boss adopt a positive attitude. It's important that you don't cross the line and start sucking up to your boss, but I trust you know the limit. If you see a photo of a dog on the desk of your boss, you can talk about your own dog. If it's a cat, you'll just have to think up something. But if you have a furry pet at home—bring it into the conversation and see how your boss smiles all the wider. If the photo isn't a dog but a little yacht, then you once went out sailing. If it's a vintage car, then you've seen a similar one on some TV show years ago.

I think you get the idea. Build a bond between you. Cultivate the relationship.

Pretend that the sun is always shining

Yellow bosses don't like bad news. They would much rather hear that the sun is shining. All the time. *But*, you might be thinking, *it doesn't shine all the time. That isn't true.*

I know. But your Yellow boss wants to hear good news. Bad news is . . . well, bad. If you can adopt a positive attitude, then your Yellow boss will continue to listen to you. If they perceive you as irritable and grumpy, then they'll cover their ears. It's no fun to listen to somebody who is in a bad mood. Your boss will be immediately affected and might very well end up in a similarly bad mood if what you say sounds too negative.

Don't come with more problems—come with solutions.

Yet another Yellow comment. This might seem close to naïveté but Yellow bosses really don't want to hear about problems. They might suspect that there are problems, but they don't want to talk about them.

However, the solution is simple. All you need do is actually focus on how you could solve the problem. Say: *this isn't really working very well, but I think I've found a smart solution* . . . Don't even use the word "problem." Say something else. Say *challenge*. Say that *it didn't work out how you wanted it to*. But don't say *problem*.

And put forward a proposal for what you can do about the mess. Then you can ask your boss if you guys should go try the new lunch spot down the street.

Skip the nitty-gritty

Neither Red nor Yellow bosses are world champions when it comes to details. They paint the world with broad strokes of the brush and are good at seeing issues in their entirety. This means that they can be insensitive about the value of details. Some Yellow bosses I've met are completely blind to small things. They just find them boring. So don't fall into the trap of giving loads of background about what you have to say. Remember that the thoughts of your Yellow boss are mostly in the future and at a general level.

If your boss asks what time it is—don't tell them how a clock is constructed.

One of my favorite examples of this is a conversation I overheard between an IT technician and his decidedly Yellow and extremely visionary boss. The technician spent a long time explaining that he had acquired a new weather station at home and could now read the temperature down to a hundredth of a degree. He was absolutely fascinated by his new gadget and delivered exact information on the average temperature the last few days. Then he remembered that he had a listener, so he asked his boss what the temperature was where he lived.

The answer?

"Winter."

It was cold outside. What more was there to say?

Allow social round-about-talk

While a Red boss is provoked by too much socializing, with a Yellow boss this is critical if you want to get anywhere at all with them. Talking football, lawns, digital cameras, or what the next big holiday destination is going to be is a very good way to keep your boss in a good mood. But again—Yellow bosses can also adapt to a strict agenda, but that little bit of softening up in the beginning of a conversation gets them in a good mood. And you'd rather have a happy boss than an irritated one, wouldn't you agree?

Of course, this can go too far, but if you keep it at a reasonable level, this is a great opportunity.

And—a piece of good advice—your Yellow boss will want to have their say. So let them talk. It's a good way of retaining their attention. Let your boss tell their own anecdote first. Not only are you being polite, but you will also be appreciated for being so attentive to your boss.

That's it. Now it's time to get to work.

Now You Know Everything About Your Yellow Boss

Well, not really. There are a few other things you need to keep track of. And these are things that you definitely must stay away from. Just like with Red behavior, Yellow bosses react rather strongly to certain things.

Here are some tips to keep in mind to avoid unnecessarily irritating your Yellow boss.

Imitate a robot

Perhaps this isn't the biggest problem—I'll admit that. But I did mention earlier that Yellow bosses like to feel their relationship with you functions well. If you don't show any feelings they are going to start wondering if everything is okay. So show a little warmth and openness and things should function better between you.

An example: if your Yellow boss comes back from her fall vacation and tells a long story about how she almost died when she fell off a stepladder because she and her husband were doing some renovation work at home, and then concludes by asking what you did during your break, you are going to be regarded as rather dull if you answer with a stone face: *I kept working on my ten-year plan.*

Criticizing your boss with others nearby

Typically, it's the boss who gives feedback—positive or negative—to their staff. But even bosses are people, and sometimes the need arises to give feedback to your boss. If your boss is Yellow, then there's a simple but decisive rule to follow.

If your feedback is positive, it doesn't matter if the whole world is listening. Your Yellow boss will suck up the praise with swelling pride. And fine, I think you should be able to praise even your boss. If you can turn on the internal loudspeaker system at the same time—why not? All you need is a plan for what you can say to your colleagues about your prank. They're going to think you are being a real suck-up, so you'll have to find a balance here.

But if the feedback is negative, then you should absolutely deliver it in private. Few, if any, Yellow people appreciate being criticized when others can hear it. It hurts their ego, and it doesn't look good. And if it's about the boss, then it's even worse. There are going to be problems with your relationship if you charge ahead.

Make sure you're sitting behind a closed door and remind yourself to smile now and then, even if the conversation is serious. And by all means suggest a solution to resolve what you think isn't working between you. Show that you want to actively be a part of the solution. If this is during your annual review, and you get to that awkward section asking about how your manager is supporting you, you might think you can just say it like it is. Oops, beware.

A clarification: even Yellow bosses must be able to listen to criticism. I am definitely not saying otherwise. This is just about *the way* of sharing that criticism.

Don't waste their life on theoretical discussions

Yellow people are interested in feelings and experiences. They want to talk about the future, they are visionary, and they sometimes don't manage to keep their feet on the ground. If you find yourself in a conversation that is far too fact based or much too theoretical, you'll lose the attention of your boss.

Details and fussiness about decimal points are paralyzingly boring. Your boss will mentally log out and start thinking about something else. Perhaps they'll even start talking about something else or pick up their cell phone and start playing with it instead of listening to you. Regardless of how important whatever you're saying actually is.

Remember that Yellow people aren't the very best listeners in the universe. Adapt your message accordingly.

Forgetting to laugh when we're all having so much fun . . .

Now we're getting close to going over the line and simply being overly ingratiating and sucking up; I thought a long time about whether I should include this heading. In the end I chose to use it, since I genuinely believe in the value of understanding other people.

While Red bosses can get angry if they think you are trying to curry favor, Yellow bosses don't find it problematic if their staff have the sense to, for example, laugh at the right place. This is more about how you yourself look at it. To clamp your mouth shut when your boss tells a joke—sometimes clumsily, that's quite likely, and the context may be totally unsuitable—is always an option. I'm only saying that you don't have anything to gain from that. Your boss is going to think you are stiff and boring. And there's always a risk that they'd rather talk with one of their more amiable staff members. Yes, we're in a grey area, I agree, and this has nothing to do with the job.

Many of us sometimes perceive Yellow behavior as somewhat immature, but we have to take the bad with the good. Do you need to laugh your head off every time your boss says something meant to be amusing? Of course not. You can simply make your own choice on this issue. Perhaps you think, *I'm going to protect my integrity.* I respect you for that. The choice is entirely yours. If you can manage to produce a hearty burst of laughter, it won't, however, harm your relationship.

{9}

Why a Green Boss Is the Best Option

In my experience, there is a particular pattern when it comes to Green bosses. This is a bit complicated since Green behavior is really about so much more than just leadership. As you've seen earlier, the Greens would rather be one of the gang than somebody who sticks out and has the spotlight pointed at them. They can find it rather challenging to make decisions, and they don't always appreciate change. In addition, Green bosses have more or less the same problems with conflict as most Greens.

But they are, at the same time, warmer than all the Red bosses, and that's a quality that many people seek in a boss. The Green trait feels more human and more caring, and they are more likely to do things for others. They'll remember the birthdays of their staff—the birthdays of their partner; for heaven's sake, I once had a boss who remembered when my cat had its birthday!

Lots of people find this character trait appealing, and that is understandable.

Besides, the team comes before the Green's ego. Your Green boss will try to protect their group. Note: *try*. It's by no means certain that they'll succeed since this can sometimes lead to a conflict with bosses higher up in the organization. But they'll do the best they can.

Then we're on the subject of *change*.

Green behavior strives for stability. If you feel the same, then you and your Green boss will share an important component in how you see your work. You will basically want the same thing. Since Green behavior is by far the most common, a lot of people want a boss who isn't planning on completely reorganizing everything every six months. So that makes for a pretty good match.

Within certain types of organizations and departments, Green leadership can flourish, while in other places problems will arise during the first week.

Now and then I'm asked why Green people should be bosses at all, considering these qualities. Leadership involves, for example, dealing with conflict. And carrying out change.

The answer probably lies in that even Green people have a certain need for power. An underlying individualistic driving force is often at the core of the Green behavior that gives us a person who wants to have influence.

Over the years I've also asked many Green bosses why they took the job. The answers vary, but they often say that it was hard to say no, that they were promised nothing would really change—they'd still be one of the gang—and sometimes there was money on the table. We'll have to accept that Green people are just as susceptible to temptation as any of us.

And sometimes I think that the Green didn't manage to get away in time when the question came up.

So How Do You Get Your Comfortable Boss to Make Those Unpleasant but Oh-So-Important Decisions?

Just like before—how can you accommodate their behavior type? If you can meet them halfway, the adjustment won't be so dramatic.

Here are my suggestions on how you can get there and create flexible cooperation with your Green boss. And how you can help your boss make decisions, which can be one of the tougher challenges you'll face.

See the person behind the title

Just like with the Yellow bosses, there is a strong focus on relationships. The difference here is that while the Yellow boss simply goes to somebody else if things are not working between you, the Green boss might feel bad if they think you've fallen out. Naturally, the well-being of your boss is not your responsibility, but it's in your interest to have a content boss, isn't it?

This means that you should focus just as much on your boss as a person. If you happen to have different opinions on an issue, you shouldn't simply say "you're the boss, so you get to make the decisions." That isn't what Green bosses want. They want to be seen as one of the work team, one of the gang. They won't get on their high horse, and they would never dream of playing the boss card if you have a different opinion about something. They will want to solve the issue by mutual agreement. And they care about what you think in this matter. They want you to feel good about what's been decided.

Treat your Green boss a bit like your friend. Ask how they're feeling, if they're stressed, if there are things you can help with. If you get the vibe that they're having a tough time at home, perhaps you should listen a while. That will create a good relationship and strengthen the basis for collaboration between you.

Or even simpler: remember that it isn't a boss sitting on the other side of the desk—it's a person.

Restrain yourself as much as you can

When you interact with your Green boss, you should take it easy. If, for example, you have a suggestion for change or improvement—calm down. Present your arguments one by one and talk it over as if you were planning a vacation.

Be observant of their body language. Green behavior often involves hiding your feelings. But the body isn't fooled. Even if the words sound nice and friendly, you can see whether their arms are crossed, a brow is wrinkled, etc.

The Green boss relies on their feelings. They listen a lot to their inner signals and also try to understand your mood. This takes time. The issue at hand can take a back seat for a while, that's a natural for Green behavior. The best you can do is play along and let the process proceed at its own leisurely pace.

What do you think?

It might seem puzzling, but it's not guaranteed that your Green boss will express their own opinion. Green bosses can be very cautious in this respect. Perhaps not as much as Blue people, but you won't get to know the opinions of your Green boss just like that. There are lots of reasons for this, but the best thing you can do is ask questions.

Ask open-ended questions, i.e., questions that can't be answered with a simple yes or no.

Instead of asking: *Can we do this?*—which requires a decision on the part of your boss—you can ask: *What advantages do you see with my proposal?*

Instead of saying: *I need an answer right away—can we start?*, you should ask: *What do you think of the possibility of starting the project this week?*

Now you're talking about your idea in a completely neutral way. No decision is demanded; nobody is asking the boss for a specific standpoint. You'll have a sensible conversation about various possibilities. And there's no point trying to exert pressure and demand an immediate decision. If your boss doesn't feel like it, you won't get a decision. If you start stirring things up, you might be seen as a troublemaker, and then you'll have made problems for yourself.

Note that there is not necessarily anything wrong with your proposal, it's certainly full of glowing improvements. And we're not talking about whether you will get your proposal approved or not; I'm not telling you to let your boss walk all over you and wait until there are two Thursdays in a week before they give you an answer. We're talking about how you will get your boss to feel good so that you can get them to seriously consider what you say.

Red people usually roll their eyes when I talk about this sort of thing. They don't have time. Though that says more about Red behavior than anything else, it doesn't make any difference whether you have time for it or not. This is how you reach your Green boss. You just have to accept it.

Otherwise the problem will be that you don't know what your boss thinks. And that wouldn't be a particularly successful outcome. Your Green boss may also agree with you during the meeting without actually being on board. Why? Because really they didn't like what you said. They were not convinced. You didn't reach them.

No decisions are made here

This is intimately linked with the previous section. If you can't coax your boss's real opinion out, then you aren't going to get anywhere. But you also might end up not getting any answers at all. If I got a dollar every time a Green person has just hemmed and hawed and nodded but didn't really say anything to me during a meeting, I would be taking my family out for a very nice dinner tonight.

But why do Green bosses behave like this? Because they don't give straight answers. They don't say yes or no. They don't spout on for five minutes about what a great idea this was. They are Green, so they murmur and say maybe.

You need to come back and follow up. If you need some new hardware to be able to do your job—make certain that the old equipment will work a little while longer. Your boss won't necessarily order the stuff right away. If you want to transfer to another group—be aware of the fact that this is a major decision for a Green boss. It could totally upset the existing balance.

So read the heading again.

Accept that this is how it works.

The solution is to go back the next day. And the day after that. And, perhaps, the week after that. The bigger the decision, the longer it will take to get an answer. Finally, your boss will reach a decision. And you'll get your answer if you don't hassle them. Remember that this is a person who values your relationship highly. If you are seen as a troublemaker, it can result in very difficult passive opposition. That would really not be good news. More on that subject later on.

So you know everything about Green bosses—now you can get going!

Just like with the Red and Yellow bosses, there are a couple of warning flags.

In fact, I have already mentioned several of them, but for the good of the cause I will nevertheless emphasize some ways you can really get yourself in a pickle. As always when it comes to Green behavior, the challenge is that you won't necessarily see their real reaction. So it's a good idea to know what you should avoid so that you won't find yourself with unnecessary problems. But if you want problems—then you don't need to read this.

Don't confuse Green with Red

There is the question of task-oriented versus relationship-oriented. Throwing yourself into a meeting, your computer already open, and starting to go through the items one by one might seem like the highest form of efficiency. And I agree—it saves lots of time. The problem is that the Green boss thinks that we've got it wrong. They prefer a gentler start to the meeting.

So take it easy and see how the land lies. Believe me—that is well-invested time.

Acting like the alpha

You've already worked out that the Red person is the opposite of the Green person. And dominant behavior can be perceived as threatening by Greens. It will lead to deadlocks between you. Even though your boss can put you in your place, you are adults. It's best for you to tone things down a little. At any rate, it is if you want to get your way.

There is a risk that your boss will come to see you in an extremely negative light. This is an instance where you need to rein it in and make an effort to listen to what your boss has to say.

Provoking an argument

This point is, of course, linked to the previous one. It's not just a matter of how you behave vis-à-vis your boss. It's also about how you behave in the group generally. Your Green boss appreciates consensus and calm reasoning. Being too loud and behaving too dominantly, even in other contexts, can be perceived extremely negatively. The risk is that your behavior creates conflict in the group, and that will not aid cooperation in the slightest. Bad news for you.

It's not just one person's fault if two people argue, you might say. But sometimes it actually is. You can get a reputation as a troublemaker and a person who has difficulty cooperating if you always challenge your environment and the members of the team. Your boss will pay more attention to this behavior than to the results you achieve.

Demand an answer here and now

You understand the pattern. There's really no big hurry. And even if there sometimes is a bit of a hurry, Green bosses don't want to be pressured into giving an answer or response to anything under duress. Because they need to think things over, and sometimes that takes a bit longer.

It's not going to work to claim (like some car salesmen do) that you must decide now because tomorrow will be too late. That customer won't come back, and your boss won't either. You'll have to accept that their thought process is different than your own. So try going about things like I've described above, and equip yourself with a decent amount of patience.

See the positive side of this: with the right amount of patience, your proposal will likely be approved.

{ **10** }

Why a Blue Boss Is the Ultimate Solution

I've met lots of Blue bosses. You'll often find them in technical professions, and by that I mean professions that involve a great deal of specialized knowledge. For example, organizations that involve lots of engineers, as well as doctors, lawyers, accountants, and certain types of IT people. Specialists.

There are many other types of specialist, but what makes these professional categories unique is that people in these fields must follow very specific rules. Medical knowledge is the result of thorough research. Lawyers abide by every detail of the law. Accountants are the same. These bosses are often assessed—and judged—on the basis of their expertise and their ability to know rules and regulations. These are professions where the boss needs to know the most of anyone in the room. It used to be that way in many professions, but nowadays most people know it's not possible. Nobody can know everything about everything. Besides, it would be extremely impractical if only the boss knew everything. Talk about a bottleneck.

With the Blue bosses, this situation is still rather prevalent. They are genuine experts. It's an integral part of their behavior. The advantage is that if you go to your Blue boss and ask a question, you will get a—detailed—answer that gives you all the information you need to move on. These Blues are precise and answer only when they have the facts at their fingertips.

The advantage with a Blue boss is that work will also be structured. Most things will roll along in good order. (Perhaps not at the highest speed, but who said that speed is everything?)

Your Blue boss will also follow the existing regulations down to the finest detail. Sometimes that will drive you up the wall—on the occasions when you would like to cut some corners. But in situations when you refer to the manual, your Blue boss is your best friend.

Umm . . . except for the fact that *your best friend* is something they will never be. The same applies to the Red bosses. Strictly task-oriented. They are less susceptible to internal politics, and they'll rarely fan the flames of any conflict at your workplace. They are solely concerned with work tasks and with ensuring that the deliverable meets with the quality standards. That's a paradox in itself when we're talking about Blue behavior, but I think you'll understand what I mean.

So How Do You Avoid the Critical Eye of This Stickler for Details?

The question is whether you actually can. If you're new to the workplace and you really want to learn the job from the basics up, then a Blue boss can be very useful. You're going to get to know exactly how everything works.

If, however, you want to do your own thing without anybody interfering, it can be a good idea to consider how you communicate with your boss. Getting your message across isn't really that difficult. We're talking about a rational person who will always listen when they realize that there's a problem. Some are good at following up on things, too. So it can be difficult to get out of their clutches once you're caught there.

Here are a few ideas about how you can interact with your boss.

Be Ridiculously Well Prepared

Prepared, well naturally, you might be thinking, *I'm always well prepared.*

I believe you. But will your Blue boss believe you? We're not talking about gathering up some papers off your desk and rushing in to your boss with the best idea in the world. No, this is about having all the paperwork with you, and in the correct order too. All the details have to be there. Why? They are going to question everything at the molecular level.

If you refer to a report you've read, you are going to be asked who authored the report. And since it was interesting, your boss will want to know if the author has written anything else. And if there are other reports as a point of comparison. And did you read the report in the original language? There can be errors in the translation. That has actually happened.

Before you say that of course you read the original version, I would remind you that your boss won't be easily fooled. There will be questions to confirm that. Just as well eat humble pie and admit that you don't speak Japanese.

Dig Out All the Details

This is part of the same thing. What your boss is looking for is proof that what you say is correct. That you know what you're talking about. If you don't know the answer to some detail or other, it's fine to say so. You don't need to answer *quickly*; your Blue boss knows that it takes time to present information that is 100 percent correct. But if you promise to get back to them at two o'clock on Thursday—make sure you do so. Your boss will already have noted that time in their calendar.

But there are better methods. You can do a thorough job *before* you barge in on your Blue boss to present your vision. Details can be all types of figures. All sorts of data that looks as if it comes from a source that might be so reliable that it's worth listening to.

I'm not saying that Excel is the answer to everything. But it will help you at this stage. If you have a proposal for some sort of improvement, do a quick spreadsheet in Excel and present it. Show that according to your figures task X will take 8.7 percent less time than before if you use your new method. Your boss will love this. You have the facts at your fingertips.

I often come across the assumption that Blue bosses don't like change, that they always drive down the same road until the mud is knee-high. But that isn't correct. Blue bosses can be very inquisitive types. What a lot of people miss is that even though they like new ideas, they will still want to have proof that what you've suggested actually works. Just spouting wild ideas without substance won't work. But if you present a good idea behind it and can back it up, you're a winner.

Stick to What We Came Here For

If there is an agenda, then stick to it. Simple—isn't it? However long the agenda, it's best for you to stick to it. And in the right order, too. You can't read it from the bottom up or start with item two when there's obviously an item one. After all, you want to look serious, somebody who knows what they're doing.

Your Blue boss will focus on the task at hand. All the other roundabout stuff is of little concern. What you did last weekend or where you think your Blue boss should spend their vacation has no place here. The same as with Red bosses—drop the small talk. You'll only embarrass yourself.

Be Thorough

This is a bit of the same theme as the focus on details. It's not a good idea to round the figures, to show averages. Only exact numbers are acceptable.

An advertisement in a newspaper doesn't cost *around 2,500*. It costs 2,487. Plus tax, which would be 27.33.

The same applies when you do your work. Thoroughness

will always be appreciated by your Blue boss. You'll get some extremely good cred if you show that you've considered all the various constituent parts of a proposal—not just the most important ones. And you've made allowances for all the possible risks that can affect the project. You're not just taking a chance that everything is going to work; you've actively looked for weaknesses and prevented future problems.

Now, *is that really necessary,* you might be thinking, *most of the things people go around worrying about never actually happen anyway.* No, I know that. Your Blue boss probably knows it too. But they will still want a risk assessment for everything that could possibly go wrong.

Better safe than sorry.

Stick to the Real World

Blue bosses, like all Blue individuals, don't want to know about any wild plans for world domination and how you will irrevocably crush your competitors. They want to know what is realistic.

Now You Know Everything About Your Blue Boss!

Nope! Not this time either. There are some very essential elements in your Blue boss that you need to be prepared for if you're going to avoid putting your foot in it. And I use that expression deliberately because the Blue boss can be quite uncompromising and may judge you harshly if you make too big of an error—in their eyes. So let's have a look at a few more points.

Show Carelessness and Shortcomings in Organization

You probably already understand how Blue bosses view carelessness. Blue people demand precision in all respects and actually find it hard to understand that not everybody thinks the same way. Since your Blue boss always checks, double checks, and might even triple check everything they do, there might be an expectation that you will do the same.

Besides, Blue bosses tend to be wizards when it comes to follow-up. This depends slightly on whether there is some Green in the picture too, because Blue-Green bosses aren't usually too hard on their staff, but if they're Blue and Red, then you can count on them carefully monitoring every step you take.

When you make a presentation, it should be very well laid out, well-thought-out, and above all—correct. If you've been careless about facts, the judgement will be harsh. And if you haven't included all the attachments and important background material (and for that matter, all the other background material) then the criticism will be merciless.

Unfortunately, your Blue boss won't forget these signs of sloppiness. There's an obvious risk that you will be under closer supervision for a long time if you've created too much of a mess. This partly depends on your own color, but if you really want your relationship with your boss to be free of friction—spend some extra time on your preparations.

Claim that Deadlines Are Important

Sometimes you need an answer from your boss. I don't think you can simply delegate tasks upwards if your boss is Blue.

They are punctilious, and delegation doesn't go in that direction. But sometimes you still need something from your boss. It might be a decision or an answer to a particular question. It might be some information you need before you can start work on a project, or you might actually want to know what your new work assignment will be.

This is a bit tricky. Your Blue boss knows what they're doing. What you're waiting for hasn't actually been forgotten. These bosses very rarely forget anything. Either what you're waiting for isn't important enough for your boss, or they simply don't want to answer your question. This can also be dependent on what driving forces your boss has, but they'll rarely miss something like this. It can also be the case that you haven't explained that this is urgent. Perhaps your boss has their own agenda that takes priority and your errands are at the bottom of the pile.

The best thing you can do is ask: why the delay?

But preferably avoid stressing your boss. They won't like that at all. "Time" is a relative concept, and it's simply a fact of life that things take time. What you need to do is to negotiate what deadline makes sense and do that from the very start. If you agree on this, then there won't be a problem. You'll get your answer in time.

Mawkish Sentimentality

On one occasion, a guy was on the way to the hospital with his wife as their first baby was about to be born. There was no hurry; they had plenty of time. At the hospital entrance, the guy—nervous and a bit starry-eyed—met his Blue boss who was on the way out. His *fourth* child had just been born, and he was now on his way home with his wife and the new baby. One might expect that they would exchange a few words. Neither of them was in a particular hurry. And the boss knew very well that this fellow was going to have his first baby. They had worked together several years. So what do you think the boss said to his colleague when they met in the doorway?

"Hi!"

That was all.

Blue bosses are not allergic to people in general or to certain colleagues in particular. They're simply not interested in socializing. It would have been perfectly normal to stop for a few moments and chat about the future baby, how the mother was doing, whether they were excited, and above all, reassure the parents-to-be that everything would go well. Logical, but not for a Blue boss.

Hi! had to suffice. No way was he going to talk about his own new baby. That was private.

For all relationship people, this is weird. At any rate, it is in Sweden where we are usually on a first-name basis with our bosses. We're rather informal. There's really nothing odd about saying hello to the CEO. But the Blue bosses aren't interested in this. And it isn't just you who isn't interesting. All of us are fairly uninteresting outside of work.

Just like the Red bosses, the Blue equivalents—or at any rate some of them—have learned to smile and nod and look as though they're joining in. But they don't want to. They don't care whether you got a new kitten. Nothing could interest your Blue boss less than your children's school progress. And if you're thinking of showing them some photos—good luck!

I'm not saying that this would necessarily damage your career, but you can easily make your Blue boss feel extremely uncomfortable. They realize that if you show them pictures of your children, you'll want to see theirs. If you can avoid all that sort of thing, it will help to ease along your professional relationship.

Keep it on that level. Professional.

{ 11 }

Why We Do What We Do: What the Colors Don't Show

Sometimes I'm challenged when I talk about Marston's studies and the DISC system. Some people I meet don't want to see what I see, and they claim that there isn't any scientific evidence. On the other hand—psychology in general is not a comprehensive science. To explain human behavior, you also need to look at sociology, humanism, neuroscience, molecular genetics, pharmacology, psychiatry, linguistics, anthropology, pedagogy, and economics, as well as a whole lot of other stuff too. Some people feel that there's something missing. And some get quite angry—*it can't be as simple as that!*

You've missed something. People can't be described by such simple categories. Of course there are more than four types of people. It's wrong to divide people up in that way.

What is this doubt about?

I am sometimes told, quite often by psychologists and other people with formal qualifications, that this system doesn't work. That it's far too simple. That it wouldn't work. That there are more than four types of people.

My answer is: But of course. Neither I nor Marston have ever claimed that there are only four types of people. But the four fundamental base elements affect who we are. And these can, as I've said, be combined in lots of different ways. Thousands of variations of behaviors can be described with this system. Remember the example with the cake?

When you measure which color or colors a person has, it often leads to slightly different types of follow-up questions. For example, when I've performed analyses on the staff of an entire company, people come up to me clutching their reports and want to talk. Often they're rather intrigued, but sometimes slightly perplexed.

A common question is how two people with very similar profiles can still be perceived so differently. For example, two Yellow-Red salesmen can be perceived as having totally different personalities. It's evident that they do communicate rather similarly, but still there's something that isn't quite right. There is something that doesn't really fit. And it *feels* wrong.

They're probably right.

Oftentimes, the answer lies in their driving forces. These two little devils might not come to work for the same reason.

What Lies Below the Surface—and Fools Us All

A driving force is what makes a person get out of bed and go to work and want to do their best—day in and day out, year after year.

Somewhat simplified, you could say that this is about your motivation.

Or even simpler: the answer to the question "Why?"

Why are you prepared to make an effort?

Why do you want to do that little bit extra?

Why is it important that you succeed at this thing in particular?

Or just as well: *why* is this chapter totally uninteresting to you?

Driving forces can change over time. Times and conditions change, and then your reasons for doing something can change too. Depending on where you are in your life, you might give different priorities to various things.

An example: if you don't have much money, you might dream of becoming a millionaire. Nothing wrong with that. But say that you win the lottery. All of a sudden you are financially independent. Now perhaps money isn't so important to you. One could say that you're safe and sound on that front. Instead, you take things easier at work and start using your time for other things, perhaps something you have dreamed about but have never been able to afford. Perhaps you want to paint, or you won so much that you want to embark upon a career as a philanthropist and donate money to the homeless.

None of this is better or worse than anything else. During different periods in our life, we simply give priority to different things.

Our need for security and stability increases when we have children, but perhaps decreases when our children have been guided to maturity and finally left the nest. Now we can relax again. Driving forces vary with where you are in your life. However, the colors do not vary in the same way.

Basically, a person's driving forces are what their heart beats for. They're things that make a difference for each and every one of us. Every time we're given a task that satisfies a particular driving force, passion and energy are brought into our lives. We want to do our best for a particular reason, and we will do a better job when the task is in line with our primary driving forces. Which is why it's a good idea to identify and understand your driving forces.

Are We Really Testing the Right Things?

Individual tests and analyses like those used during recruitment, for instance, have been around for a long time. We can go way back to before the First World War. During the 1920s these kinds of tests became very common, and gradually these various tools became more sophisticated and thus more accurate.

In a recruitment process, for example, most people first look for experience and competences. Then after that come behavior and driving forces.

In my opinion, it should be the other way around.

If a person lacks competence, we can always train them. We can arrange in-house courses. There are other people who know what needs to be done. We probably already have someone with that knowledge in the building.

But if a person has values (and thus driving forces) that don't agree with yours, or with the organization's, there's no training course in the world that can change that fact. You won't be motivated by the same things, and in the long term this can trigger stress in all concerned.

How About You; Why Did You Pick Up This Book?

Take this book, for example. I'm of course pleased that you've chosen to read it. But the reason you chose this particular book is actually interesting. You could be reading it for lots of reasons, and whether or not those reasons match up with the book's actual content will partially determine how satisfied you're going to be with it.

- Perhaps you're reading it because you think new information is exciting; you'll learn new things; you'll discover information you weren't aware of. Knowledge is, in itself, sufficient reward for you to invest four or five hours of your youth here. If you're not the slightest bit wiser after 400 pages, then this is a really useless book.
- Another person might be reading the book because they think the content is beneficial. He or she intends to use the knowledge to, for example, become so good at their job that they can negotiate their way to a hefty pay raise. If they're not able to use the content in practice, then they've wasted several hours of their precious time. Not good.
- A third person might read the book as part of their personal development. They want to be a better and more complete human being. If you don't grow (either as a colleague, staff member, or in your leadership role) after having invested many hours in reading, it's going to be a disappointment.
- A fourth person might see the book as a helpful

selection. A boss can support lots of people by using the information the book contains. If it turns out that nobody can make use of the good advice (based on the contents of the book) that the reader hands out and that people weren't actually helped by the contents, then the book will end up in the trash can.
- The fifth person might see the book as an important way forward in their career. By making use of the insights in these pages, not only can you earn money—you can even get promoted. If it turns out that the advice in the book makes everything go sideways and you risk being demoted, well, then the book will get a very bad rating from this reader. (This might even result in some angry emails to the author)
- There are those who read this book and notice that what I've written agrees with their own values. The author seems to understand the priorities in life. But if, for example, our values collided on the question of leadership, then the book will not be well-thought-of. *That author simply didn't understand—why should I listen to him?*

All of these readers devote the same amount of time to the book. The contents are the same regardless of who is reading. But all of you get different things from reading it. Consider this insight in addition to your main color, and you will realize that you're going to see everything in a slightly different way depending on what motivates you. Besides—you were probably motivated by two of the six reasons above to read this book.

The Three Levels of Driving Forces

You can think about driving forces in slightly different ways. There are basically three different levels to consider.

There are *personal driving forces* that are deeply embedded in the innermost core of a person. Fundamental values that are learned in a positive way over a long period. Things that give immediate satisfaction when they're fulfilled.

When we are influenced by *values* that come from *outside*—for example, values that exist within the organization where we are working—our own driving forces become weaker. These external values are still significant, but they're not as important as the ones that come from inside. We can easily go along with what other people say, but what comes from a person's innermost core will always have priority.

If the organization's driving forces and values agree with your personal driving forces, they can provide extremely strong motivation. If they don't, a conflict arises between what you value and what others value. Suddenly we disagree. Even though I can understand that what the organization stands for is important, and even though I can see the logic in it, it doesn't necessarily appeal to me. Friction is going to arise.

Then there are *inactive driving forces*. They are deep inside us, and sometimes we don't even know what they are until we find ourselves in a given situation. Sometimes they lie there, waiting just below the surface for half a lifetime until the right opportunity turns up. And sometimes they're actually repressed, deliberately or otherwise.

If you've met somebody who has made an abrupt change of career, or radically changed their lifestyle, or who has suddenly sold everything they own to "find" themselves—well, then you've met somebody who discovered something inside themselves that they hadn't known about earlier. Some things need to develop to full maturity.

What Are the Various Driving Forces?

There are lots of driving forces. In life in general there are all sorts of reasons why something is important: love, sex, power, money and so on. If we look at Eduard Spranger's studies of driving forces in work life, you could say that there are basically six driving forces:

Theoretical Driving Force—a Passion for Knowledge and Truth

This driving force is defined by a passion to learn and to acquire more knowledge. As a rule, an individual with this driving force adopts a thinking attitude. They tend not to judge things and circumstances on the basis of appearance or utility; rather, they'll attempt to understand the context and draw conclusions from that. Since a person with a strong theoretical driving force is usually critical, rational, and bases their judgements on experience, they can be perceived as intellectual. Systematizing knowledge might be one of their major interests.

Utilitarian Driving Force—a Passion for What's Useful

The utilitarian driving force manifests itself in the form of a considerable interest in money and things that can be practical and useful. For these people, the security and freedom that economic assets can provide are important—for themselves and for their family if they have one. People with a strong utilitarian driving force usually understand the inner workings of commercial activities. They often consider material assets and status objects important.

Aesthetic Driving Force—a Passion for Balance and Harmony

Those who have a strong aesthetic driving force usually have a deep interest in form and harmony. As a rule, they appreciate objects, experiences, and events for their aesthetic qualities and design. People with a strong aesthetic driving force can be observant of, and appreciate, unique details that are often missed by others. A strong aesthetic driving force doesn't necessarily mean that a person has a talent for artistic expression, but they will at least appreciate aesthetics, beautiful objects, balance, and harmony.

Social Driving Force—a Passion to Help Others

Those who have a strong social driving force typically have a genuine interest in people. These people appreciate others and are perceived as friendly, sympathetic, and unselfish. They can, in turn, experience people with a strong theoretical, utilitarian, and aesthetic driving force as somewhat cold and hard. As opposed to people with an individualist driving force, a person with a social driving force thinks that we humans are created to help one another. People with a predominantly social driving force are often self-sacrificing by nature.

Individualistic Driving Force—a Passion for Personal Success

The chief interest behind this driving force is some kind of power, and that doesn't necessarily mean political power. Research has shown that leaders in most areas have a comparatively strong individualistic driving force. Many philosophers believe that power comprises the most universal and most fundamental driving force, since competition and struggle are found to a varying degree in all areas of life. For certain people, this characteristic is especially prominent. These people commonly strive for personal power, influence, and success.

Traditional Driving Force—a Passion for One's Own View of the Meaning of Life

Harmony and unity, order, and a system for life or perhaps tradition are all at the core of this driving force. Individuals with a strong traditional driving force usually seek out a system to live by—something they believe in that offers guidelines for how you should live your life. This might be a belief in any number of spheres, not necessarily a religious faith. This system can consist of a religion, political party, or any other guiding outlook where there are clear rules and principles for how you ought to live.

Those are the basics. But—we can also divide the six different driving forces into two subcategories: strong and weak.

A Matter of Conscience

The combination of driving forces can affect how you evaluate what you encounter in your everyday life and how you choose to interpret what you see and hear.

Depending on what your two strongest driving forces are, you will experience your work in different ways. And you'll respond to the leadership of your boss in extremely different ways, especially if he or she has different driving forces than you do.

Before you read this text—were you aware of your strongest driving forces? Are you theoretical, aesthetic, or individualistic? Or do you have more of a social, traditional, or utilitarian driving force? And what does the combination look like in your particular case? What are your two strongest forces? And just as important: what are your weakest? That, too, impacts what you give priority to in your work and what motivates you. Did you have any idea of how these forces affect your view of your job?

And the most important question: has your boss tried hard to find out what your driving forces are and adjusted their leadership accordingly? No?

Then how will you be able to fully understand one another?

When I mediate conflict in some workplaces, I almost exclusively find the reason behind the conflict in the analysis of driving forces. And, as usual—if you're going to solve a problem, you need to know what that problem is.

What driving forces does your boss have? If your boss earned their role thanks to their focus on results, but you think that customer service is more important, then it won't help if you have similar colors. You'll find it hard to understand each other's priorities. Sometimes you have to simply sit down and discuss these things.

{ 12 }

The Author's Profile and What You Can Learn from It

Now you're going to be privy to a well-kept secret. The answer to a question I'm asked hundreds of times every year. I usually give a vague, evasive answer. But here you're going to get the truth.

On the next page, you can see two graphs. They depict my communication profile. The left-side graph shows my adjusted profile, i.e., how I behave when I'm working. The right-side graph is my basic profile, which means that I have a somewhat different character when I'm not working. My colors are mainly Red, Blue, and Yellow. Quite a lot of all three, mainly Red and Blue and slightly less Yellow, but considerably less Green. Hardly any Green at all, in fact. The difference in the two graphs is—as you can see—not especially dramatic, but there is a difference. Since the right-side graph shows the real me without any proper adjustment, one could say it's the most *me*.

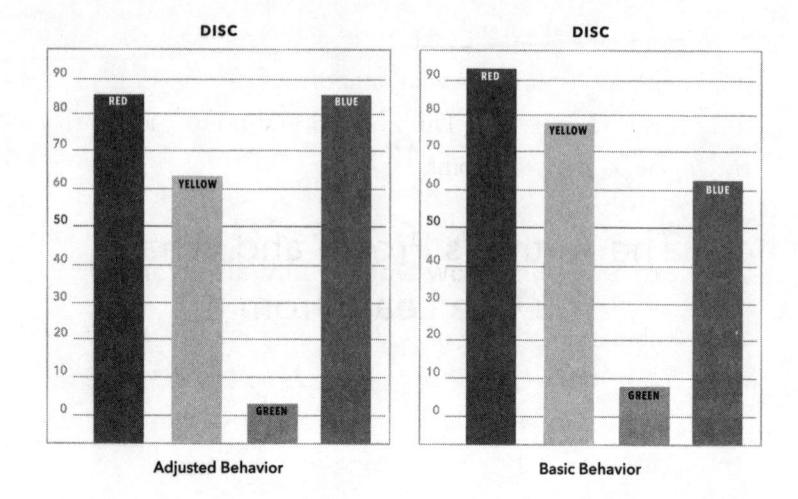

DISC — Adjusted Behavior: RED ~83, YELLOW ~55, GREEN ~2, BLUE ~80

DISC — Basic Behavior: RED ~90, YELLOW ~73, GREEN ~5, BLUE ~60

The Difference Between Me at Work and Outside of Work

According to those graphs, I am less dominant when I work, but also less inspiring. On the other hand, I'm more analytical when I'm working. What does this tell us? Not that much, since the difference doesn't tell you if I need therapy. Joking aside: too large of an adjustment, i.e., dramatic difference between your basic behavior and your adjusted behavior, can lead to problems. Quite simply, it's good if I can be myself to the greatest extent possible in my work.

But my profile does lead to specific behaviors that I now understand very well. I can be incredibly impatient when the Red element has its say, but I can also be actually quite analytical (read: *slow*) when the Blue part takes over. Ask my wife. She has even more Red than me—but hardly any Blue.

Sometimes I plan too much and look for holes and weaknesses everywhere. And there are still occasions when I come to a dead stop in a task. Besides—with so little Green, I can be careless about listening to what others say. It requires some effort. This isn't something I'm proud to admit, but I accept that this is one of my weak points.

So, This Mix—How Does It Actually Work?

The combination of a lot of Red and a lot of Blue sometimes makes me a somewhat less sensitive person, I realize that. But it also helps me do the job the right way. It's particularly useful when I give advice to senior bosses as a consultant. For example, when I'm advising a managing director in a large company (this is dangerously close to boasting, and that's because my Yellow column is also rather high) who asks me how they should handle their motley management group. These people have painfully little time and are already surrounded by yes-men. The last thing they want is to pay lots of money for a consultant who just sits there and agrees with them. They want to hear the truth. If they don't appreciate me giving it to them, well, I can live with that. It's my job to be uncomfortable.

All of that is entirely logical, and I'm sure it's similar for you. You know your own strong sides, and you are more or less aware of the pitfalls.

Yeah, right, so you simply have to observe yourself and correct whatever isn't working!

If only it were so simple.

Imagine this: you often find yourself in a situation you don't like. Or that is about to go off the rails. And you know exactly what's lacking. You need to do something concrete: make an adjustment, take something away or add something else. You know what you need to do, but nothing happens.

Why?

Simple. You don't want it to.

Even though I've got better at this, I am not a world champion when it comes to getting a grip on myself. Sometimes I know perfectly well what the solution to a certain problem is, but it doesn't help. I know that I need to change something. Perhaps I need to learn something new, need to listen to somebody besides the people I usually listen to. Perhaps I ought to get some regular exercise.

But it simply isn't one of those days. So none of that happens.

Sometimes we have days like that. We drive along on the same old track and know it will probably all go wrong. Logical? No, not in the slightest. But we're human and our brains fools us from morning to evening. We often do what feels best in the moment, and sometimes that means withdrawing into a cocoon and refusing to hear what those around us are saying.

When this happens, I have to go back to my driving forces and have a serious think. My natural behaviors are not enough. The above profile based on colors alone isn't going to help me go further. I need to look at my motivation factors and see whether I can find the energy to move further.

The Tired Old Men

Not so long ago, I was sitting in a seminar and trying to listen to a whole pack of British psychologists, one after the other. I say "trying" because the whole thing was horribly dull. They were all dangerously monotonous, the very opposite of entertaining. I had to force myself not to pick up my phone and start busying myself with something else. Personally, I hate it when people do that, and I consider it disrespectful. The knowledge that these psychologists possessed—and there was a lot of it, nobody doubts that—wasn't so fascinating that I could just sit there for fun and listen to them talk about their research. And after having suffered through four or five of those old men, I was so desperate that I was prepared to flee the premises.

But I stayed because I finally found a reason to do so. By going back to why I had even come there in the first place, I reminded myself that I would be able to use the information they were sharing. There must be something useful in what they were saying. And that appealed to my utilitarian driving force. That's how it works. My theoretical driving force is weaker. Paired with my utilitarian driving force this means that I would rather only learn things that are going to be useful to me.

Hmm. There's something in that. I purchase quite a lot of books about psychology, behavior, and everything about how people really function. Often, I see an interesting title—or a provocative one, like *Surrounded by Idiots*—and I think: *I'm going to read that. It sounds fascinating!* This happens many times every year, and now I have a comprehensive library with subjects that relate to my job.

But I don't read all of those books, far from it. Some of them I just thumb through; others I read a few chapters of; others I do actually read from cover to cover. That happens when I believe that the contents will actually be useful to me. Reading three or four hundred pages because it's fascinating isn't my style. It takes too long and life is too short.

But some people do exactly the opposite. They read any book at all because it's an interesting subject. It doesn't bother me if you read this book for that reason, but that isn't how it works for me. I don't have much time. How do I know that? Easy, my utilitarian driving force tells me. It strives for efficient use of time. You can't read specialist literature the same way you read a novel. I'm not saying this is the right method, I'm simply explaining what I do. If I want to be entertained, I read a thriller.

But it doesn't stop here.

The Mystery of the Unknown Driving Force

Many years ago, I worked in a bank. In many respects it was a good job. I got to see a lot, do some travelling, and be a part of important projects. I gave people across the country training in sales skills; I built a career and the pay was pretty good too.

All those activities stimulated my utilitarian driving force. What was most important to me was creating results. I needed to see with my own eyes that the work I did really was profitable. Actually, I'm not really talking about money, even though that was part of it.

Except there was something that didn't really feel right. However hard I worked, I liked it less and less, even though I was doing most things right. I was praised, I was regularly promoted, I got pay rises and a fancy title. I vaguely remember getting some sort of bonus towards the end.

But something felt wrong. My motivation declined, and however hard I worked it just got worse. Finally it got so bad that I found it hard to get out of bed in the morning, and that had never been a problem before.

By chance, I started to try something that had long been a dream of mine—writing books. Why this was my dream isn't relevant, but I've always found the idea of creating something completely new on a sheet of white paper to be deeply appealing. I find it easy to see things in images and I like being able to use my imagination. This is partly why I prefer to read a book rather than see a film. In a film everything is finished, with a book I can create my own images founded in my own imagination.

And to write a book yourself. *Wow*!

As soon as I started writing, life felt a bit more pleasant. I started to get my motivation back, to regain energy for all sorts of things. The fact is that I felt more harmonious. All of me felt better.

At that time, I hadn't really understood how things were connected. But then I did a driving-force analysis. And suddenly all the pieces of the jigsaw fell into place. When I understood that my second strongest driving force, almost as strong as the utilitarian one, was aesthetic, I realized why I had lost interest in my job. At my job, I wasn't really creating anything, everything was regulated, and there was no space for creativity. Everything had to be done the same way.

The weird thing was that when I wrote during weekends and nights—with young children at home and a lot of travelling for my job—I started to feel better even when I was at work, despite the fact that the work tasks had not changed at all. But the writing made me a more complete person. The aesthetic force motivates people to strive for harmony and balance. And that's exactly what I got. My entire existence became balanced.

The aesthetic driving force also explains some other decisions. For one thing, I can't drive the same car as my neighbor. My car doesn't need to be fancier or more expensive than all the others, but it needs to be *different*. This is because aesthetes want to feel unique. If I were to shell out for a really fancy car, then I would prefer a Jaguar or a Lexus—just because they stick out a bit—rather than a Mercedes or a Volvo.

Although I am fifty-plus years old, I still find it hard to choose the same option as everybody else—regardless of what it is. As much as possible, I want to feel unique. Logical? Nope, not in the slightest.

If there is any moral to this story, it's that you ought to follow your heart if you want to feel good. Before we all start getting nauseated from the cliché-sounding advice, what I mean is that driving forces are more important than many people think. To do what you really like doing and what actually interests you is more worthwhile than you might believe.

And what about you? What can you do about this?

If you are going to find your own motivation in your job, you need to understand your driving forces better. If you know what they are, it will be simpler for you to enjoy your job. And if you come to realize that you can't find an outlet like the one I had the luck of finding—then give your notice.

Life is too short to be spent in the wrong place and with the wrong people. Or with the wrong boss.

So again—do your driving forces align with those of your boss? Of course, it's not absolutely necessary, but it undoubtedly makes things easier. But an even bigger question is whether your driving forces match those of the organization. Since driving forces are often connected with our fundamental values, challenges can arise if the organization you work for often acts in a way that clashes with what you yourself give priority to.

The best example I have here is a time when a salesperson in a company left her job because the owner of the company didn't think it was important to turn a profit. The owner was a theoretician, he thought it was fun to try out new technology and search for exciting innovations. And he could afford to allow the company to take a loss year after year. But the salesperson had a strong utilitarian driving force, and she hated the way her business deals weren't given priority. When the owner told her to sell less, she just walked out. That was probably the best solution for everyone concerned, but rather a shame since she was so good at doing business.

{ 13 }

Distinguishing Between Colors and Driving Forces

On the next page you can see an example of a person who is mainly pragmatic, receptive, effective, and investigative. That is what drives him or her. The way she or he acts this out can be found in their colors, but the reason for the behavior is rooted in the driving forces.

Let's look at the first driving force, the theoretical. This person is pulled less to the intuitive side and more to the investigative side. How can you strive for knowledge?

In principle, none of this is really connected with the colors.

Theoretical Driving Force vs. Blue Behavior

We need to understand the difference between a driving force and a behavior.

Behavior: *being thorough, exact, and analytical*
Driving force: *Seeking knowledge and wanting to learn new things*

Intuitive	Theoretical - knowledge	**Investigative**

Natural	Utilitarian	**Efficient**

Pragmatic	Aesthetic – surroundings	**Harmonious**

Selective	Social - other people	**Generous**

Cooperative	Individualist - influence	**Controlling**

Receptive	Traditional - values	**Principled**

As you can see above, it's necessary to distinguish between behavior and driving forces. To strive after knowledge is a driving force, while being thorough with facts and details is a behavior. But there is no connection between these two. A Blue theoretician is going to want to know everything and they will put a lot of time into finding it. A Yellow theoretician will also want to know how things work, but they might do it another way. They would probably rather see a film than read a book. And instead of writing down everything they've learned, they'll phone their friends and force them to listen to how fascinated they are by the age of the moon, how to build apps, or whether there really are alligators in the New York sewage system. The same desire for knowledge drives both—but they have different methods of finding it.

Talkative Peter

I have in mind a client I had many years ago. Peter was the sales manager in a fairly large company. He was almost a caricature of Yellow behavior—always talking about everything and nothing. Muddled and irritatingly unstructured, but at the same time irresistibly fun to be around. Few people can tell a story like he can. The interesting thing about Peter is that he's also a theoretician, which meant that he didn't fail to do his homework as badly as you might have thought since he was Yellow. He did actually learn about things, but he did it in his own Yellow way. He told me that he could never simply throw away anything that arrived in his mailbox. Advertisements, information from the local council, free newspapers, and so on. He had to look at them first to see if there was anything of interest.

This drove his wife mad since he left piles of all sorts of stuff all over the house. He couldn't throw it away, and he didn't really manage to organize it all. All that happened was that he messed up the house with piles of old papers until it looked alarmingly like a recycling center.

Early one Sunday morning, many years ago, he called me. Since I'm always up at the crack of dawn, it wasn't particularly disturbing, but you can't help wondering if something has happened if somebody phones you at seven in the morning on a Sunday . . .

Peter shouted: "Thomas! Did you know that the moon . . . is older than the Earth?!?"

He was shouting because he had been sitting up all night long with headphones watching Discovery Channel—I suspect that immeasurable amounts of coffee were also involved in this—and learned that the Earth was a little younger than its own moon. Fascinating indeed. I had to admit that I hadn't known this before. Since Peter had now learned this fact and since he was so Yellow, he was immediately forced to tell somebody about it. And who did he know who might be up and about at this time on a Sunday morning?

Hi, Thomas.

Theoretical driving force—Yellow behavior.

The Creative Who Loves a Spreadsheet

But there are other interesting combinations. Take, for example, the Blue translator I once met at a publishing house many years ago. She translated German computer manuals into Swedish.

Naturally she worked very calmly and methodically and left nothing to chance. And I really do mean nothing. She made excel spreadsheets for everything that needed to be dealt with. All the details ended up on those spreadsheets. Interestingly, she not only put all the information there, she even made sure the spreadsheet looked good. That there was a system for which colors she used for different types of information. And when she used different colors, there was a system there too. Since she was extremely Blue, this was well-thought-through. She not only used different colors; no, she had the colors of a rainbow in gradient shades. All the fonts had to be exactly right, in size and form. If she needed headings, there was a theory behind them too.

When she put together a page being translated, she always

looked at it afterwards to make sure it looked good. Did it feel *right*?

That's interesting, isn't it? *Feel right*—that doesn't sound so Blue, does it?

But this woman wasn't only Blue—she was also an aesthete. Which meant that the appearance and experience of her work was important. She had a need to create a certain type of harmony. The method she used to achieve that was all Blue.

To want to create harmony in the manuals is the aesthetic driving force. To do it by using—elegant—Excel spreadsheets is a Blue behavior. As you will certainly understand, it would have looked different if the translator had been Yellow, or Green for that matter. To start with, there wouldn't be any Excel spreadsheets in the first place.

Aesthetic driving force—Blue behavior.

It isn't enough to just interpret your own colors or other people's colors. There's more to keep track of. The more you learn about this, the better the tools you'll have at your disposal to achieve a really good dialogue with the people around you. And with your boss.

Do you remember the example about learning to install electrical wiring? This is the same thing. If everybody does their homework about basic electricity, they will all learn a bit more about the subject, and that makes everything a lot easier, even if it doesn't turn us all into full-blown electricians.

Reflect for a moment on your own driving forces. By being aware of those driving forces, you can gain a greater understanding of your own behavior in many different situations.

And the fact is that when you become aware of what you are passionate about, you will find your motivation much more easily. I personally feel much better and am happy with my life in a very different way than before I understood my own driving forces. Perhaps the same applies to you?

If we consider leadership, it's clear to me that there are bosses who have taken on the job for the wrong reason. And this is where we find a whole bunch of bad, and even superfluous, bosses.

The Identical Bosses Who Were Completely Dissimilar

In leadership, driving forces are even more important. After all, what the boss does affects so many other people.

Here are two short examples:

These are Tina's two profiles. She is a boss. Tina is lightning fast at understanding problems, and she's highly focused on finding solutions.

Tina has a reputation for achieving good results, and she is

146 SURROUNDED BY BAD BOSSES

Tina's Profiles

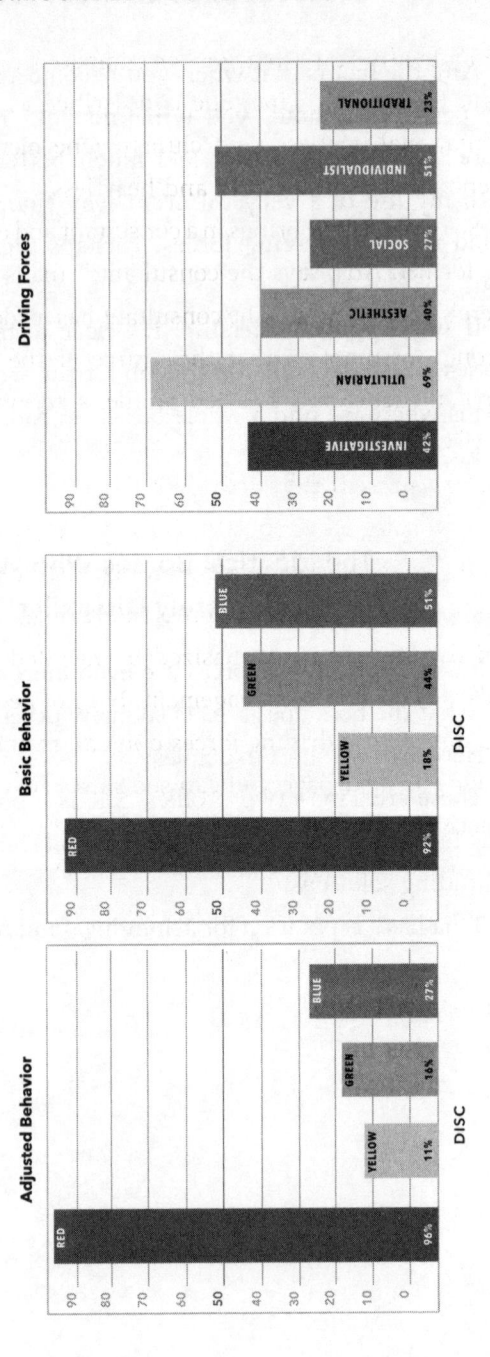

Adjusted Behavior

- RED 96%
- YELLOW 11%
- GREEN 16%
- BLUE 27%

DISC

Basic Behavior

- RED 92%
- YELLOW 18%
- GREEN 44%
- BLUE 51%

DISC

Driving Forces

- INVESTIGATIVE 42%
- UTILITARIAN 69%
- AESTHETIC 40%
- SOCIAL 27%
- INDIVIDUALIST 51%
- TRADITIONAL 23%

undoubtedly respected for her competence, but people don't want to work for Tina. She is described as demanding, confrontational, tactless, and clumsy. One member of her staff even describes her as cold and heartless.

So the company brings in a consultant and creates a DISC profile for her. Aha, says the consultant, Tina is extremely Red—there's your problem. The consultant has made a common—but wrong—assumption that the source of the conflict between Tina and her team is her Red profile. A serious mistake.

If we had Tina's driving-force analysis, we would see that she has an extremely strong utilitarian driving force and an exceptionally weak social driving force. This means that she values financial results much more than helping others. This combination drives her to press her team to earn more money, and her attitude is emphasized by her Red behavioral style. This is good for the management, but not necessarily good for the staff whose driving forces don't all match Tina's.

On the next page you can see Sara's two profiles. She has exactly the same DISC profile as Tina, but with a big difference.

Sara's team adores her. She's good at getting things done,

Sara's Profiles

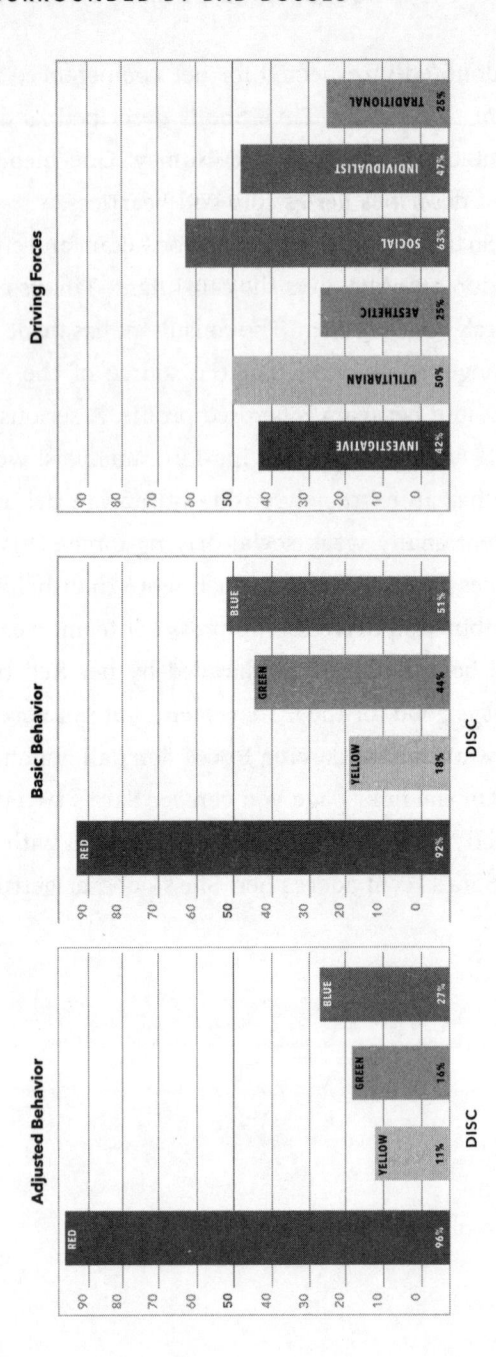

Adjusted Behavior

- RED 96%
- YELLOW 13%
- GREEN 16%
- BLUE 27%

DISC

Basic Behavior

- RED 92%
- YELLOW 18%
- GREEN 44%
- BLUE 51%

DISC

Driving Forces

- INVESTIGATIVE 42%
- UTILITARIAN 50%
- AESTHETIC 25%
- SOCIAL 63%
- INDIVIDUALIST 47%
- TRADITIONAL 25%

and she holds everyone responsible for their own work. But she also values their input, is democratic when it comes to decisions, and takes an active interest in every person as an individual. Her strong social driving force means that she supports her team and helps them be better, and this is reinforced by her behavioral style. Her problem is totally different than Tina's: she's far too tolerant of underachievers. She simply finds it hard to put her foot down—despite her Red style. And this is going to be good for some people, while others will find it irritating.

The driving forces are the real source of conflict. Behaviors are relatively easy to understand, but many people need a framework to discuss driving forces and values. When it comes to leadership, just like with private relationships, people can overcome basic behavioral differences—but values and driving forces are harder to compromise on.

The conclusion is that Tina and Sara need completely different coaching to be able to help their respective teams. And if you had the opportunity to actually choose your boss: who would you work for? Tina—or Sara?

{ 14 }

The Difference Between Your Personality and Your Behavior

Do I have to become a different person to satisfy my boss?

I really advise against that.

Your personality is something that goes considerably deeper than your behavior. It's based upon your driving forces, what motivates you, what you like, your upbringing, your experiences, and your intelligence, plus lots of other things.

Different researchers have varying definitions of personality, and it depends on which theory they base their research on. Most psychologists use the term "personality" to refer to psychological qualities that contribute to an individual's permanent and characteristic pattern of emotions, thoughts, and behavior. This means that the facets of your personality are relatively constant over time and in different situations. "Permanent" in this case means several years. Perhaps many, many years. "Characteristic" refers to what distinguishes one individual from another. Different individuals are simply perceived differently depending on their personalities.

So Why Did You End Up the Person You Are?

Most of us have probably thought about that question at some time or other: what made me the person I am today? Not that you can do anything about it, but simply because you want to know. Now we come to the question of heredity and environment.

A long time ago heredity was thought to be the key factor. Who you are is decided by your DNA. If you're born with it, you'll have to live with it. Bad luck. Few things are harder to correct afterwards than which parents you have.

Then it became generally understood that it was probably the complete opposite. Somebody discovered that people with the same parents could have extremely different personalities, which must be because of environment. By "environment" I mean everything that influences a person outside of their genetic and hereditary makeup.

On the other hand, that didn't seem to be completely right either. Individuals with a similar upbringing and pattern of learning can nevertheless end up very different. I can well imagine that the researchers were scratching their heads when they tried to understand how it all fit together.

Nowadays there is a fairly strong consensus that 40 to 50 percent of our personality can be explained by genetic factors. The shared close environment (your family) can explain about 5 percent, while the remaining 45 to 55 percent can be explained by unique environmental effects (i.e., effects in the external environment). This builds upon decades of research. Don't take the figures too seriously though, because sometimes opinions change as to the exact percentages. I'm not going to go into the details, because only the Blue theoreticians can stomach that.

The only way to fill in all the gaps would be to carry out serious and very long (at least twenty-five years) analyses of identical twins who were separated at birth. Then you can eliminate lots of other factors that could disturb the result, like differing genetic profiles.

What Then Can We Conclude from All This?

Your personality is there, whether you like it or not. You will probably try to interpret other people's personalities as you go along. But you do so based on what you observe.

You see a certain behavior and make your evaluation.

That guy is so boring. Why? Because he's totally bogged down with the details. However, your analysis is not based upon his personality but on the *behavior* you observed. Besides, he only behaves like that on certain occasions because he too is influenced by outside factors.

Behaviors are one thing. Personality is something else.

Imagine that you are sitting at a dinner and listening politely to the nonsense of the person next to you. You nod and smile, laugh a little when it seems suitable. Why? Because you've learned some basic principles of social adaptability. You're never going to be especially enthusiastic about the municipal tax situation that seems to fascinate your fellow diner, but you can play along. You've adapted your behavior according to the situation, but you haven't changed your personality.

Or you have a boss who's really quick. Who likes to get

quick answers all the time. Who always wants to know the fastest way to get from A to C. So you try to satisfy him or her as quickly as you can. You adapt your behavior and almost garble your words, but you're still you.

This is important:

If everybody adapts themselves to everybody else all the time, then nobody is their real self in the end. Everything just becomes a game. What if you completely lose yourself in this mess?

Can't We Ever Just Be Ourselves?

It's obvious that most of the behavior you observe in others is simply a game—all of us adapt ourselves all the time, often without even thinking about it—but what I am offering here is a particular way to do it. By making use of the DISC language, you can guess right more often. There will be considerably fewer seriously wrong moves on the slippery social playing field. And communication will work more smoothly. There will be fewer conflicts. Your job will be simpler. Fewer arguments around the dinner table; easier to recruit the right person for the job. Better team-building.

But that's manipulating other people and manipulating me. I'm not going to do that! . . . you might be thinking.

Fine by me. Everyone does what they want. You can save time by stopping reading here and now. That would really say a lot about your personality.

All joking aside, there are many motives for adapting at a particular time. It's about what you find lacking in your dialogue with your boss. Regardless of whether you like it or not, your boss affects your everyday life. And if they don't, then we have a different problem. Invisible bosses are quite another challenge. More of that later on.

Does It Make Any Difference What Colors You Are?

Definitely. If you've read *Surrounded by Idiots*, then when you opened this book you already knew roughly what your strongest colors are. And they do, of course, play an enormous role when it comes to which adaptations you could make in different situations. And my guess is that you've already seen a number of faces in your mind's eye, perhaps indeed even your own face, as you've read about the colors.

We've already gone through the general characteristics for bosses with different colors, and that's a good start. Now we'll try to ascertain whether we should all adapt ourselves in the same way to our respective boss.

My short tip is that we should not.

If your boss is Green and you're Yellow, your adaptation is simply to slow down and talk less.

But if you're Blue, your adaptation will be to show more interest in the person behind the "boss" title. The same boss—different adaptations.

So let's look at some specific points to keep in mind that take into consideration our own profiles.

{ 15 }

How to Adapt Effectively to Your Boss's Color

First, Your Red Boss

If you have a Red boss, it matters whether you yourself are Red or not. If you're Red, you'll have no problem understanding each other. You'll have short and, on some occasions, loud discussions. You will probably quickly agree on something and then go for lunch. Neither of you will be grumpy a long time if you can't come to an agreement. And the people around you are going to wonder how it's possible to have a loud argument at eleven o'clock and then have lunch together at noon. Let them wonder. But you won't have to make any enormous changes when it comes to communication with your boss. He or she will cope with your . . . uhmm . . . direct manner.

If you are Yellow, you and your Red boss will work surprisingly well together. The Red person likes the way that Yellows have a certain physical liveliness, and Yellows will often find the decision-making ability of the Reds beneficial. Being Yellow, you can just keep talking in circles around every decision, but together you will move forward. Being Yellow, you will soften up your boss a little, and they in turn will probably make you a bit more result-oriented. Not a bad combination, if you think about it. The only adaptation you need to make here is to hold your tongue. Talk less, act a bit more. Come on, you can do it!

If you are Green, you might have greater difficulties with your Red boss. That direct focus on the task can be hard if you are a subtler master of relationships. On the other hand, a boss who likes giving orders and a member of staff who is perfectly happy to receive a—politely formulated—order, what can go wrong with that? You need to put your feelings to the side. You shouldn't ignore them, but you'll gain nothing by venting them in your meeting with your boss. You might also need to be considerably clearer, stick to the point, and use fewer words. Red bosses rarely try to bulldoze people deliberately, but there is a risk that you are going to feel you've just been flattened if your boss doesn't understand what you actually think. Silence is often taken as a sign of agreement. The only way to alter that interpretation is to say it like it is and explain your viewpoints directly and clearly.

If you're a Blue and have a Red boss, then the recommendation is very simple: stop stepping on the brake and press the other pedal instead (and I'm not talking about the clutch). What you have in common is that you stick to the subject in your conversation. Neither of you gets bogged down in any emotional sloppiness, and neither of you wants to know what the other person is planning for Christmas. But you put far too much effort into talking about background and details. Your Red boss doesn't want any of that. He or she wants to know what you're going to do about it. So focus more on what's ahead. And accept the fact that while your boss likes it when things get done properly, the priority is that they get done in the first place. You won't get any bonus points for making plans that stretch into the next century. Talk faster and, above all, use fewer words.

Adapting to Your Yellow Boss

If your boss is Yellow, and you're Red, you will still actually be quite a good match. You like a bit of go, your boss likes a bit of go. Things will always happen when you work together. What you need to think about is restraining yourself slightly and accepting that your boss uses more words than you. While he or she can probably inspire you to great new exploits, it will be done in a slightly less succinct way than you might wish for. What you need to do is ask some concrete questions about the task, then it'll be okay. And accept that there might be some clowning also.

If you're just as Yellow as your boss, you'll have a really great time. There will be lots of fun and laughter most of the time. Depending on how self-aware you are, there's a risk that in all this positivity you'll forget to write down what you actually agreed on. Because both of you are great talkers, but perhaps not as good listeners, there's also a risk that you won't hear what your boss says. It will work best if you try to keep your mouth shut a little bit more than usual, and actually listen. And your boss does actually expect you to do just that. Listen, because your boss has brilliant ideas too.

If you're a Green, you will share the relationship-focus that your boss has. Your Yellow boss—the good speaker—will speak eloquently about their own opinions, and for you—the good listener—the important thing is to keep track of everything they say. Your boss will talk in the first person. If they remember their leadership training, they should include a few questions about what you think. And then the best thing for you to do is to get involved in the conversation. If your Green column is extremely high, there is a risk that you'll remain too passive in the conversation, and in the worst case your boss won't even notice that you've hardly opened your mouth. So take a step forward and make your presence felt. And accept that your boss tends to talk about themselves even if the conversation is actually about you.

What if you're Blue and have a Yellow boss? Hmm. You should bear in mind that you need to make a considerable effort. You like facts, details, and you think things over before you open your mouth. Your boss mainly goes on feeling, quite often talks without a point, and avoids details the same way politicians avoid the truth. On paper it looks like you complement each other. And you will be able to! In order for that to happen, you need to allow yourself to be a bit spontaneous. You don't have to smile all the time, but it wouldn't hurt to make things a bit less formal. And you'll probably have to accept that you most likely won't be able to mention all those details you wanted to include. In addition—your focus on looking back will clash with the way your boss focuses on the future. You need to remind yourself to look ahead more often. Your boss is not just considering next week, but might already be considering next fall.

Adapting to Your Green Boss

Uh, oh, yeah. A Red person with a Green boss will often express themselves very clearly about the merits of their boss. Your desire to rush ahead will be a good complement to your Green boss's desire to stay where you are. You'll probably talk rather quickly and only about things that are—in your mind—relevant. You aren't afraid to use strong language, and your boss is your total opposite.

The challenge is that your boss is . . . your boss. So now and then you'll have to tone things down a bit. Lean back, use open body language. Use words like cooperation, together, jointly, security, and stability. (The response that just popped into your head says just as much about you as about your Green boss, remember that).

And remember that you can't just take over, simply because everything is progressing too slowly for your taste. If you think you can do a better job than the boss—well, apply for that job instead. And take the responsibility.

What if you're Yellow and have a Green boss? That doesn't imply any major problems. Both of you like talking software and relationships. You'll tend to dominate the conversation, which can be a problem for your boss. So don't immediately say everything you're thinking, and bear in mind that your boss will likely remember everything you *do* say. Especially if you express feelings. Take a couple of deep breaths, ask questions, and since you're neither the best listener nor have the best memory—why not take a notebook with you to the next meeting?

Try to avoid saying nasty things about people unless it

concerns serious violations. I'm not going to try to convince you that Green bosses never spread rumors and gossip. Nor do I mean that you should keep quiet about potential conflicts within the team. But your Green boss will not like it if you express yourself in a way that causes friction within the group. Your boss doesn't want to have to deal with that, so it's a good idea for you to maintain a positive attitude, which of course you already have. You are Yellow, after all.

If you are Green person with a Green boss, you'll feel understood and safe. You and your boss will both agree that it's okay that things take time and won't hurry if it's not necessary. The boss feels more like a friend than a colleague and boss.

Now we'll move on to those of you who are Blue and have a Green boss. This is going to work out quite well. Neither of you really thinks there's any particular urgency about anything. You both appreciate quality more than speed. Where your Green boss is, however, very caring and perhaps a bit too personal, you strive to keep your relationship strictly professional. Nothing wrong with that, but if you discourage all attempts to talk about free-time activities and the like, your boss might feel slightly rejected.

If you can loosen up a bit and be slightly more open about who you really are, you have a lot to gain. And your relationship will definitely benefit.

Your boss does trust you, so you *don't* need to list all the details every time. Your Green boss is, of course, equipped with considerably more patience than both the Yellow and the Red bosses down the hall, but there are limits. And make sure to ask what your boss thinks about what you've just said. But don't expect a straight answer right there and then.

Adaptation to Your Blue Boss

If you are primarily Red and your boss is primarily Blue, the two of you do, in fact, have quite a lot in common. You don't need to be overly cautious about what you say, as long as you don't criticize what your boss does. This is probably never a good move, but if you suggest that your boss doesn't maintain an appropriately high standard, then your relationship is going to sour.

But you are going to discuss concrete issues completely neutrally. Remind yourself, however, that where you want to accelerate out of the curve, your boss will want to slow down. Your preferred speeds are where you differ the most. You think that you can do the prep afterwards, while your boss would rather do it in advance. Apart from the fact that your boss is probably right on this point, it would be best for you to ease up on the accelerator if you want to stay on their good side. They won't necessarily get grumpy or irritated at you for stressing them. But they might become very tense if they think you are being careless.

Now some thoughts for the Yellows. You still with us? Good.

You know, a Blue boss could be the best thing that's ever happened to you. But it can also be the reason you finally clear out your desk and start a career as a circus performer. You have nothing in common. Sorry.

Apart from the fact that you both work in the same place and are in some way dependent on each other. And think about it: even though it gave you the shivers to read the chapter about the Blue bosses, you can learn a great deal from this relationship. And you can see how much you actually complement each other. The only thing you need to do is to steer yourself a bit in the Blue direction. Reflect on whether you really need to talk so much about yourself. Whether you must tell that story from last spring. Whether it's relevant to discuss your recent hospital visit when you're all having a coffee break.

It'll do you good to be a bit more thorough in your work. I know that you don't want to talk about such boring things, but later on when no one is listening you can admit I'm right. And, sure, it would be really nice not to have to keep everything in your head; not to have to worry what you've forgotten and to have a system for everything. Your boss can help you with this. If you're brave enough to ask.

Since I'm hoping your boss, too, will read this, you can encourage them to loosen up a bit and not to be totally fixated on decimal points. Together, you can achieve miracles!

Okay, you're Green and you've got the Blue boss. You both have the same need for peace and quiet, the same desire to proceed with caution. Of course, your boss is more concentrated on the task at hand than you are, but that needn't be a problem. For the most part, they won't interfere with what you do. At least, they won't as long as you deliver high quality work. And you want to do that, don't you?

What can be a bit tricky is that Blue bosses can sound rather critical when they notice things they don't like. Then they'll sometimes mercilessly criticize what you've done, and unfortunately your Blue boss will probably have very good reason to do so. What's important here is that you don't take what they say too personally. It isn't about who you are, but about what you have (or haven't) done. For your Blue boss, there's a big difference, but it will nevertheless probably feel rather unpleasant to you. But your boss isn't after your head; they only want you to be more thorough about details in the future. And that's not really so bad, is it?

If you get negative feedback that you know is fair—don't say it's not your fault. Don't try to claim that you didn't know. Your boss will simply pull out the notes from the meeting when you both agreed on the specifics. You're not going to just slip out of this. Blue bosses don't want to hear evasive answers. They want the job to be done properly.

So what's it like for you if you are Blue and have been blessed with a Blue boss? Well, congratulations are in order! You both care about details and you both know how important it is that everything is correct. Both of you appreciate having a clear rule book concerning how the job should be done. Both of you like collecting data and finding out every tiny thing before you make a decision. This means that you'll understand the decision-making process of your boss better than other colors. Just like you, your boss doesn't like taking risks. And you won't have to deal with any nonsense about feelings and that sort of unpleasantness.

However, your perfectionist tendencies will not necessarily facilitate cooperation. You might find that you have different ideas about what "exact" actually means. That can sometimes bring things to a total halt. If both of you slam on the brakes—who is going to take the next step forward? So help your boss leave the starting line. And don't forget that you too need to move forward. You can't all be defense; someone's got to kick the ball.

Where Do I Start?

The same as usual; you start by reminding yourself which colors are in your own profile. If you only have one color—simple. If you've got two, hopefully you know which they are. Think about your strengths and your weaknesses for a few minutes and consider whether your boss perceives you in the same way you perceive yourself.

After that, reflect on how the dialogue between the two of you works. Think about situations that could have worked better, but also of times when it works like it should.

If things have always worked well between you and your boss—can you see the pattern in the examples I gave above? And similarly, if the dialogue between you has gone wrong—are there explanations that are connected to your colors? And in that case—have you interpreted your boss correctly?

{16}

The Missing Piece of the Puzzle: When Colors and Driving Forces Aren't Enough

If we've grasped the colors and have learned about the driving forces—are we home free? No. I hate being a wet blanket, and I wish it was that simple. But the colors, the behavior profile, are just one of many dimensions. The driving forces that we've discussed are also an important factor. Experience, motivation, general background, and culture, plus loads of other aspects, all play a role in how people act. There are lots of things to take into account if you're going to be able to call yourself an efficient communicator.

Leadership is a communication process, so things can go very wrong if your boss hasn't understood any of this. And bosses who just keep on heading down their own road, regardless of what that road may be, miss something important. It's naïve and sometimes simply stupid not to consider the differences of other staff members. This is a central part of leadership, and if a boss ignores it, one needs to ask whether that person is in the right role.

Some people have gotten the message, other haven't. Many bosses probably try to do their best, but without the right tools it's difficult to build a house no matter how enthusiastic you are. With a bit of luck, you'll have a boss who considers both your color and your driving forces. That alone will get you a good part of the way.

Then, of course, we've got the question of development levels.

Just When You Thought You Had It All Figured Out . . .

Let's have a look at a situation where both colors and driving forces fail to help us.

Imagine that you are going to tackle a task on your long to-do list. Sometimes you can do it in five minutes, while other times it can take you several hours to deal with something that shouldn't really be complicated. Sometimes you'll be sitting and staring at your computer screen trying to work on something you know perfectly well how to handle—but you can't make yourself do it. On other occasions, the same task is as easy as pie.

How does this fit together? What causes this?

It's dependent on your level of development.

This is a model that was originally developed by the Americans Paul Hersey and Ken Blanchard way back in the mid-1970s. Based on their research into learning styles, they drew several conclusions that finally led to the realization that there is no single "best" way to lead people. Instead, the correct approach is determined by a whole number of

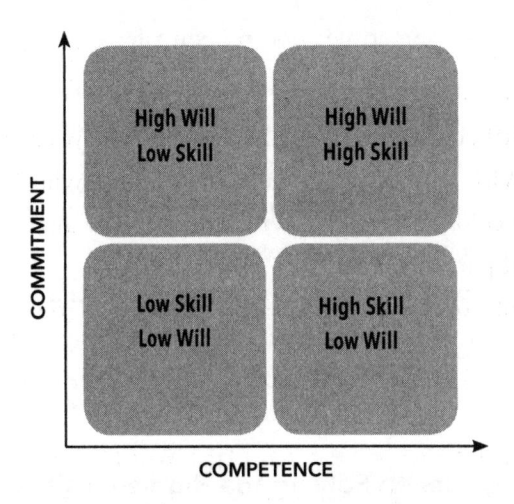

COMMITMENT	High Will / Low Skill	High Will / High Skill
	Low Skill / Low Will	High Skill / Low Will
	COMPETENCE	

different factors. Effective leadership is partly task-oriented and partly commitment-oriented. Hersey and Blanchard said that the best bosses are people who manage to see every member of their staff in the situation that the person finds themselves in at a given moment. And I agree 100 percent with that.

They looked at competence (ability, knowledge, skill) and the person's commitment, which they divided into motivation—*do I want to?*—and self-confidence—*can I?* If your boss knows how much of these respective factors you have when facing a particular task, then they'll also know what sort of leadership you require. This is a smart tool to avoid a lot of guessing games.

Hersey and Blanchard called the model "situational leadership." Effective leadership thus varies depending upon the task, commitment, and competence.

That's the theory.

If you understand this, then you'll also understand what your sometimes-uninterested boss hasn't grasped. This is why your boss sometimes doesn't contribute anything at all to your development. The good news is that if you identify the challenge, then you can also solve the problem yourself. You won't even need your boss. You'll be able to fix most of the issues entirely on your own, regardless of which color you are or what your driving forces are.

Your boss will be, essentially, superfluous. And you'll be in charge of your own development. The only thing you need do is to decide to take active responsibility for your own future.

A Step Closer to Solving the Riddle—This Is What Happens When You're New at Your Job

Imagine that you are going to start a new job. You applied, and you know what?—you got it! Congratulations! But what happens now? Full speed ahead? Or are there a couple of things you should consider? Yes, there are, and we'll look at them now.

The first phase—high will, low skill

High commitment (motivation + self-confidence) but low competence (for this particular task).

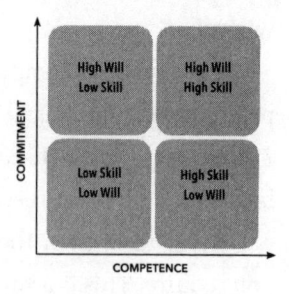

THE HAPPY BEGINNER WHO SHOOTS AT EVERYTHING THAT MOVES

If you start at a new job and you don't have any previous experience in the field, then you'll generally feel a strong commitment to your new job. You're motivated and you feel very self-confident as you start tackling everything that needs to be done. This is going to be really fun. How hard can it be? You just have to get on with it! But somewhere at the back of your mind, you're well aware of the fact that you've never done this before, which ought to make you stop and think. But even if you do realize that you might have *low competence* for your new work, it doesn't worry you. You'll get on with the job regardless. Why? You have such *high commitment*! Everything feels great.

You call your friends and relatives, you talk to your neighbors and your family—you've got a new job! Perhaps it's your first managerial position? You are starting a new career here. You're inspired! Everybody congratulates you, of course.

Someone might ask you what the job entails. You reply that it consists of lots of things and you're not exactly sure what they are yet, but it's going to be great fun to get your teeth into it. But what will your day be like? You don't know that either, but you'll be sweeping in there like a tornado with your boundless energy. After all, what's the worst that can happen?

You take on absolutely everything and throw yourself into every project since they all seem interesting, and you don't have any idea how long anything is going to take. You work evenings, nights, and weekends—because this is all such amazing fun. And absolutely nothing can stop you.

This is referred to as *unconsciously incompetent*.

The second phase—low skill, low will

Low commitment (motivation + self-confidence) and low competence (for this particular task).

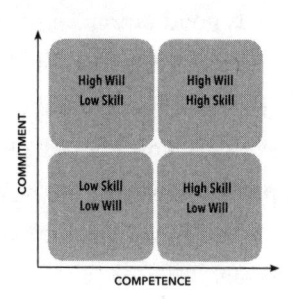

THE PERSON WHO REALIZED THAT NOTHING WORKS AND IS ABOUT TO GIVE UP

You start your new job with all the energy and motivation and self-confidence you can muster. You're everywhere. Join every project. Have a hand in every single process.

But after a while, you run your head into a brick wall a few too many times. You've discovered that things aren't quite as simple as you thought. It's difficult to find time for everything, you don't really have the right tools, you don't know who to ask, and the people you think you might be able to ask all seem to be fully occupied with their own work. You can't even find your own boss, and you start wondering if you might have bitten off more than you can chew.

After a while, you realize that you're working on the wrong things, you can't get a proper routine going and soon you're tired of the late evenings. What was inspiring at first is now simply onerous. Everyone else seems to know how to do it, but not you. This wasn't the job you applied for, the boss is stupid, and on top of that it's raining outside. There's no end to the problems.

There's a risk that you'll starting blaming others and look for scapegoats. On some days you are going to feel like you're surrounded by idiots. But most of all you feel confused. What little work you manage to get done is wrong, and nothing feels good anymore.

In the worst-case scenario, this will happen before your trial contract becomes a permanent employment contract. Perhaps you should just give up everything, anyway. This probably wasn't the right job for you.

You have become what is referred to as *consciously incompetent*.

The third phase—high skill, low will

Low or medium commitment (motivation + self-confidence) but high competence (for this particular task).

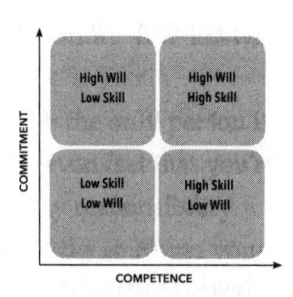

	Low Competence	High Competence
High Commitment	High Will Low Skill	High Will High Skill
Low Commitment	Low Skill Low Will	High Skill Low Will

THE PERSON WHO HAS BEGUN TO UNDERSTAND, BUT HESITATES ANYWAY

No choice but to give up? Time to throw in the towel? Not quite. You simply need to be aware of what's happening. The trick is to not give up, but to struggle on, hopefully with the professional support of the manager above you. This is a natural phase, and we all end up in the ditch now and then.

When you battle on—and resist that acute desire to just abandon everything and arrive late, take long lunches, and leave early—you'll notice that even though it's tough going, you're learning little by little how the job should be done. It's a question of looking for the positive. For example, now you probably know about all the things that don't work.

But, after a while, things will get easier if you don't give up. Keep at it, and you'll notice how the pressure slowly relaxes. You'll gradually get your motivation back since each task will go along a little smoother. The quality of your work will get better, and things will be a bit more fun again.

There are, of course, still tasks where you feel unsure. They might be small things. It might be something like finding a note on your desk that says: PHONE JANELLE. You get a sinking feeling in your stomach because you know perfectly well what it's about. Under the heading it says: *She's really pissed off with you.*

Sure. Fine. It was time to sort out that unpleasant item. You know what Janelle wants. Unfortunately, you know what you're going to have to say to her, and you have the competence to dial her number.

It's just that . . . you need a cup of coffee first. You can call Janelle a bit later.

Perhaps after lunch. Or why not tomorrow?

The reason for this behavior is simple—your self-confidence isn't strong enough for you to deal with an angry Janelle. In other situations, this might not have been a problem. But today . . . no. You don't trust your own ability enough to be actually able to pick up the phone.

You are what is identified as *unconsciously competent*.

The fourth phase—high will, high skill

High commitment (motivation + self-confidence) and high competence (for this particular task).

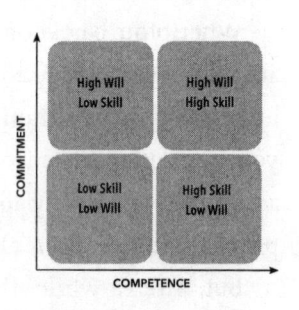

THE PERSON WHO MANAGES ON THEIR OWN AND BECOMES MORE CREATIVE

And finally, it turns out alright. Since you aren't the sort of person who gives up easily, you've struggled along and done your best. You've worked on enough projects, and so much has turned out well that not only has your competence and motivation increased—even your self-confidence has returned. Now everything feels okay again, and you might even find it hard to understand why you were so dreadfully dejected earlier.

You get things done in the time they were meant to take, you even look for more things to do, and you sleep well at night again. The stress has released its tight grip on you, and you're now feeling strong and creative. You might even start looking around for a new job because you're feeling ready for fresh challenges.

You are what is noted as being *consciously competent*.

How Long Does This Process Take?

One can't say how long it will take between the first and the last phase. It depends on how difficult the work is. There's a big difference between learning how to sell to the market in Poland versus understanding the new coffee machine. And in the description above, I've described a person who is *new at their job*. The situation is usually much more complex than this.

But what's important is that you understand that this is a logical process that takes place virtually *every time you learn something you didn't know before*. Putting in a lot of effort at the very beginning indicates that you're committed to carrying out the task; there's nothing wrong with that. And if, in the course of things, you mess some stuff up in the process, well that's part of the package.

It's important to note: there is nothing wrong with you.

You react negatively to setbacks, and that can lead to frustration. And as you learn your job, your commitment will return. You only need to retain your faith that this will happen.

There are studies in this field, and it's clear that once you've lost motivation and perhaps even your self-confidence—the second phase—you then need to build up your confidence first. It is hard to feel strong when you know you lack the competence for a particular task. It needs to be developed before you'll start to feel good again.

As usual, there are always exceptions to the rule, but it's also good to know that if you do lose momentum when you're working on a particular task, the solution is fairly simple: learn the job from the beginning. Don't cheat. No short cuts, don't ignore the task, and don't dump it into somebody else's lap. Learn the job from the very beginning. Then you'll feel a lot stronger when you start on the next task.

So What About the Days When You Just Want to Pull the Covers Up over Your Head?

If your boss reads this and thinks that they have several staff members who have been drifting all over the place, perhaps the reason is that those staff members are simply moving between development stages. There isn't necessarily anything wrong with them. (Now and then, I get a call from bosses who say that they've recruited the wrong person. I usually remind them that this might be a part of an extremely natural process.) Even if the new staff member has promised the moon and the stars (the first phase), and the boss actually believed their questionable promises of perfect delivery, they're going to end up in the ditch sooner or later. That is part of the process, and it's the boss's job to pick them up again.

Not everyone can manage this all on their own. They need help. And this is where a really good boss can be enormously useful. If you let them. You can't be led if you don't want to be led.

I won't be too long-winded about this, but you should be able to see a certain logic here.

A more complex problem arises when your boss doesn't notice that you're moving between development levels and that, even though you said you could manage the job, you actually lack the tools to do so. Bad bosses take the easy way out here.

Fred said he knew what he was doing—now it's up to him.

But who the hell wants to admit that they lack motivation or self-confidence? How much fun is it to go to your boss and admit that you're dropping the ball?

Good Bosses Solve This; Bad Bosses Don't

The thing is that you don't really need your boss to help you move on. There are ways to move on all by yourself. To start with, you need to identify where in the process you are, but once you've done that you can identify what you're lacking. Perhaps you need new knowledge, or you might need someone to encourage you. Sometimes your boss has the answer, but surprisingly often you'll have it yourself. Or the solution will lie with one of your colleagues. Together you can analyze some of the difficulties just as well as an absent (or even an indifferent) boss.

If you can talk with your team and be open, you can support and share things with each other, probably just as well as any boss. It's highly likely that you'll even do it better, since you'll see a problem much sooner than your boss would. Imagine how much time you would save if you don't need to wait for your boss to have time to listen.

With the right approach, your boss will actually be superfluous.

Does This Process Only Happen at Work?

In fact, this happens every time you take it upon yourself to do a new task. And not only work-related ones. You can see this development process play out even in the activities you do in your free time.

Just consider some people's gardens. Or in their homes! They started enthusiastically, but now there are unfinished projects all around. Why? People start something without really realizing how hard it's going to be, and once they get stuck, they lose their focus and begin somewhere else. You can go on like that for years unless a magical lifestyle TV program appears to fix your DIY nightmare.

How You Drive into a Ditch

This is one of my favorite examples borrowed from one of my good friends. George is a Red businessman who often tells the following story: he'd had a driver's license for more than twenty years and considered himself a very good driver. (Since I've driven with him, I can add that he's also a sensationally *fast* driver.) He'd driven a sedan for decades and thought he knew exactly how it should be done.

Then the family bought a second car, a very large SUV. And what do you do with a huge SUV? Of course, you go off-roading. That's what it's for. George has always been a man of action, so he jumped in and drove right out to a large field to take it for a spin.

Confident in his new vehicle, George gunned the engine

expecting to go straight over the first ditch he saw. The SUV's chassis caught on the edge. Stuck.

Curtains.

I wasn't there at the time, so I can only guess what words were said in that car. But according to George, he had a very clear insight as the vehicle hung on the edge of that ditch. He had thought he had been in the fourth development phase when it came to off-road driving. He hadn't considered that driving a huge SUV over a ditch is a bit different than driving a sedan on a highway. It's actually not the same at all. They both involve driving a vehicle, but the challenges are so very different.

Anyhow, that realization not only sent him straight into the ditch, but also straight into the second development phase. He swore and shouted and called his new SUV all sorts of names. How can you make a giant SUV that can't deal with one little ordinary ditch? No matter what he tried, he couldn't get loose.

After a while a farmer came by with an old 4x4 from the 1970s and towed him out. George was also informed that he could use the center differential when he drove off-road, and that it was better to cross a ditch diagonally than to cross straight through the mud. This was the third phase. He started to learn how to drive an SUV, but since the episode had damaged his self-confidence, George just drove home.

Later on he took the same road, but took it gently. This meant he could avoid the worst obstacles in the field. And now you could say that he's in the fourth phase in his development curve. He has recovered his motivation and his self-confidence and he's fairly competent—as long as we're talking about a fairly flat field.

So What Does the Map Look Like?

How do you know which development phase you're in? It isn't as complicated as you might think. Take a look at the picture with the four phases on page 166. Then answer the following questions:

- What is the task?
- What competence do I have for that particular task? (An honest answer, please. Boasting here would only be fooling yourself.)
- Do I feel motivated to deal with this task? Will it be fun? Will I get energy from thinking about it, or does it simply make me tired?
- What is my self-confidence like? Do I genuinely believe that I'm going to manage this task without any major problems? Or do I feel weak at the knees at the very thought?

It starts when you make this short analysis. The purpose of going through these four points is that it will help clarify what sort of support you need to be able to move forward with the task.

For example, if you find yourself in phase one, you don't really need a pep talk, but you do need some clear instructions about how the task should actually be carried out.

If you've landed in phase two, angry words and cheerleading are both unhelpful—what you need is somebody who cares about your situation and who calmly and methodically helps you along.

In phase three, the one where you actually know how to handle the issue, but for whatever reasons don't do it, you need to hear that you have the competence, that you've got this. You need to reinforce your self-confidence.

At the same time, if you've reached phase four, you'll almost be irritated if people tell you you're clever. Now you want to hear what good results you're achieving and how you contribute to the company.

{ 17 }

Surrounded by Superfluous Bosses

But What About the Bosses? Don't They Have Any Responsibility?

Without a doubt. The bosses have the greatest responsibility. They ought to guide you through this sometimes-troublesome loop. But your boss doesn't know what it looks like inside your head. After all, the aspects of the cycle that concern your motivation or your self-confidence have an emotional basis. And what's going on under your skin won't necessarily be visible on the outside. It's almost impossible to work out how you feel and experience the situation. Even if I've been pretty tough on your boss, we still need to find a way to approach the central question:

Should you be dependent upon your boss to achieve success?

I have already said several times that it isn't necessary. Sometimes waiting for your boss isn't going to be the solution. You'll be forced to deal with the situation yourself.

Leadership Is Not the Same Thing as Mind Reading

That the boss *ought* to have known, that it would have been *better* if the boss had been able *to see inside my head* and understood my concern—that might be true. But since the whole concept of mind reading is probably a myth, we'll have to find other solutions. Do you feel that you're not seen, or are ignored, or just generally undervalued—but you'd like to have help from your boss? Well, there is an almost ridiculously simple solution:

Go to your boss and say: *You know, this isn't working. Can we talk about it?*

The very second that you actually do that, you will show that you are an adult person who is prepared to be a part of the solution. For me, it's proof of personal maturity to take full responsibility for your situation. And sometimes full responsibility means being able to ask for help.

We're talking about your situation, about your job—a job where you might spend eight or nine hours every day. What would it be worth to actually untangle all the knots that are causing problems?

What Can You Do Yourself? Can You Help Here?

If you have a good boss, then they will come to you and propose some options. They've noticed that you're struggling with certain things, and they're there to support you so that you can move on. But, and this is incredibly important, if you have a boss who doesn't offer help the way you would have liked, that's not the same thing as your boss being an idiot.

Perhaps they're simply having a hard time seeing what you're struggling with.

Give your boss a chance.

Ask for a conversation.

Sit down.

Explain what's happening.

And then you say: *I need your help.*

With a really good boss and leader, you're on your way to a solution. The problem is that a frighteningly large number of bosses aren't going to listen. They're going to think: *another whiner who can't think on their own.*

I've given up on some bosses. They can say the right things; they can declare that they believe individuals need to be seen and supported. But in practice they do nothing about it. They either don't have the energy, or they don't make time for it. Or they don't actually know what they can do to help. Talk about burying your head in the sand.

These are the people that I call the unnecessary bosses.

They have a job with specific expectations, and they're getting paid to take responsibility for things they're actively ignoring. This is not acceptable. And some of them won't change before it's too late for you.

When I meet this gang during my leadership programs, they often say everything they know I want to hear. They are clever pupils, and they know that it's in their own interest to do well in the program. As a leadership coach I've met literally thousands of bosses—some good, others frighteningly incompetent. Some of them have bettered themselves based on what we've worked on. Others haven't bothered. Far too many have evidently liked what they heard but still haven't succeeded in bringing about any sort of change. They continue to do what they've always done. They continue to be the boss without giving any leadership. And this category of bosses will always exist.

What do employees need from an organization? They need to be motivated when things are tough, they need to build up self-confidence, they need input and education to raise their competence. What's interesting is that all the answers are already there within the organization. Since the boss isn't the ultimate specialist, they shouldn't be the bottleneck preventing a particular member from moving further. And many bosses don't give their staff what they need. They hardly exercise any leadership at all. So why are they even bosses?

It's Still Your Decision

What conclusions can we draw from this? That different people will have to tackle the problems they're facing in slightly different ways depending on what the goal is. As usual, your own personal insight is what counts. You can't change what your boss is like, you can only change yourself—that's the reality here.

As you may have noticed, this book can be read from two angles, so there's hope. I plan on giving your boss some insights too. But I want to strongly emphasize what I wrote in the beginning:

You also have a responsibility to see that the dialogue and communication works as well as possible. We are all adults and we can't just point a finger and say that *it's all on the boss. I don't care.* That's the same as giving up.

At the end of it all, if you're sitting there with a wrecked career and a ruined bank account, it's not going to help if you just realize that you could have done something yourself. If you have a really bad boss, you need to make a decision. For your own sake. Stay in the ditch and hope for better times, or start taking responsibility for the solution?

Hopefully, you'll now have some sense of what is lacking in your work dynamic. Now you can go to your boss and say those magic words: *I need* . . . , and then you fill in what you lack.

Start just like that. *I need* . . .

Nobody is going to be able to answer: *No, you don't need* . . .

Within your team, your group, your department, or unit, you can give each other what each of you need ninety-nine times out of a hundred. You can simply lead yourselves. And you can lead each other.

My Own Conclusions

If I had had these insights the first time I was a boss, would things have ended differently?

You bet! To start with, I would have understood much earlier what knowledge and competences I lacked. I stepped into the new job in phase one. Lots of energy, and I didn't have a clue. If somebody had told me that I didn't know the lay of the land and that I needed clear instructions to be able to be a boss—I would have listened. Nobody said anything to me. Everybody—including me—expected me to just handle it.

My bosses ought to have said that it was my responsibility to do my job, and they ought to have made sure that I had understood and acted accordingly. Instead they just left me to take care of myself, but I actually didn't have a clue as to what I was doing. That was, without a doubt, my own fault. Unfortunately, it affected a lot of other people in various ways.

When I lost my motivation and then finally my self-confidence, it was too late. Nothing could save the situation. I said I didn't want to lead those thirteen unfortunate people. If somebody had coached me and explained what useful leadership looked like instead of what I was doing, it would have helped.

> *Thomas, stop telling people to just fix things. Listen better. Make suggestions. Explain what they need to do instead. Learn to see the difference between motivation and a lack of competence. They are completely different things.*

Somebody ought to have sat down with me and demanded that I get my act together. Made sure that I, too, took my share of the responsibility. But also given me the tools I lacked.

Am I sitting here and blaming others? Perhaps I am.

But there is an important point here: if I'd understood the development process, then I would have gone to my own boss much earlier and asked for a meeting.

Sat down.

Explained the situation.

And then said: *I need your help.*

At twenty-four years old, I was a bad boss. Worse than that: I was one of those superfluous bosses. The staff managed much better without me.

I learned in the end. I started looking at myself in the mirror and looked for solutions there. And, in the end, I think I became a good boss.

Don't make the same mistakes I made. Don't wait for somebody to see you. Evaluate the situation based on what we've talked about so far and draw your own conclusions. Take control of your own development. Everything you manage on your own will strengthen your self-confidence and your motivation. And whatever is missing, go to your boss and ask for it.

And start off with that simple phrase: *I need* . . .

Remember what I said at the beginning of this book: *choose your boss*. Life is too short to waste working for a bad, mean, ignorant, or just generally uninterested boss. You deserve better.

Now it's up to you.

Warning!

If you don't have a managerial position today, the second part of this book isn't for you. Because now I'm going to reveal the leadership secrets that only a boss ought to know. If you delve into this part, it will open a door that you will never be able to close. You might find out what your bosses really think about their staff.

You read on entirely at your own risk.

PART II

Surrounded by Lazy Employees

{ 18 }

Why It's So Hard for Your Staff to Get the Job Done

Welcome to Part II. As you'll certainly have noticed, this book is written from two different perspectives, since I wanted bosses as well as employees to be inspired to see things from different angles. If you're a boss, this will absolutely help you develop your leadership skills. The fact that you even picked up this book shows that you are curious, that you realize there are many challenges to being a boss, and that you have enough personal insight to understand that you can become even better at the craft of leadership.

And perhaps you might be faced with the same challenge as many other bosses: your staff just doesn't get enough done every day. I know that it's sometimes frowned upon to criticize your team, so let me do it for you: certain people on your staff don't put in enough effort to do their job properly. Some staff members are top performers; no problems there. A study carried out by a large number of companies in the EU a couple of years ago revealed the following harrowing statistics:

- Only 10 percent of all employees can be classified as top performers
- Approximately 70 percent can (with a bit of optimism) be considered average performers
- And around 20 percent are without a doubt underachievers

Hard facts, I know. But are you going to contradict me? What's it like in your group? Do you even know what they get done every day?

If you lead a sales team, you have a particularly big challenge. According to a report—admittedly American, but it is doubtful whether it differs very much from Europe—an average salesperson works on marketing (conversations with customers, visits from customers, writing quotes, following up on quotes) for about ninety minutes a day. What do they do the rest of the time? Well, you tell me. For some of them it takes a couple of hours to even get started on their workday. Others get bogged down in administration, and others probably couldn't even explain what happened to all those work hours.

Perhaps you're one of those bosses who's taken your leadership position extremely seriously, and you actually have a higher percentage of top performers. And sure, that's perfectly possible. Naturally, there's enormous variation between different types of organizations. But perhaps you know that certain members of your team could speed up considerably. If you just glance at them, it looks as if they're busily working, but if you look properly you can see that they're really just shuffling along. In fact, a couple of them look like . . . complete slackers.

The Remarkable Phenomenon with Slackers

You've explained what the job entails. You've read the workplace guidelines and expectations to them. They've nodded and said they understand what's expected of them. Everything seems to be alright. And yet . . . the commitment you were hoping to see from your staff member just isn't there. After a while, you realize that the person concerned isn't doing what they should be doing at all.

How does that happen? What's actually the problem?

You've almost certainly read various types of management books before. Perhaps you were trying to develop your own leadership skills, or you wanted advice on what was up with the reluctant members of your staff. Reading books about leadership—or going to lectures—is a good way to get new ideas and allow yourself to be inspired to try new approaches and to apply better methods in your leadership. Nothing wrong in that.

I've read an incredible amount on the subject since my work entails supporting bosses in their leadership. That is my specialty. I've worked in this area for more than twenty years. I don't claim that I know all there is to know about leadership, but I know quite a lot. Above all, I've made many mistakes of my own, which has helped me gain certain insights. Some of them were a bit painful, to be honest.

There's a natural problem built in to how our companies are

structured. If you want to have a good career, it's all about becoming the boss. Of course, our view on this has been modernized over the last twenty years, but it's still more common to move linearly upwards within an organization than it is to move laterally, if you're interested in building a successful career.

What Are You Actually Doing Here?

It's very evident to me that a lot of bosses today haven't actually sought out that position as a conscious choice. It just happened, and I hardly need to point out that that isn't the optimal reason to shoulder the responsibility of being a boss and all it implies. The excuse, *I didn't manage to sneak away when they asked me*, isn't good enough. You need to know why this is a job you want. Because when you feel surrounded by bums who don't love their job as much as you do, it's helpful to know why you took on this challenge in the first place. And if you consider all of your staff members who aren't performing as strongly to be lazy, then you actually do need help. Of course, there are lazy people who don't contribute more than absolutely necessary. But the reasons behind this behavior are often more complex than you can imagine.

The reason you accepted the appointment as boss could lie in your driving forces. Perhaps you thought that the pay increase was a carrot; perhaps you like the power it gives you over others. It is possible that you think you actually can make a difference if you were to hold that power. You can really add something. There's nothing wrong with any of these motives, but from experience I know that far too many bosses can't give an honest answer to the question: *why did you accept the job?* Sometimes I'm drowned in empty phrases when I ask it:

> *It's important for me to make a difference.*
> *I wanted to make myself superfluous.*
> *There are things that I can contribute.*
> *I want my staff to grow.*
> *I want to reduce the inefficiency in the group.*
> *My managers thought I ought to accept this job.*

The true answer, albeit slightly mercenary, is quite often:

> *I took the job because of the pay rise.*
> *It would have been wrong to say no—what would that have looked like?*
> *My wife/husband/parents thought I ought to start a career.*
> *I like the perks.*
> *It's fun to call yourself a boss.*

Or—perhaps the worst answer of them all: *I don't know.*

Mission Statement

Even in Swedish I use the English term "mission statement." I haven't thought this up myself, but you can define it for any function at all: salesman, customer service, or boss, for example. The purpose of creating a mission statement is to explain the purpose behind a particular role. And you really do need to find the answer! It's incredibly important in your role as boss and leader. You must be able to say to yourself: *This is the reason why I got out of bed this morning*!

As I mentioned earlier, if we can't even explain to ourselves the purpose of what we're doing—how will we be able to explain it to anybody else? If you don't know why you personally get out of bed every day, why should anybody else care?

I know there are other examples, but let's take a sales team to start with. If they can't explain to the customer why the salesmen are there, then everybody could just as easily order everything online. Why, after all, do you need a salesman in the 21st century? They'll only prove useful if they offer something more than the price of the products.

The same applies for bosses within an organization. It's quite a useful process to sit down together and try to define some goals. What are we actually trying to provide here? Should we be good models, should we be professional, should we be good listeners, or should we be at the forefront of everything?

Regardless of what the goals may be, it's a good idea to write down a few lines. Here's an example from one of the organizations that I've had the privilege of working with:

> *As a boss and leader, I should be committed to taking responsibility for inspiring and developing my team in order to help them achieve the goals we have set.*
> *I want to be perceived as a straight-talker and a credible and professional leader.*

This particular goal was created during a number of meetings with a management group designed to deal with obvious shortcomings and the negative climate in the division. The bosses were not seen as role models, and the staff members didn't think that they took enough responsibility. There was no inspiration, and the leadership felt that communication was vague. The whole time, we returned to this question: *How can we motivate our staff to listen to us? Why are we here?*

Do you have your own mission statement? You don't need to do it as formally as this, but if you don't know why *you're* there—how will your staff have any direction? How will they know what they can expect from you, if you don't have a clue yourself?

Think about what you want to demonstrate in your role as manager. Write down who you want to demonstrate it to and a few words describing how you want to be seen.

Imagine that you walk into a restaurant one evening with your family. In one of the booths sits a member of your staff with her family. She doesn't see you, and just as you pass her booth you hear her say to her family: *My boss is so . . .*

How would you like her to finish that statement?

My boss is so *clever, competent, experienced, forward-looking, inspiring, loyal, positive, a good listener, thorough, visionary*—what?

You have to want something, so think about how you want to be perceived. That can be a part of your mission statement.

You need to know this. If you don't want to be perceived as a bad or even a totally superfluous boss, you need to have some overarching goals. And it's a good idea to start with yourself. The worst that can happen, of course, is that you conclude that you don't actually have anything to offer your team at all. Then it's really time to start taking your leadership role more seriously.

And what's interesting about this is that once you start doing that, you're going to see considerably fewer slackers in your office. I promise.

Liked—or Respected?

So when the going gets rough and there are more demands made on you, it becomes a question of reminding yourself why you stepped into this job. This isn't something that should be done without at least an evening's reflection, perhaps together with your partner or a mentor you trust. I'm not trying to frighten you, but this is good advice. Figure out what motivated you to take on the job, to become a boss.

Inexplicably many bosses, far too many if you ask me, feel a need to be liked. Especially if they've been promoted to become the boss of their former colleagues. And who doesn't want to be liked? Most bosses would answer *be liked* when asked whether they would rather be *liked* or be *disliked* by their staff. Of course, if you have to choose, we all prefer to be liked!

But such a wish can undoubtedly create more lazy employees. Think about it. If your decisions and your standpoints are governed by a concern over how your popularity is going to be affected, well, this is going to be a rather bumpy ride. You'll back down when somebody loses their temper or shows dissatisfaction with you as a boss. If you're afraid that people will suddenly stop talking when you enter the breakroom, then you've got a problem. (Hint: you're already cut off from a lot of information about what's happening in the group. It comes with the job.)

Some staff members will make use of that. A person who doesn't want to bother doing a good job might get away with it. They'll badger you with requests about everything from odd working hours to who should actually get to park closest to the entrance.

Don't misunderstand me. I don't have a problem with you wanting to be liked in your role as boss. But if that steers your decisions too much, *you* are going to have problems.

Why? Because you're not always going to be liked. You can't please everybody all the time. That is a fantasy and an impossible pipe dream. Forget it.

Respected—or Liked?

If we switch perspectives and look at what it means to be respected, we'll find some interesting psychology under the surface. What does it mean to be respected? I'm not talking about the idiotic attitude where "respected" means "feared"—that's simply stupid and nothing you want to have anything to do with.

No, to be respected means that you are esteemed for your competence and that you have a reputation as a skillful and fair leader. That you're appreciated for what you do and that your staff have faith in you. For example, you make those difficult decisions and then you stand by them.

To be motivated by a desire for respect is to be aware that

you must sometimes make decisions that your staff aren't going to like. Sometimes you must have the courage to put your foot down and confront certain members of the team. For example, the folks who come in late, who take long lunches and leave early. To be respected you need to be prepared to demand more from underachievers and to roll up your sleeves and do things yourself when necessary.

Think back to your school days. Think about the teachers that you now appreciate for what they did.

Who comes to mind? The cool teacher who sat with his cap on backwards and tried to be nice to all the freshmen kids? Who allowed an awful lot of chaos during class because *boys will be boys?* The one who didn't care whether you really did your homework or not?

Or do you remember the teacher who was firmer, or even strict, and who demanded some discipline? Who was prepared to give negative criticism if you didn't behave properly? Who said *stop* when it got too noisy in the classroom and who was even prepared to phone your parents if you behaved badly at school?

If you're like most people, now that you're grown up, you'll feel most appreciative of the teachers who pushed you and made sure you left school with the highest possible grades. I realize this is a bit of a generational issue, but I think you will agree with my point.

To be motivated by wanting to be liked as a leader is a dangerous path to tread. Think about why the approval of others is so important to you.

To strive to be respected—in the positive sense—is a safer

path to take. And the funny thing about this is that if you become respected, you will be liked, too. It just doesn't come in the order you might think.

An Example

Imagine that you get a new boss. What are your expectations? *I hope it's someone nice!*

The new boss arrives. He makes it clear that you will be given whatever you ask for. Face time is nothing to him. He's laid back about work hours and is flexible about people actually delivering what they should. Deadlines aren't taken seriously. He's satisfied as long as everybody is happy. People should have fun at work.

He praises everybody, and the flattering words rain over you too. He highlights everybody who has succeeded in even the smallest of achievements. Everyone gets cheers and compliments. Ice cream and balloons every single week. You hardly need do anything to get a pat on the back from this lovely guy who really does seem to see everyone as the individuals they are. You're overjoyed. What a great guy! How did we get so lucky?

But fairly soon, problems appear. People start doing things their own way; nobody takes full responsibility since it isn't expected of them. You can do whatever you think is the most fun. What a fantastically nice boss you've got who really does let you choose whatever you want to work on. And who doesn't have any issues when you decide to "work" at home on Fridays.

Suddenly, your boss notices that things are slipping out of his hands. The whole department threatens to collapse like a house of cards. Perhaps the management reacts and wonders what his team is actually getting done during work hours. He changes his tone, quick as a flash, and suddenly he becomes very thorough and starts to demand discipline and quality. He follows up on everything, he's always on your back, and he demands that you pick up the pace. You can forget Fridays at home, and you'll no longer have time to pick up the children from preschool. Suddenly your once cuddly boss has been transformed into a real dictator.

What happened?

Do You Get a Second Chance?

We'll try again. So you're getting a new boss. She talks to everybody on the team and becomes fully acquainted with what each and every person does. She interviews everyone, and she notes down everything. You talk about her behind her back when you have your coffee break. Ugh, she is sticking her nose into every detail. It feels invasive. She wants to know what isn't working well at this workplace. She sorts out those issues straight away. She has a hold on everything and follows up in detail every week. She adapts these follow-ups to the particular staff member's competence and experience, but she keeps close track of everyone. She gains full control. Every time there's a departure from what should happen, she talks to the person concerned and solutions are laid out. The lazy employees are told to look sharp the same day.

During a meeting, you guardedly ask her whether she distrusts all of you; she answers no. But also that she takes her task extremely seriously. After the meeting, and when she's not around, you start calling her names I don't intend to repeat here. Now all of you are stressed and wondering if she cares the slightest about the feelings of her staff.

But after a couple of months, the work of the team starts, funnily enough, to run a bit smoother. You realize the things that you were irritated by, poor routines, internal communication, or whatever it might be, suddenly work properly.

Then your tough boss says that she's treating all the staff to dinner at a luxury restaurant since you've worked so hard to get everything into order. During the dinner, she expresses her genuine appreciation for your commitment. She says that she knows she's been a bit tough now and then, but that she's proud of you.

After this, she lessens the pressure a little since everything is in better shape. Everyone follows the routines you've all agreed on. She takes a step back. What she does, is she adapts her leadership to the situation.

Believe me, you're going to see the new boss as a heroine. You're going to feel privileged to work under such a professional. You respect her, and because of that you will also like her.

What About the Bums?

The conclusion is obvious: it works to put the pressure on in the beginning, and then to loosen the reins a little.

Doing it the other way around doesn't work nearly as well. People just get angry. It's a psychological effect that has always existed. We simply have to accept that it works like that.

When it comes to dealing with lazy employees, a deeply consistent attitude is required. You simply have to be a bit of a bother for a while. But it will pass. That's how you deal with people who likely know what they should do, but who might have started to feel a bit too comfortable in their job.

{ 19 }

How to Read Your Staff's Colors

I'm guessing that you've read this book from the beginning. In which case, you know what I'm talking about when I mention somebody's colors—Red, Yellow, Green, and Blue. Perhaps you might even have stumbled across *Surrounded by Idiots*. That, too, should have given you—as boss—certain guidance.

But I would nevertheless like to emphasize some tips on how you can quickly and relatively easily recognize the various behaviors that each color displays.

We'll take an example. Let's say that you have an employee who is reporting on how the latest project is proceeding. You have an inkling that the news is not going to be totally positive, but you've decided to give the person in charge of the project the chance to express their view on progress.

Sara's Red Report

"It hasn't gone at all the way I wanted. We're on schedule, that's true, but we ought to have reached the next phase by now. We should be able to meet the deadline with a week to spare, but not if people drag their feet like they're doing. Some real slowpokes. No matter how much I try to nudge them on, I can't get them to speed up. But I've got some ideas.

"This should be a profitable project. I've managed to negotiate so that there are no fines, and it wouldn't surprise me if you could save at least 12 percent on the last line.

"Incidentally, have you got anything more you need me to work on? I'm in a bit of lull right now."

Your analysis: Sara's way of delivering her report is comparatively concise. She covers what she considers to be most important: schedules and budget. She says they're on schedule and are way below budget. But she would have liked a better result. She seems rather demanding. and she keeps the pressure up. She is critical of some members of her team but sticks to the point at hand. How the team is feeling, or if somebody thinks they're overloaded with work—we don't know anything about that. Sara probably hasn't asked them, and if that's the case, then it hasn't reached her ears anyway.

You're going to get a profitable project, which sounds great. Sara does seem dissatisfied with progress in the project, but nevertheless so she wants more to do. Since the others are dragging their feet, she's getting bored. The best thing you can do is to give her some more work. If it turns out to be too much for her—which isn't very likely—she'll get back to you.

Besides—if there are any problems with the project, she doesn't mention them. She counts on having sorted out the situation before she needs to talk to you about it.

Bertil's Yellow Report

"We're all busy on this, and everybody is extremely committed. Are we going to have a break over Christmas? I thought I'd go off to the Alps if the Christmas bonus comes through. I really like the team dynamic. I've got a few ideas about a side project; can we have a chat about it? But I think we should be able to take what we've learned from this initiative and take that in a totally different direction. We should be able to achieve even better results in the future. You never know what can happen at the end of such a large project. You know, I'm working 24/7 with this. My wife thinks I work too much, but that's what it's like when you are as committed as I am. Actually, perhaps I ought to take a holiday in the sun over Christmas instead. Some of the team members work a bit slowly, but I usually go in and get them going with a pep talk. There's a guy in the group, I can't remember his name. Chris, perhaps? He doesn't really seem to feel at home here, so I thought I'd have lunch with him some day . . . or is he Peter? Do you know who I mean? The guy with the Excel spreadsheet on his forehead? I tried to sound him out and he just stared at me as if I had something on my face, really weird, but anyhow—Björn, perhaps?—he doesn't like sitting with the group. I haven't gotten the latest updates, but I reckon we are sticking fairly well to budget, more or less. Have you been in the Alps?"

Your analysis: Okay . . . Bertil thinks out loud. He opens the hatch at the front of his face and out comes a whole mess of words. He's terrified of silence. A second can't pass without something being said. Bertil uses about 80 percent more words than are really needed. Despite the fact that he talks a lot more than Sara did, you know considerably less. And what you did learn—you can't even be sure it's correct. Bertil doesn't know either.

In addition, he seems to randomly jump from one subject to another, and you find it hard to follow his thoughts. Everything you hear is just one long stream-of-consciousness monologue. You listen to a whole tangle of thoughts that effectively camouflage any bad news there might be.

Bertil is fairly certain that they'll finish in time, that's what it feels like anyway, but he can't say that for sure either. He simply isn't well-informed. The guy whose name is completely unclear probably knows exactly what the situation is. But since Bertil thinks that this guy—George—is a bit of a weirdo, he probably doesn't ask him.

Bertil perhaps does just as much work as Sara. The difference is that while Sara didn't mention this—it's self-evident when you work hard—but instead asked for more, Bertil manages to make his wife become the spokesperson for his long workdays. He manages to convey—somehow in a slightly elegant manner—that he's beginning to feel overworked, but he isn't one to complain.

Margareta's Green Report

"Yes, I feel like things are going fairly well with the project. I'm not really sure; haven't had time to sit down for a proper talk with everybody. But they seem to be having a good time and like what they're doing. They all seem to have found their role within the project, and as far as I can tell they get on well together. Even though there's an awful lot to do—everybody is working very hard—the atmosphere is good. We're taking it nice and easy and working methodically. I try to go around as much as I can and really listen to all their needs. The only person I am worried about is Stefan. He looks to be under a bit of pressure; perhaps I can take over some of his assignments if it becomes a problem. After all, I don't work every Sunday, so I can fit in a little bit extra."

Your analysis: Hmm. What is it you are actually hearing here? An extremely nurturing project leader whose greatest worry is that the staff members in the project might suffer from occupational burnout from the unbelievable amount of work. Margareta sneaks in that, just like Bertil, she too thinks she has too much work to do. But instead of saying that her family is worried, she exhibits signs of a victim mentality when she says that she still has some free Sundays. She's hoping that you'll say that it isn't necessary. She doesn't dare ask for more resources. On the other hand, we don't know how well this project group is actually getting on; since she's very empathetic, she will interpret every sigh from a member of the group as a sign of imminent burnout.

Besides: how is the project itself actually going? There wasn't a word about what you're probably asking about—schedules, budget, efficiency. You'll have to ask.

George's Blue Report

"The figures that I emailed to you this morning comprise all the data up to yesterday evening at nine o'clock. After that, I can only give you an estimate. New reports come in around three o'clock. In my judgement, we're slightly behind schedule since so many new parameters have been added, and it has been impossible to allow for them.

"So I have emailed the client and asked them to do better. It's impossible for us to do a good job when they incessantly change the conditions. After seven reminders, they've promised to create extra resources for quality control. And they did so—you can see I copied you in the emails—but the person they appointed has no experience with our report system. I've suggested that I meet to explain it to him on Friday at four o'clock.

"The budget discrepancy on row 12 is about returns. I've allowed for possible returns on the latest material. I've included a follow-up point for next year to keep track of this $159.00.

"Lena finds it rather difficult to manage her tasks, so I need to train her. An external course for the software we're using costs about $200, excluding tax, and I count on being able to talk them into giving us a bit of a discount. Perhaps $178. Is it OK with you to invest in this? She's worked here more than ten years. It would be appreciated if you could sign the order for this in your capacity as her formal manager in the hierarchy.

"Furthermore, I can note that . . ."

Your analysis: Tick, tock. With that, we can leave George.

George only talks about details, and he double checks everything. For example, he has a note about a future $159 somewhere. And he wants to try to get a discount for Lena's course. He's checked her background, and she's worth investing in.

I can't possibly comment on everything, but if you read the example again, you'll realize the following: George doesn't really care very much about the people in the group. Compare this report with how Margareta expressed herself. He expects somebody to come to a mini software course at four o'clock on a Friday afternoon. When this person cancels the meeting, George will be very surprised.

Details, details, details. But how is the project progressing in its entirety? You don't know. I don't know. Does George know? Perhaps. But his big picture view is missing. All he really talks about are the details. And the problems.

This Was Complicated

What can we learn from this? In your group you probably have a lot of different people who prioritize things completely differently.

Since you're likely a very busy person, the checklist below outlines what you can expect. If you can keep track of these things, you'll go far.

	RED	YELLOW	GREEN	BLUE
BEHAVIOR	Has drive and is direct	Optimistic and spontaneous	Considerate and understanding	Thoughtful and correct
IS	Business-like	Visible	Discreet	Formal
WORKS	Diligently Ambitiously Formally Effectively Precisely	Is committed Personable Flexibly Is stimulating Is eloquent	Warm Relaxed Friendly Informally Low key	Structured Organized Specialized Methodical Taciturn
WORK PACE	Quick and decisive	Quick and spontaneous	Slow and stable	Slow and systematic
PRIORITIZES	The task and the result	Relationships and influence	To retain good relationships	The task and the method of working
AFRAID OF	Losing control	A loss of prestige	Confrontation	Making a fool of himself
ACTS UNDER STRESS	Dictates conditions and becomes dominating	Attacks and becomes ironic	Gives way and agrees	Withdraws and avoids
WANTS	Results	Inspiration	Stability	Methods
WANTS YOU TO BE	Direct	Stimulating	Nice	Precise
WISHES HIMSELF TO BE	The person who decides	The person who is admired	The person who is liked	The person who is correct
GETS ANNOYED BY	Inefficiency and indecision	Passivity and routines	Insensitivity and impatience	Surprises and gimmicks

	RED	**YELLOW**	**GREEN**	**BLUE**
WISHES FOR	Success and control	Status and flexibility	Peace and quiet and close relationships	Credibility and time to prepare himself
ACTS	Business-like	Elegant	Friendly	Law abiding
LIVES IN	The here and now	The future	The past (when everything was better)	His thoughts
TRUSTS	Gut feeling	Recognition	Himself	Specialists
FINDS DIFFICULT	Sit still	Loneliness	Unpredictability	Urgency

{ 20 }

Whip or Carrot—How to Motivate Your Staff

One of the things I always deal with when I'm coaching a group of managers through leadership training is the question of having responsibility for other people. And how they see their present or future staff.

In 1960, Douglas McGregor wrote a book called *The Human Side of Enterprise*. Among other things, he tried to ascertain how work motivation, leadership, and management worked. He developed two theories that he called Theory X and Theory Y. These describe two different attitudes when it comes to work motivation.

According to Douglas McGregor, there are two contrasting sets of assumptions about how people are motivated, based on two types of management. Theory X emphasizes the importance of strict supervision, external rewards, and penalties, while Theory Y highlights job satisfaction and encourages workers to approach tasks without direct supervision.

Theory X says that:

- People have an instinctive aversion to work and try to avoid it if they possibly can;
- People must be forced, controlled, governed, and threatened with punishments to carry out work;
- People prefer to be led because they lack ambition and want to avoid responsibility.

A Theory X leader thus assumes that their workforce is not committed to the results of the work they're doing, that they need clear instructions and close supervision, and that they only work hard if they absolutely must. The only way to get them to carry out their work is to control them the whole time, prodding them with a stick and never letting up. You can't trust anybody, and if the boss turns his back, then work will come to a complete halt.

Here we have the definition of a lazy employee. And with this set of attitudes it's obvious why there are so many of them.

What do you think of this theory? Does it feel modern? No?

Of course, this attitude feels horribly outdated. When I mention this example, most bosses just shake their head. I usually ask *Who thinks that this is a good attitude?*

Nobody holds up their hand. Nobody wants to be associated with this.

But note: this is about an attitude. This is how *you choose to see your staff,* it's not about what *they're actually like.* Naturally, there are people who are in the wrong place in work life; it's self-evident that not everyone is good at their job.

There are some people who are completely unsuitable for certain tasks. And some of these people are unmotivated and lazy. Absolutely. There are people everywhere who don't know how their job should be done and many of them are simply incompetent.

But that isn't what Theory X is about. It's about how you regard your staff. *Your* view of *them*.

Theory Y says, instead, that:

- People can, under beneficial circumstances, seek and want to take responsibility;
- People value communication and commitment;
- If people can govern and control their own work, you don't need control and punishment.

A Theory Y leader assumes that their staff can be motivated to work with a minimum of instructions, that to a high degree they can supervise themselves, and that they want to do a good job. The leader's role is to help them do that. There is imagination and a richness of innovation here, if only the boss is willing to let it loose.

This is fundamentally about whether you, as the boss, actually dare to let your staff solve their own problems. If you give them a little freedom, their creativity will find an outlet.

Yet again—this isn't about all your employees wanting to take responsibility if only you give them the opportunity. Or that they want to be successful and have an instinctive nose for what is a job well done.

No, not everyone is so good at what they do, we all know

that. But your attitude towards them is going to influence how you handle them.

Your view of your staff shows in your leadership.

When I ask bosses what they think about Theory Y, guess how many of them say that they follow it?

You've guessed right: *all of them*.

And why not? Bosses are just as smart as anybody else. They know that there's only one answer unless you want to look like an idiot.

Then we work our way through the leadership program for perhaps ten or fifteen days over a twelve-month period, and little by little the truth comes out: their support for Theory Y is often just lip service. A lot of people trust nobody but themselves. They control, supervise, and in general mistrust everyone they meet. If you want something done well, do it yourself!

So I'm asking you to put this book aside and find the nearest mirror. Take three deep breaths. Look yourself in the eye and think about: *which theory is closest to my own attitude—Theory X or Theory Y?*

My task is not to get you to change your opinion. You can think exactly what you want. All I want is for you to be clear about where you really stand on the issue.

What you need to realize is that, regardless of which understanding you have, regardless of whether you believe in Theory X or Theory Y, it's going to be evident in your leadership. Your staff are going to feel the effects. And perhaps you need to prepare yourself for that.

If you assume that you're leading a bunch of tired slackers and unprofessional sleepy-heads, they're going to notice what you think of them. And that is going to result in more underachievers than you ever imagined. It's a self-fulfilling prophecy.

Nobody wants to be a failure. Nobody wants to do a poor job. There are, of course, some people who do. But very few people go to work in the morning and think that *today I shall cause as much chaos as I possibly can. It's going to be fun.* When things go wrong, it's rarely deliberate. They simply haven't learned the job.

Assume that everybody *wants* to be good at what they do.

When You Haven't Had Any Leadership Training

Have you attended a leadership course? You haven't? Then you know what I'm talking about. How can you know how the job should be done if nobody ever told you? Besides, a lot of senior bosses have such poor awareness that they can really only teach bad behaviors.

Some of them like to sound tough and say things like: *here we practice management by growing mushrooms!*

They want you to ask what they mean by that.

The answer is going to be something like: *throw some shit on them, and keep them in the dark!* This might possibly be followed by a snorting *ho, ho, ho!*

None of that is going to help you. And if you make the poor decision to share your brilliant comments with your staff, you can count on embarrassed silence the next time you step foot in the lunchroom. They're going to think you're an insensitive idiot.

And if you've been on one or more leadership courses, you'll know that a lot of what they focus on doesn't have anything to do with leadership. You learn how to draw up business plans, plan your calendar, and how to deal with your own stress; time management, recruiting, employment law, and lots of other stuff. Good things, no doubt about that, but they're not really about leading other people. Of course, it's fine to be a good role model, but that isn't enough. You need to know more. A lot more.

Leadership is not for weaklings. It really is an uphill battle.

How Can You Do a Job You've Never Been Trained For?

We all need instruction, training, inspiration, ideas, and thoughts from people with more experience than us if we're to figure out our role in an organization. We need something to use as a starting point.

It would be dishonest of me if I were to claim that it's enough to read a book. You need to meet other bosses, talk about everyday challenges, share experiences, and learn from one another. But you also need to solve a number of scenarios, to contemplate situations from different angles, and to listen to the views and ideas of different people. After all, there's more than one way of solving a problem.

Pedagogics is another aspect.

There are three things you remember from a training course: the beginning, the end, and what you've said yourself. Above all, the latter.

When you actively take part in a course, you're going to have a far greater chance of learning. The more active you are, the more you're going to benefit from the course. That's why it isn't enough just to read a book. You need a course that does what it's meant to. If you haven't had any training in leadership, you need to put this book down, go to your boss and express the need. Give them my regards.

"I Don't Have Time for a Leadership Course! Isn't That Obvious?"

You have lots to do. Okay. But if you think you can't be absent from your workplace for six or eight days over the course of a whole year—well then, you've got problems. Real problems. But not the ones you think.

Memorize the following: what's important is not what happens when you *are* there, but what happens when you *are not* there.

But what would happen if they hear that I've been attending leadership training! It would be really embarrassing!

Yes, what would happen if your staff notices that you've been attending a course to learn how you can be of more use to them? They're not going to like that, are they? Come off it!

Managing to Deal with Everything and Everybody All the Time

There is not less time. That is a myth. Forget all about that. *Oh but*, you might be thinking. *It was easier to manage to get things done before. There was more time before.*

No, no, no. There was just as much time before as there is

now. The difference is what we do with our time. Your success as a boss is dependent on your ability to prioritize your time. You're not going to manage to do everything anyway, so forget that idea. What you need to sort out is what should be deleted from your calendar. And there's probably lots; you just have to start looking.

Jonas, the Caring Boss

Let me tell you about a guy I met a few years ago.

Jonas was stressed on a stratospheric level. He came to me with his big problem: he didn't have enough time to do his job. Could I help him?

He described his workday like this: he got out of bed at 5 A.M. so he could check his emails in the early morning because there wasn't going to be time during the day. He arrived at work at 7 A.M. Then he started figuring out what issues had arisen the day before and corrected things that some of his staff had done. When the first staff members started to arrive at 8 A.M., a queue soon formed outside Jonas's office door. The line of employees who needed him was exponentially growing. There was no end to the problems that needed solving. Everybody had questions, and Jonas solved everything as it came in. He took it upon himself to fix a lot of things. He promised to look at this thing and that one. He would get back about question X. He promised to examine issue Y. He guaranteed that he would definitely make phone call Z.

He did have almost thirty staff members to keep track of, and that was far too many. But that wasn't really the problem.

The problem was his attitude about his own leadership, to his role as their boss.

When things started to get a bit quieter at around 4 P.M.—which was when the staff went home—it was time for Jonas to get on with his real job. He sat in his office until at least 7 P.M., while most of the staff went home when they should. Since he had taken over most of their problems, they all went home right on time.

If you're a boss, this might have made you feel a little queasy because you recognized something in it. If you're not a boss, you might think that Jonas only had himself to blame. He's been well paid to work hard.

But Jonas was not actually paid to do the work of other people. Yet that was indeed what he was doing, partly because he'd never taken a step back and looked at what he really spent his time on.

I asked him if he had any ideas to help solve the situation. With deep, blueish-black shadows under his eyes, he confided in me that he was contemplating getting to work at 6 a.m. All he needed to do was to get up a bit earlier. That way he'd have a bit more time to manage his own job before all the others arrived at the office. Perhaps he might get home before his children went to sleep.

I heard something entirely different from what he said. I asked him what he thought the problem really was.

"Too little time," he sighed, dejectedly.

Instead of telling Jonas a few hard truths—that he was using the time he had for the wrong things—I asked him what he thought his job was as the boss. And his answer was amusing and frightening at the same time.

"I have to do everything for everybody all the time."

I remember that I stared at him. I didn't really know how to react. When I got over my initial surprise, I asked him to go up to the whiteboard and write down what he had just said. Jonas was an obedient boss, accustomed to reacting to every request regardless of who it came from.

He wrote in capital letters: I HAVE TO DO EVERYTHING FOR EVERYBODY—All THE TIME.

When he sat down again, I asked him what was wrong with him. He wondered what I meant. I pointed at the whiteboard and asked him to analyze his own statement.

Jonas scratched his chin and admitted that perhaps it wasn't entirely reasonable after all.

I got up and underlined some of the words.
I HAVE TO DO EVERYTHING FOR EVERYBODY—ALL THE TIME.

One Heartbeat Away from a Heart Attack

Jonas sank back in his chair like a punctured balloon. I remember that he—he was probably in his early thirties—put his hand over his chest when he said that he simply had to work harder.

But sometimes hard work isn't the solution. It's about how you choose to see your role as boss and leader. What your job actually is in the chair you're sitting in now. You need to find the answer before you can know what the right thing to do is. Picture it as a goal. When you can see that, you'll know how to use your time.

Can your job be to do everything for everybody all the time? Of course not. That's an impossible way of looking at it, and nowadays Jonas knows that too.

One thing Jonas was really good at was doing the work of his staff members. Sometimes even the boss must roll up her sleeves and give a helping hand. Absolutely, you can't just sit there and be the boss. But if you have staff members who have specific tasks to perform—isn't it better that they are the ones actually doing them?

"But," said Jonas, "they don't have the training. They don't know how to do it!"

Ah! There at last we have a task for Jonas. Make sure that they know how the job should be done. That would be better than having to do their tasks himself. They won't learn anything from that, will they?

Jonas was particularly upset about one member of staff, Kenneth. I asked what the problem was with him in particular. "Well, you see, Kenneth, he doesn't do his job at all." He doesn't? How has that come about?

Jonas threw out his arms and exclaimed loudly, "Exactly what I ask myself!" It turned out that Jonas really had tried everything with Kenneth. He had coached him, tried to explain, given criticism, and finally taken over loads of Kenneth's work tasks. Remember that Jonas had almost thirty people under him. Imagine that each of them has their problem areas. That makes for an awful lot of tasks to take over, besides your own work.

I decided to shorten Jonas's suffering as best I could. I asked him, "If I call Kenneth now and ask him to tell me his five highest priorities at work right now—what is he going to tell me?"

"I can tell you," said Jonas. "He's just going to mumble nonsense. He isn't even going to be able to answer that question!" The look on his face said: *Now you can see what I have to deal with.*

"So he doesn't know what he should be doing," I said.

"Exactly."

"Okay, and that makes you angry."

"Yes, it really does."

"All right," I said, "then I'll ask you, Jonas: what should Kenneth's five highest priorities be?"

Then Jonas looked at me, blinked a few times . . . and started mumbling nonsense.

Curtain.

I said: "Okay. *Kenneth* doesn't really know what he should be doing. *You* don't really know what he should be doing. But you're very angry about the whole thing? Have I really grasped this correctly?"

Jonas's answer: "Well, I hadn't thought about it like that."

When I asked him how long this had been going on, I really did have to control myself so he didn't see my reaction to his response: "Seven years."

Seven years!

This is exactly the kind of thing I'm talking about. Sometimes you have to step back a bit and look at the situation afresh. It isn't my intention to sound haughty here. Of course, it's easier for me to do it. I wasn't involved in the daily work. Jonas started creating a list of Kenneth's priorities. Kenneth was really pleased with this, and suddenly found more direction and purpose in his job—and no longer had to put up with lots of criticism for things he (unknowingly) ought to have done long ago.

The conclusion of all this is simple: let each person do their own job. Your job as boss then is about making sure they have what they need to do just that.

{ 21 }

Leader—or Specialist? Your Job as a Boss

Like I experienced in my first managerial position, it can happen that as the boss you inherit an expectation from your staff that you will solve all their problems. That it's the job of the boss to be there for the staff.

This is both right and wrong at the same time.

Right in the sense that the boss should make sure that every member of staff gets the very best conditions to be able to carry out their work. The correct instructions, the correct training, the correct follow-up, a reasonable amount of time to do the job, good feedback, sufficient praise, and the necessary tools, to name just some things.

But this attitude is also wrong because it's not the boss's job to do other people's work. It's your job to do your job. The job of the boss is to make sure that everything in the paragraph above happens smoothly. But to actually do the job will always be the work of each individual member of staff, however dull it might sometimes be. You cannot negotiate who is actually going to do the job.

Bosses, as well as their staff, sometimes get caught in an unfortunate trap that means the staff delegate tasks to the boss and then check that they've been done. This is not acceptable, and, above all, it's not particularly efficient. If everything is going to be done by a single person, then in the end everything will collapse, since we'll all be waiting for the boss. And if the boss is going to do everything—then what do we need staff for?

A lot of bosses—like Jonas in the example above—have completely misunderstood their task. I want you to understand me correctly here—there are reasons why they haven't realized this, but now it's time to break this deeply unfortunate pattern.

Take a look at this picture:

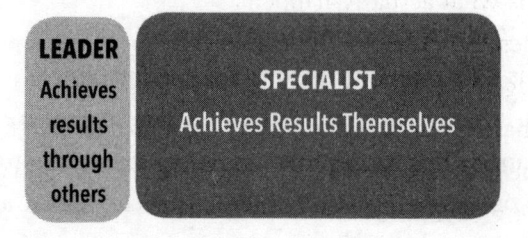

LEADER
Achieves results through others

SPECIALIST
Achieves Results Themselves

The everyday life of a boss can be simply divided into two parts. (To all the management consultants who are reading this with growing irritation: I am perfectly aware of the fact that the picture above can be made considerably more complicated.)

On the left side everything is about leadership, that is, activities such as instructing your staff, training them, following up, having personal conversations, leading group meetings, building motivation, showing support, listening to problems, helping when the staff ask for it, giving feedback—

positive as well as negative—and more. The purpose of all this work is to allow the staff, instead of the boss, to do the actual job at hand.

Many people still maintain that the boss should be the best at everything. I often see that in various types of workplaces, particularly with relation to technical questions. That's unfortunate because it turns the bosses into colossal bottlenecks—the only one who can answer these sorts of questions. They interfere in everything and control lots of details since they see themselves as the only people who understand the problem.

Let's Just Do What We've Always Done—That's Safest

But this is what actually happens:

The best mechanic becomes the head mechanic and finally the manager of the workshop.

The best administrator in the accounts department becomes the head of the department with responsibility for ten other administrators.

The best doctor becomes the senior consultant and ends up as head of the clinic.

The best consultant becomes the head of the consultants.

The best cleaner becomes team leader for the cleaners.

The best engineer becomes the technical director.

The list can keep going, and probably there are also lots of examples where the worst specialist somehow ends up in charge of the group. The circumstances around certain managerial appointments are so shadowy that one can only speculate as to how sensible the top management really is.

But the point is this: In everyday life, the wheels spin fast. It's no longer possible to do everything that should be done. Nowadays I hardly know anyone who has everything done by five o'clock when the whistle sounds. There's always more to do, and then you have to prioritize.

Only you can decide what the balance between your time as a leader and your time as a specialist should be. Where are you in the annual cycle? Do you have deadlines? What about goal levels? How many people do you have at your disposal? How competent is your staff? How experienced and independent are they?

Do you even know the answer to these questions? If not—find out. You'll find some help further on in this book about how you can go about it. But for God's sake, take it seriously.

The risk with an incorrect focus is that you'll find yourself in this situation:

LEADER	SPECIALIST
Achieves results through others	Achieves Results Themselves

Perhaps your division is 50/50. Or it might be 40/60. Perhaps it's 60/40. It depends. Perhaps you can't even answer. What I want you to do is to think seriously about this and try to set up some sort of goal as to how you want to use your time from now on.

What is the optimal division in your particular situation? 50/50? 60/40? 30/70?

Go back to your mission statement and reflect upon it. What's important is that you personally look at your situation and make an active decision: *this is how I want it to be.*

That is always better than *it just ended up like this.*

Note this, however: I'm not saying that you should have as *much* leadership as possible in your agenda. But you ought to have a *sufficient* amount.

What Happens if You Don't Find Balance?

I'm glad you asked. Because the following will happen:

- There will be loads of ad hoc solutions—a new fire to put out every minute—and you'll be the team's permanent fireman. Congratulations!
- You also run the risk of becoming a universal problem-solver. You're going to answer the same question from the same person many times. Nobody is ever going to learn anything properly. Your staff will use your brain instead of their own.
- You will be extremely active but not especially proactive. You're going to react instead of act. You are going to be criticized for not looking forward. But how could you do that? You can hardly keep your nose above your desk.
- You solve your staff's problems—that's good. But when you're sitting on all the answers, they will

become totally dependent on you, and you can never leave the office without checking your cell phone all the time. You don't give your staff the space to take initiative and grow.

Still not convinced? Here's the best reason to deal with the situation here and now: you are going to *work too much*. You're going to be the first person to arrive at work—and the last to leave. The only thing you need to do now is to ask your loved ones what they think about that scenario.

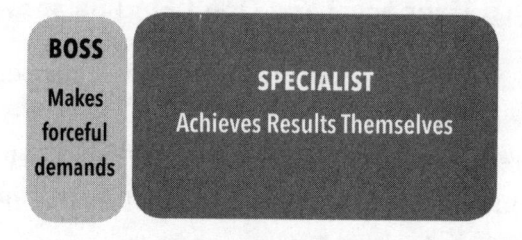

BOSS
Makes forceful demands

SPECIALIST
Achieves Results Themselves

You'll end up having no time left over for any thoughtful and motivating leadership. You'll only have time to be the boss. There will be lots of shouting and stern instruction but there will be no encouraging measures, and you can forget the idea of being a sounding board. Nobody is satisfied with the situation. You probably aren't either. If you even have time to think about it at all.

How You Make Yourself Superfluous

Many years ago I had a boss who really understood this. When I held out a piece of paper and asked for his help, he put his hands in his pockets and gave me an inquisitive look.

Then he wanted to know if I had any ideas of my own. Every time, the same thing. A few times I really did have to bite my tongue to stop myself from shouting out loud. It was colossally frustrating. Sometimes I just wanted a quick answer. Couldn't he simply give me one?

He could. Probably every time.

But he was smarter than that. He said to me that if we were two people who worked on the same thing, then one of us was superfluous. And he assured me that it wasn't him.

Hard? Possibly. Not very charming? Perhaps. But many years later I understood that he was completely right. He taught me to get as far as I possibly could with every task before I went to him. I realized eventually that if I just routinely went to him to get a quick answer and to avoid having to think myself, then I was making myself dependent upon him.

What would happen if one lovely day I needed help and he wasn't there? What would I do then?

For me this was an important lesson.

My job was to get the task done in the best way possible. His job was to guide me. And that's what he did. But he refused to take over my work tasks.

I got much better at my job when he gently "forced" me to do it myself. He was there all the time, he rarely abandoned me—but I was always the one to do the work.

Do you see the difference?

By doing all these things myself, I continually improved my ability. If the boss had said *give me those papers and I'll sort it all out,* it would have helped me at the time, but I would only have learned one thing: that it was okay to dump difficult things onto his desk.

So even if your staff huff and puff because you refuse to deal with things that they need to learn, you should stick to your guns. You won't help them by falling into the Jonas trap.

Whose Lap Is This Problem Really Going to Land In?

You're stuck just as much as anyone else.

Your staff can't tell you if you're doing the wrong things. They sense that something is wrong, but they don't always have the language to express what it is. How should they know what you ought to be doing, if you don't know yourself?

The next level—your bosses—don't know either, and they find themselves in exactly the same situation—just higher up the ladder. Nobody's told them what the solution is either, and besides, they don't have time for all this. They have a company to run.

The number of management levels varies, of course. But fairly soon, we might reach the managing director level. The MD is also busy with more important questions. She is often being an ambassador for the company in the market. She either makes the really big business deals or she is a representative for the company in other contexts. Sometimes, the MD is just as useless a boss as her intermediary managers, and she's especially indifferent when it comes to these questions.

The HR department then? Don't they have some responsibility here? They must have the know-how. For example, the boss of the HR department might have studied management at university. But then we're talking about leadership on such a theoretical level that it's pointless to even try to apply it to real people.

For that matter, the question isn't landing on the desk of the HR boss either. HR should be dealing with problems that arise in negotiations with the union, staff policies, sick leave, employment law, other legal matters, the people who secretly drink at work, and a whole lot of other things. Experienced and ambitious HR bosses can undertake major projects aimed at creating a leadership culture, but without the approval of the entire top management group, nothing will come of it. In many cases, the HR boss isn't even a part of the top management group, and thus doesn't really know how the decision process works. The question is a dead end from beginning to end.

But don't worry—you'll get an answer. But you need to be aware of the problem to be motivated to take the rather unpleasant medicine.

You also need to be prepared for the fact that a lot of your staff will react strongly and negatively when you change your attitude here. Some of them are used to you handling everything for them—and are thus rather spoiled. It's been colossally comfortable to be able to go to you to get certain things out of the way. But don't be too hard on them—both of you have had a role in creating this situation.

If You Hadn't Been Able to Ask Me— What Would You Have Done?

To avoid the risk of taking over your staff's responsibilities, I'm going to give you a simple tip. It works eight times out of ten. When you realize that you get the same question from the same person repeatedly, both of you have a problem.

This is the solution. Don't open your mouth.

Instead, take some deep breaths. Count to three.

Then ask a counter question: *If you hadn't been able to ask me—what would you have done?*

The purpose of the question is to get your employee to think about the problem and develop a plan for how she or he could deal with it. Strangely enough (you'll find this out when you test it, starting tomorrow) your staff member will often answer: *Oh right, well I'd do this.*

This is an incredibly important insight you need to understand. They almost always have a suggestion for a solution. Now you can calmly lean back in your chair and listen to their thoughts. In the best case, you just need to say, "that sounds like a good idea. I wish you luck."

Perhaps the suggestion isn't going to be exactly what you thought, but who says that you are the only one with good answers? If you immediately start babbling on about what you would have done, you miss the opportunity to hear a different solution you might never have thought up yourself. What do you say to that?

If you hadn't been able to ask me—what would you have done?

This is excellent counter-fire against all types of shortcomings in responsibility or just ordinary laziness. It puts the finger on something essential: If you'd been away from work this particular day, then everything wouldn't have come to a halt. The problem would have been solved in some way, one way or another.

So why does somebody come to you with a question about something they already know the answer to?

That's simple: They don't need to think. You answer quicker. The power of habit.

And you go home convinced that you're the only person in this office who uses their head. You might even feel that you're surrounded by slackers who never take any responsibility.

But, you know what? Sometimes you have to blame yourself.

You create the problem by helping everyone the way you do. Every time you solve problems for a staff member, you are the one who is taking the responsibility. You might actually believe in Theory X. Perhaps you don't even trust your staff.

Your staff might also know that their boss—they're probably wrong—needs to be in control. They know that you interfere in everything all the time. Besides, there are a lot of people who don't want to take responsibility for this and that.

And think about it. If you point in a certain direction and say that's where your staff member should go—who is responsible if he or she gets lost? You—or your staff member?

We Need to Do Some Sorting, and It Depends Somewhat on Your Colors

Why you, as a Red boss, take on the task yourself

It's a lot quicker. Everyone is so slow that you couldn't be bothered to ask again. If you want a thing done well, do it yourself. Your need for control messes things up for you. If you do the task yourself, it will be done exactly how you wanted it done. You're simply best at doing this.

Why you, as a Yellow boss, take on too much and try to do the task yourself on top of everything else

When somebody asked you how to do some task, you thought that it might just be simpler if you did it yourself. You feel instinctively that you can do it! Unfortunately, you have no idea how many hours of work you have just taken on, because you don't actually know how long anything takes. Your attitude is that everything goes quickly. But, in fact, it doesn't.

Why you, as a Green boss, take on too much and end up sitting up all night doing other people's work

Your staff looked so pained and stressed that you wanted to give them some help. Or you didn't have the heart to give them more work. You find it hard to make demands on them. You are far too considerate and you ask far too little of them. The consequence is that everyone else goes home in time for dinner and you get to eat a snack at your desk. You are simply too kind.

Why you, as a Blue boss, take on too much and just do the work yourself

You're the only person who can do this task to the appropriate standard. After all, it was you who created this system. You see yourself more as a specialist than as a leader. And you like the actual work. Besides, sometimes you forget that you have staff. It's so easy for you to open a document and be immediately caught up in it instead of letting it go on to the right person.

Summary

Think about which pitfalls you might have in your leadership. Do you take on too many of the wrong tasks? Or do you dump everything on somebody else's desk? You must be somewhere between those two. Think about whether you're in the right place.

You need to have these realizations now. Otherwise you're not actually doing your job.

{ 22 }

If You're an Efficient Red Boss

A favorite question asked during the annual performance review is how the staff sees their boss. The question often comes during the discussion part of the review and the boss feels rather uncomfortable asking it, because it's included in the document that HR has produced together with some polished consultant or other.

The idea is good. Even bosses need to get some feedback. So there will be a few questions about how smoothly you cooperate, what the boss can do differently, and perhaps even something about the strengths and weaknesses in leadership. It will be hard for your own boss to answer these questions since he or she doesn't see you in leadership situations particularly often. So you'll have to ask your staff.

And there are, of course, cases where employees of all color combinations have such good self-confidence and feel sufficiently secure in their position that they'll actually tell you the truth. But—and this is a rather large but—it takes quite a lot to get this to work.

Openings for bosses with big egos were sold out long ago. Far too many don't like being criticized, especially by their subordinates. Good intentions fly out of the window, because what do you say to a pompous boss who also regularly displays a bad temper when something doesn't go their way? Many staff members choose politeness before honesty in these situations.

But we can help here. As bosses we can work to build up our staff's confidence. We can be good role models throughout the year, and when that damn annual performance appraisal comes along, there doesn't have to be an embarrassing silence when the miserable question is asked. Perhaps you'll have a fruitful discussion where you, as the boss, actually feel stronger and inspired from the feedback.

Unfortunately, there's a whole list of alternative outcomes from such an appraisal conversation, and to a certain degree it depends upon your own personal insight. If you have an idea as to how your staff see you, you can make your questions a little more specific. Instead of asking questions that are far too open: *How well do you think we cooperate together?* the Green boss asks: *how well do you think I have succeeded in creating unity in our team?* The Yellow boss might ask: *What tips can you give me to create a good atmosphere in the group?*

You get the idea. More specific questions help your staff get on track quicker.

So how do they see your leadership? As usual, your style of communication is an important piece of the puzzle, although not the only one.

Let's take a look. As usual, we start with Red.

Your staff's view of you as boss

Now you know that if your strongest color is Red, you like speed and you don't hesitate to give concrete, very specific orders. You want to see results and you're fully prepared to roll up your sleeves and dive in when necessary. You suspect—if you stop and think for a moment—that some of your staff think you are in too much of a hurry and that honesty is an overrated tool.

But if we look at your staff based on their colors, we begin to see interesting patterns:

Your Red Staff Members . . . (Match: Good)

. . . like it that you are direct. In fact, you match each other quite well. Red staff members appreciate your clear communication and the way you don't hide even bad news. They also like that there is a certain structure in what you do, and that the goals are probably clear and sufficiently challenging.

There are many reasons why Red bosses recruit other people who are Red. There is less bullshit and you don't have to sugarcoat everything all the time. On the contrary, it's fine to just get on with things. And if the Red boss can, on rare occasions, be a bit too hard, the employee will just shout back. It can't really be much simpler.

ON THE OTHER HAND . . .

. . . Red staff members sometimes think you're a total idiot. Why? Well, you *steer* them and Red persons *hate* being steered. Since you are a strong person, you demand that everybody does the job in a particular way—your way. Here it doesn't make any difference whether you're right and they're wrong; they don't like being told what to do.

You only need to look in the mirror to realize that you know what I'm talking about. Why the hell is there any need for orders from higher up, when I already know what's best for the company? But employees who think that you limit their freedom and control can be annoying since they cause problems when they are dissatisfied. They mess up everything and can create enormous disorder in the group.

DO THEY WANT A FIGHT? NO PROBLEM!

Continue to be direct. Continue to say what you want done. But provide alternatives for possible solutions. If you have a conspiratorial nature it could be said that there's value in letting your Red staff members think that they're the ones who make the decisions. It's in their egos. So provide a couple of alternatives that they can accept—and let them then decide which way to go.

If you don't agree—and that's going to happen—then stick to the facts. Don't complain, don't criticize, but continue to point out facts. Fight for it. Accept that things can become pretty heated before you reach an agreement. Remember that Red staff members are happy to challenge even their boss. They're just like you. So you'll have to put up quite a lot of resistance, but you shouldn't smother them.

A dramatic conflict can very well flame up, and it won't benefit anybody who isn't Red. Others are going to think that you're about to fight.

In the same way, it's pointless to try to become friends with your Red staff. They'll only be irritated. You're not at work to find a tennis partner, so forget about that. Perhaps you might be thinking that this is an unnecessary warning, but I know that you would try something like that if it would help you to get your own way. Don't do it.

But do continue to make quick decisions. Act quickly. Continue to move from thought to action as quickly as somebody else sneezes. That is popular. That will win you respect, and it will make your Red staff members work harder.

Your Yellow Staff Members . . . (Match: Very Good)

. . . like it when things are always happening. They're particularly keen on the way you don't give them detailed instructions but let them run around and be creative. They don't spend any time *inside* the box, and it's good that you accept that. They know that you're more focused on when the target is to be reached, than on interfering with exactly how they get there. Your reluctance to rummage in details suits the Yellows very well, especially considering that they could hardly describe these details anyway.

It's logical that Red bosses recruit Yellow staff. Both parties like action. Things happen and neither of them is bothered about the details. Besides, the Yellow is such a skillful communicator that he or she knows how to get through to their sometimes peevish Red boss. Sure, the Yellows tend to use a lot of words, but they can restrain themselves and only say what their Red boss wants to hear.

ON THE OTHER HAND . . .

. . . the Yellows don't find you especially stimulating. After all, they want to be inspired and they like to talk about feelings. None of this is part of your repertoire, and that grieves the Yellows. They like having fun at work, too. You only talk shop and don't want to know what happened last weekend.

Since relationships at the workplace are a necessary evil for you, the Yellows feel ignored. And you don't laugh at their fun and games, either. They want to amuse their boss too, you know; in that respect they can be like children who fool around to get a little attention.

Another thing that can stress Yellow staff members is your ability to paint extremely gloomy pictures about what will happen if the team doesn't succeed in meeting its goals. Even if you were only being direct and explicit about the forthcoming closure, and even if the Yellows understand perfectly well that no one can run an unprofitable business very long, they still don't want to hear about it. They would rather be inspired to great deeds, and that isn't really your strong suit. Your habit of raising your voice and demanding that they look sharp doesn't help.

BUT, FOR GOODNESS' SAKE, I HAVE TO DEAL WITH A BUNCH OF CHILDREN NOW TOO?

Take it easy. If you notice that your Yellow staff members are looking a bit dejected, try to give them something to look forward to. Inspire them, give them energy. Think up something to do that's fun. If you don't have a clue what that might be—ask one of them to think of something. They won't have any problem coming up with something.

Let them arrange an activity of some sort, book an after work get-together. It doesn't need to cost very much, and you don't have to stay the whole evening. But it will add energy.

A sure way into their hearts is to be personal and friendly. Ask questions about how things are going for them, what challenges they're facing, if they're okay with the timeline. And by all means ask about their personal life. Not what they do when the lights are off, but talk about their children, their garden, their vacation. And if you manage to commit some of this to memory, so you can ask some follow-up questions in a week—well, all the better. That shows that you really care about them.

It's a good idea to make jokes and have some fun together. Try to ignore the fact that your desk is about to collapse from the weight of all the papers you need to deal with. It's time well spent to fool around with the Yellows, because then they'll do a better job. If they don't feel comfortable, there might be nothing to show at all.

Give them time. They aren't as quick as you. They need to talk a bit before things start to happen. Remind yourself that while you go from thought to action, the Yellows go from thought to talk. They think aloud. If you learn to filter through all the words, you might actually hear something useful.

Make sure you give them your approval, due recognition. If a Yellow person has done a good job—then you can certainly say so in front of the group. Inflate their egos as much as you have time for. Let them shine. They lap up the praise like a kitten with cream. I know, you don't think like that. But do it anyway.

Finally, I want to raise a finger in warning. The Yellows are skillful communicators. They have a talent for making almost anything sound absolutely fantastic. One of the reasons that you work so well with them is that you like what you hear. They say the right things. And they agree with you. And that saves time, of course. Just make sure you keep track of what they actually do. What a member of staff says and what she actually does in the end are not the same thing. Yellow individuals can talk you into the ground and make you believe everything is great. That can be a mistake. Always ask a couple of check-questions and listen very carefully to the answer.

Your Green Staff Members . . . (Match: Not Too Bad)

. . . like to have something to lean against when the wind starts blowing. Having got this far, you'll know that Green personalities are very different from you. The good news is that you complement each other. You are quick; the Greens give themselves more time. You keep track of the concrete issues; your Green staff keeps the relationships going. You like handing out orders, and the Greens are quite okay receiving a—politely worded—order. This is going to work really well, don't you think?

The Greens appreciate you because you are precise. They like security, and if you really understand your boss, that creates stability. You might very well be the rock that withstands the storm, and the Greens will want to hide behind you.

There are some grounds for the claim that you and your Green employees are going to work quite well together.

ON THE OTHER HAND . . .

. . . you are light years away from each other in a number of areas. The Greens feel their way forward through all decisions—they navigate by gut feeling—and you just push things along. They sometime feel that you're totally insensitive. You don't listen. If you go into your Green employee's office and ask how things are, the answer won't come straight away. First, they must think about it, about how they feel. It can take a few seconds. And if you've already left the room with a shrug of your shoulders, this will simply be further proof to the Greens that you don't care about them. Not really. And now they have something to whisper about by the coffee machine.

Besides, you're clumsy and aggressive. How do I know that? Well, you look them in the eye when you say that *this isn't good enough. Work harder.* I'm not saying that you're looking for trouble, but Greens shy away from conflict more than anything else. Even just a slight sharpness in your tone or a stern look, and the Greens will feel your displeasure engulfing them. They will clam up, and you'll never find out what they think.

And why do you change your mind all the time? Can't things be like they always have been? Your Green staff members want to feel predictability in their workplace. They want to know what's going to happen, which is exactly what bores you. They don't want to know about problems and difficulties, which is precisely what gives you energy and motivates you to sort things out.

This is Too Much! Can't People Just Pull Themselves Together at Work?

Oh yes. And as the boss you can help them. Here's some good advice to get things to work how you want them to.

Every time you meet a Green employee—slow your pace. When you think you are taking things nice and easy—slow your tempo another fifty percent. I really do mean that—you must slow down. When you speak, when you think, when you make decisions. You're seriously stressing your Green staff members. To just pop your head in and shout: *Are you coming to the conference in October?* Doesn't work. The Green person's mental functions will jam, and they'll start to stammer. What, for you, is a simple decision, the Green sees as a major decision. Accept that you will get a *hmm* in answer. Ask again in two days.

And you need to make sure you get a bit of genuine confirmation en route. You can't simply interpret the lack of an answer as a "yes." Nor can you assume that "yes" always means "yes." It might even mean "no."

Illogical? Absolutely. But now we're talking about Green behavior. You need to realize that these staff members try to give you the answer they think you want to hear. Eventually you'll notice whether this particular individual actually does turn up at the October conference. What you need to do is to build up the Green's confidence, and you can do that by making the effort to coax out their true opinions. That shows that you're prepared to invest some time in them. You will benefit from doing so. Believe me.

Give them a reasonable amount of background information. Not extreme quantities, but enough to create a feeling of security. The Greens like thoroughness in decisions; it simply makes them feel better. Think about what type of facts these Green individuals would like. All the facts that support their needs are valuable. Find these, and then deliver them in a calm and orderly manner.

Listen to everything that is said. The words can be extremely cautious. A Green person doesn't say: *The whole project is about to collapse*. They say: *I can see some challenges here, but things will probably sort themselves out somehow*. You need to learn the Green language.

But listen, too, to what is *not* said out loud. Silence is *not* the same thing as agreement. Plato was wrong. Remember that your Green staff members want to please you; they'll say what they think you want to hear because they don't want any arguments. Listen to the rather long silences, too. Observe their body language. A Green person might say *that's going to be fine* while simultaneously shaking their head. You need to learn how to interpret this. You need to learn how this particular Green functions.

Before you claim that you haven't time for that sort of stuff, I would point out that it doesn't matter. Your job is to reach out to your staff. Time or not—this is how you reach out to the Greens. You'll have to work harder. Your "winnings" when you succeed will be considerable. If you can display enough patience, you will win their loyalty for many years ahead.

Your Blue Staff Members . . . (Match: Bad)

. . . see you as fairly okay since you are at least focused on work. You're both interested in the task at hand. For the

Blues, that earns you points. They appreciate that you don't ask about their personal life. It would never occur to them to spontaneously describe what they did last weekend, how their wife is, or ask you what you think about the spring weather so far. That would not be professional, after all.

And it's also positive that you haven't fallen into the *give-everybody-you-meet-a-big-hug* trap. They don't like to touch people. They also appreciate if you express yourself unambiguously. The Blues like it when they understand an instruction. Even though the instructions weren't totally comprehensive, they were at least crystal clear. Good.

ON THE OTHER HAND ...

... they'll see you as a professional good-for-nothing. You ignore things that are important and you lack focus. Orders and counter-orders. You're not consistent and you lose your temper over things that don't matter at all. Not that they really care about that. Yell all you want, nothing could be less stressful for the Blues. They'll simply wait until it's over, then they'll return to what they were doing before. You don't have a clue about the quality of the team's work, and your inattention to details makes them feel a little ill.

They realize that you're in a hurry, but they don't understand why. Time is a relative concept and has nothing to do with quality or doing a job properly. Your desire for quick results clashes head-on with their search for perfect, and I can tell you right now that all Blue people consider your approach to be wrong in the long term.

And speaking of long term. You might think that you do have a long-term approach. Well, *you* might think that it's a long time before it's Christmas again, but for the Blues that is just one decimal point in the wrong place in the calendar. To think long term—that means bearing in mind what's going to happen over an entire economic cycle.

How long is that? On average, about seven years. Any questions?

I'LL SHOW THOSE DAMNED STICKLERS FOR DETAILS!

Yes, you do that. But first read the following before you get to work. Remember that these staff members love information of every sort. Facts, details, evidence. I know that you're task-oriented, and that does make it easier. But the amount of information and depth of detail that you'll need to work with is going to tire you. They'll never be really satisfied. You don't have a chance even if you try to obtain all the necessary basic data.

What's the solution? Point out where the details can be found. Then you let the Blue staff members dive in on their own. Present the report, but don't try to quote it or summarize it. That won't suffice. Hand it out. Ask them to read it. Asking them to read it *closely* is stating the obvious.

But let them absorb the information at their own speed. It's a waste of time to ask them to hurry along. What you need is an ocean of patience. The feeling of urgency that you always have is about as useful as a bicycle is for a fish. The difference from the Green employee is obvious. While Greens get stressed if you hassle them, the Blues will mainly react with surprise. Has the boss gone crazy? Thinking you can shout at a tree to grow. So stupid.

You'll have to try to retain control some other way. One method is a standard follow-up. You really need to think way, way ahead here. Since the Blues are going to miss every deadline and justify that by saying that things aren't quite perfect, you're going to need a plan. One way is to describe in detail what the task entails, define in advance what standard is required, and then jointly set a deadline. You can, of course, put a bit of pressure on—we take that for granted—but the trick lies in the fact that Blues tend to honor a mutual agreement. Once they've said yes to something, they want to stick to it. It's a question of honor. They don't want to mess things up unnecessarily. So if you've got a deal—follow it up.

Basically it's the pace of work that's the problem here. You're the accelerator and your Blue staff member is both the brake pedal and the emergency brake and maybe the check engine light. If you press all the pedals at once, you'll drive very erratically. You need to agree on what pace you shall stick to. The Blues will obviously need to speed up a little. But you'll be forced to slow down. There is no other way out in this case.

What Do We Do with All This?

So what do you say? That wasn't so bad, was it? The most important point is that you, as a mainly Red boss, realize that the different colors see you in slightly different ways. They'll probably agree on certain things, but far from everything. Of course, your staff—as I've already written several times—are also responsible for ensuring that the dialogue between you functions smoothly, but you—the boss—have the greatest responsibility. In the end, you need to show that you're prepared to make the effort.

And of course as a Red boss, you are, since you want to achieve your ambitious goals quickly.

{ 23 }

If You're an Inspiring Yellow Boss

You know that if your strongest color is Yellow, then you're a natural inspirer, and you spread good vibes around you. You're a skilled communicator and find it easy to convince other people about the validity of your ideas. Your creativity leads you to test new concepts. You aren't afraid to take command when necessary, and being in the spotlight doesn't scare you in the slightest. When you start reflecting, you might suspect that there are those who think your prognoses are a bit too positive and that you sometimes find it hard to stick to the agenda.

Let's take a look at what your staff have to say about you and your leadership.

Your Red Staff Members . . . (Match: Very Good)

. . . think that you have an aura of energy and go. They like how you have ideas and aren't afraid to test new things. They agree with you entirely that it's impossible to know exactly what everything will lead to anyway. They like the way you see things from a broad perspective, none of you think that details are super-important.

Yellow bosses have a soft spot for Red staff members. The reason is simple—they are sufficiently like the boss for the relationship to work smoothly. And the Reds like to go first, which can appeal to Yellow bosses. Let them take the worst battering. But the Reds don't want to be managed closely, which the Yellows can sense. This is mainly good news, since the Yellow bosses are going to miss two out of three follow-ups anyway. They simply forget, and that gives the Reds sufficient freedom.

ON THE OTHER HAND . . .

 . . . your Red staff think that you often behave like a complete idiot. You're too flamboyant for them to feel confidence in you. All this silliness and fooling around is incredibly irritating. And why must you be on their backs the whole time? Stop that immediately.

Nor do they like the way you're so personal, that you go on about things that don't have anything to do with the job. What you did last summer doesn't interest them. They realize that you need to talk about yourself, but they respectfully ignore what you say. They have learned to smile and nod—you are the boss after all—but really they want to leave the room and do something else.

It can also be a problem that you don't stand by what you say. You've said a whole number of things at different meetings, but since you never write anything down, that invariably means a whole lot of unfulfilled promises. They'll soon stop listening to you if you don't start delivering.

I know that this doesn't soothe your ego. Perhaps you're the person who finds it hardest to change yourself since your thoughts about yourself aren't particularly modest. And you do have lots of good qualities; nobody can say otherwise. But your Red staff members are irritated by some of them.

THAT'S THE THANKS I GET FOR TRYING TO BE NICE! WHAT JERKS!

There are ways of changing this—all you need do is to think about Red behavior. They're not here to have fun. They didn't come to work to be pals with the boss.

The Reds want results. So it's better to talk about goals than about inspiration and visions. Pie-in-the-sky visions are of no interest. To say that we're going to be the best in the country is one thing. But best at what? And what are we going to *do* to get there?

Your Red employees are action-oriented. That is fantastically good news! They talk a little, and they do a lot. Make sure they put their efforts into the right things, and you'll achieve miracles. But don't get in their way.

Be businesslike and professional the whole time. Stick to the subject and avoid letting thoughts leave your mouth if they're too vague. Get directly to the point. Forget the football match yesterday. And the weather. Don't soften up your Red staff members with a bit of cozy chit chat. You'll only make them angry.

Trying to be funny can be a mistake. If you make too many jokes at your workplace they're going to think you aren't serious. And note—it isn't about you not being funny. I am sure you are, but the Reds don't care about that. If they want to be entertained, they'll go to stand-up comedy on Friday night.

And in the midst of all this, you need to display a rock-solid self-confidence. You need to express yourself as if you know exactly what you're doing. The Reds react partly on instinct here. They can start to doubt when you're hesitant. It makes them uncertain about whether they can rely on you. If you start hesitating, you show them that you can be influenced. This can lead a Red staff member to challenge you, often in front of all the others, which can result in an unpleasant struggle for power that you might lose. So you should radiate impregnable self-assurance.

Stick to your guns. But playing the *I'm-your-boss* card is an effective way to completely lose their respect. Don't fall into that trap.

But—an important but—you must keep your promises. If you've said that the money is on its way, it's best to make sure that happens. If you've promised them a day off between two holidays in May, you ought to make a note of it. If you've delegated a task to somebody and promised to talk to the others in the group—then book a meeting straightaway. If you break a promise to a Red staff member, that person will confront you. He or she is not going to suck up to you. You're going to hear that you haven't delivered. That you've broken a promise. And everybody is going to get the message.

Your Yellow Staff Members . . . (Match: Very Good)

Yellow works glowingly well with Yellow. In most sales organizations I've worked with, the Yellow trait has been completely dominant. The reason is that Yellows are positive, creative, sharp at talking and persuading: they're on the whole fearless and like to have contact with strangers. They're simply cut out for the job of selling.

What has this got to do with leadership? Quite a lot, actually. Yellow salespeople become Yellow team leaders who become Yellow sales managers who round off their careers by becoming sales directors. Yellow people often recruit others they can identify with and like—people with the same qualities they themselves have.

And the Yellow staff members also like it that you're entertaining, easygoing, inventive, and you let people have a bit of fun at work. They like how the atmosphere is really great, and it suits them especially well that you very rarely ask for their reports or whatever they're expected to be evaluated on. They love the freedom you allow them. The ones you hang out with in your free time know that that in gives them considerable advantages.

ON THE OTHER HAND . . .

There isn't room for too many stars on the same stage. All Yellow people think they deserve to be in the limelight. If you, as the boss, take up too much room—which a lot of Yellow staff members think you do—they can find you quite irritating. Perhaps they're after your job, since it evidently entitles you to an awful lot of attention.

This is a bit tricky.

You need to let your Yellow staff members talk more than you, even if you think that what you have to say sounds better. They must have room to express themselves.

THESE PRIMA DONNAS! WHO DO THEY THINK THEY ARE?

The path forward is slightly twisting here. On the one hand, you have a lot in common, on the other hand it's those small idiosyncrasies that create problems.

All Yellow people, including you, would like to have fun at work the whole time. The problem is that not everything can be superfun all the time. You need to allow the lovely atmosphere to exist, but at the same time keep an eye open so that things don't get out of hand. You're probably familiar with the expression *Lots of talk, little action*. The Yellows often talk a lot more about what they're *thinking* of doing, what they *will* do, what they are *going* to do—instead of actually doing it.

Thought and action are not the same thing when it comes to Yellow behavior. And there's an obvious risk that you'll be sucked into the cozy feeling in the office without taking a close look at what's been achieved. So you must keep track of what actually happens with all the wild plans.

Make sure you're generous with praise and recognition of every type. Remember that your Yellow employees appreciate praise just as much as their boss. There's no upper limit to how much sunshine you can pour over a Yellow person. The slightest little thing that's positive—show them that you've noticed it. It won't cost much of your time. Remind yourself that they work better when they're in a good mood. You've only got to look at yourself. If it works on you, it'll work on them.

Yellow staff members often react to the mood in the room. If it's energetic and inspiring, they will be infected by it. If the air is full of conflict and bad news, they'll react with drooping heads. Some of them will feel sorry for themselves. It's not their fault you're in a bad mood. The good news is that they quickly forget all the unpleasant things, and then everything is fine again.

You need to keep an eye on the fact that your Yellow workers talk with everybody. About everything. If you make a fool of yourself and behave stupidly, that is going to spread quicker than a film clip of the cutest kitten in the world. They'll have managed to inform people in the next state before you're even back in your office.

Your Green Staff Members . . . (Match: Good)

. . . probably like you. They like the way you talk with them about things that aren't always connected with work. Since the Greens want a familiar, slightly personal form of communication, they appreciate the fact that you don't press them too hard. They know that you, too, like good working relationships and they notice that you make an effort to ensure that they feel good.

Since Green staff members on the whole don't have any problem carrying out those small, rather boring tasks, you complement each other fairly well. What bores you is perhaps exactly what the Green is perfectly happy to take on. The task that you tried to give to a Yellow staff member, and that was never given the attention it deserved, may be just the task to transfer to the Green.

It suits the Greens just fine that you enjoy the spotlight

because they don't want it to shine on them. It isn't that they want you to steal their ideas and brag in front of them, but they don't want to be at the center of things. If their boss can manage that, it makes life easier for the Greens.

. . . ON THE OTHER HAND

—the Greens think you take up too much room. You joke and fool around, and sometimes they wish you could step down off the stage now and then. I know, that doesn't agree with what I wrote in the previous paragraph. The Greens don't want to be at the center of things, but deep inside they don't want anyone else to be there either. They can express envy when you get all the attention, but if you offer to stand aside, it's not at all certain that any of the Greens are going to step forward.

I know. It's complicated.

Besides—you talk far too much. The Greens don't feel the same need to express every idea that comes into their head. Even if you can be really quite entertaining, you tire out your Green gang rather often. Sometimes they wish that you'd just be quiet and let them work in peace. As usual, they're not going to say this to you. If, after reading this chapter, you suspect that you have just this problem, you might get the bright idea to actually ask them. The problem: they won't necessarily give you an honest answer. They don't want to hurt you and they don't want any arguments.

Apart from this, you cause far too many problems. Your creativity and your desire to continually think up new things irritates the Greens terribly. They are against change *by default*, and the best approach is not to change anything at all. You, on the other hand, enjoy change for the sake of change. While you're quickly bored by routines and predictable workdays, that's exactly what the Greens want.

OH DEAR, OH DEAR! DON'T THEY HAVE ANY IMAGINATION?

They do have imagination, but not as much as you. And besides, they use it for totally different things. There is an expression: *If it ain't broke, don't fix it*. A Green person could have minted that. Don't change something if it works.

You need to further adapt your message to your Green staff members. Exclaiming at a meeting: *I just had an idea! Wouldn't it be great if . . . ?* is only going to make them feel ill. Apart from showing a total absence of long-term planning, it's the last thing they want to hear. They won't be inspired, they don't want your ideas. You make them nervous.

Build up their faith in you; show that you care about them both as individuals and as a group. Remember that the team is more important than one person's ego. All your crazy sudden ideas and silly pranks are seen as a threat to the stability of the group. You already have a relationship with your Green staff members. They like you; they just want you to calm it a little.

Think through your message. Don't just exclaim about how your new completely un-researched idea is brilliant. Think instead about how you can convince your Green staff members that this (as yet) unplanned change is helpful. There is nothing wrong with your idea, but if you don't get through to them, you might as well scrap it.

I'll take an example: the workplace needs to be moved to a new location. Don't start a meeting by announcing the imminent move and that you've already found really fantastic new space on the other side of town. Get them directly involved in the process from the start. Ask what they think about the office you're sitting in today. Ask if they think the ventilation works satisfactorily and if they think there's enough space in the breakroom.

At the next meeting, tell them you've been looking into this and you think your current space has a number of issues. The air flow is bad, you're all squashed together like sardines, and it's hard to find a parking space out on the street. You can even sneak in the fact that the rent is too high, but the Greens don't really care about that. Better to ask them for their opinion, seek confirmation in the group. Look for hesitant nods.

Meeting number three. Now you say that you're thinking of looking at alternative office spaces. Is anyone in the group willing to go along to tour some possible new locations? Make it clear that this is just a possible idea. You don't really think you're going to find anything.

Week four. You and some of the staff go off and look at a couple of alternative office spaces. You ask open questions the whole time and listen closely for all types of emotions in the people accompanying you.

During the meeting the fifth week, you can mention in passing that you've found an office space that looked really nice, and ask what the people who saw it thought? (You've of course already scoped this out during a couple of short meetings in private.)

Now you have an opportunity to get the Greens to agree to a future move. Don't claim that you don't haven't time for all this, that everything described above will take forever. It's only about whether you involve your staff in the process.

By listening to their views and not denying their worries over the idea of moving, you've earned their confidence. You've created enough consensus along the way. However impatient you are, you're going to notice that it was smart to slow down the pace of the process. If you've done everything right, there'll be surprisingly little muttering about the move.

Your Blue Staff Members . . . (Match: Catastrophic)

There is no way to make this sound good. Your Blue staff members accept you. They might respect you on a personal level, but you might never know that. Besides, we're at work now, so it doesn't even make any difference.

The Blues with some personal insight will naturally realize that you add new ideas and thoughts in a way few others do. They've noticed your creativity and ability to think outside the box.

Yellow bosses probably do recruit Blue people on occasion, but presumably without being fully aware of it. For a Yellow boss, Blue behavior is well-nigh unintelligible. You might realize that you need a few more orderly people in your group, but an active thought is necessary to do anything about it. The very idea of how these people, if you were to hire them, need to be led can give anyone nightmares. Most likely, you're going to follow your gut feeling here, and nothing will come of it.

ON THE OTHER HAND . . .

This didn't start out so well. The Blues listen to your ideas but they think that you let them blow away in the wind. You don't do any proper research and you only actually do a fraction of what you talk about. When they ask questions about what you mean by one thing or another, and how it will all happen, you rarely have any intelligible answers.

Ouch.

They're right. And you know it. If your own strongest color is Yellow, I'd venture to say the likelihood that you should lead a team of advanced technicians or a similar group is rather low. I do realize, however, that you perhaps have a couple of Blue people in your team, so they're the ones we're going to talk about.

The whole idea of speaking one's mind is something that Blue individuals find rather disturbing. They think you should only open your mouth if you know exactly what's going to come out. And that requires a whole lot of serious thinking in advance. Since you generally think aloud, you've got a bit of a problem here.

When you're in a good mood, you might like to hug or high five your staff. Be extremely cautious about who you do that with. If you have some irrepressible inspiration to suddenly hug a Blue staff member, I can tell you now that you've made a fool of yourself. They want you to keep your distance—they really do.

You must bear in mind one thing about the Blues: they remember everything.

BUT DAMN IT! HOW FORMAL AND CONVENTIONAL CAN YOU BE?

Think about this: do you have the energy and the stamina necessary to really handle the Bluest of the Blue? If the answer is *yes*, then read further.

As usual, both of you have a responsibility to ensure that the communication works, but you—the Yellow boss—will be obliged to make the greatest effort. The Blues already know that they're right.

When you spontaneously think of something—stop and really think it through before you open your mouth. Consider what you want to convey. By all means write it down on a piece of paper. Evaluate whether you can make it even a little clearer.

Asking them to *solve the problem* doesn't work well. Say that for Task X you would like to see that *this and that* are considered. If there are problems—report back with questions. Report when it is finished. And—important!—say when it must be finished! Otherwise it will end up at the bottom of the list of priorities. Blue staff members prefer to work on one thing at a time. If you want them to put aside what they're doing at the moment, because something else is more important, then you must say this explicitly. Telling them that it must be finished before they go home on Friday might work. It's even better to give an exact time and check they've understood this. If you claim something, regardless of what it is—make sure you have read and absorbed all the details and facts. The Blue will be thinking: how do you know this? Is there any proof? Be well informed. Then you'll be seen as serious. You need to be aware that what you say will also be checked later on. Blue people love to find that other people have made mistakes. Make sure that doesn't happen to you. If this is going to be too hard for you, you can always follow the advice I gave the Red bosses: point out where the information is, and ask the Blues to read it themselves.

Don't wander around at your workplace and talk about random things. Remember what I said: they accept you, but not much more than that. Avoid all personal comments.

It's not just that you should refrain from asking your Blue staff member about her family and her personal life. You should also refrain from talking lots about your own personal life. The Blues are completely indifferent when it comes to your garden, your ailments, what you ate for breakfast, who you know and how that came about, and they don't want to hear anything about your wife's job. Pictures of your children might interest you, but they certainly won't interest them. They can't see the need to spout on about your personal life to people you hardly know. In fact, you make them feel uncomfortable.

It's enough to behave in a friendly manner and to remind yourself to stick to the subject. That's all.

{24}

If You're a Caring Green Boss

You are gentle, friendly, and care about your staff. You're a good listener and you would never try to take the credit for other people's ideas. You can stand proud. You have many enviable qualities, and your staff know it. Sure, some of them might wish that you were a bit more clear and that you made decisions quicker, but you can work on that, can't you?

Let's look at which staff members you'll find the most challenging.

Your Red Staff Members . . . (Match: Fairly Good)

. . . think that you're a nice guy. Somebody who lets them get on with their own stuff and who doesn't disturb them too much and is appreciated by many. They think you're good at putting a team together even though they don't really see themselves as a part of it. They realize that you make an effort to create a good atmosphere in the group.

If you, as a Green boss, are looking to hire new staff, the

question is how you react when you're faced with a really good Red candidate. You know by now that you are very different from each other. That partly depends on how you see your leadership role. If you want to be one of the gang, somebody who's liked by their staff, well yes, the Reds can then present a challenge or two.

Your gentle and friendly side is actually wasted on the Reds. They don't want to be rubbed the right way. The good news is that you can invest more time in other members of your staff.

ON THE OTHER HAND . . .

. . . your Red staff members think you're a weakling. You never stick to your guns and they can steamroll over you as easy as pie. For the Red, of course, this is good news. It's not uncommon that Red staff members simply ignore the recommendations of their Green boss. (Who am I trying to fool? They do actually ignore you sometimes.)

Besides, you take far too long to do anything. If a Red staff member comes to you with a question, he or she will want an answer immediately. They hate waiting. If you don't have an answer, they'll do it their way. If you manage to prevent further action, perhaps you ask for an extension until this afternoon for the answer. And when is that? Straight after lunch of course. At one o'clock, the Red staff member is back with their demand. And now a bit irritated, too. Why is it so difficult to get a simple decision? That it might cost an awful lot of money or affect twelve other people in the firm, well, the Red couldn't care less. For him or her, this is not a big deal. Now let's go. And you feel stressed.

THOSE RUDE, ARROGANT . . . I'M GOING TO . . . GOING TO . . . GOING TOO . . .

What? What are you actually going to do? Here you've got to keep two ideas in your head at the same time. While you think that Red behavior is really bothersome to deal with, you're also well aware of the fact that the Red staff members actually get a lot done. Sure, they cross the lines about as often as you drink a cup of coffee, but they get the job done. They like tough challenges and they can handle a lot of unpleasant work—if only you know how to handle them. And for you—as a Green boss—there are specific things you need to do to proceed with the Reds.

The Reds like talking about results and achieving targets. They don't like it that you waste their time and devote your energies to things of no consequence. Don't tiptoe around and whisper—express yourself clearly and distinctly. That's how you get their attention.

Clarity. You are far too vague in the way you express yourself. You need to be considerably more direct. No foreplay here, if that's easier to understand.

Don't say: *It would have been great if you could find a moment to take a quick look at area X. I know you have a lot on at the moment, but I really would appreciate it if you blah blah blah . . .*

Say instead: *I want you to solve the problem with area X as soon as possible. Will you do that?*

Fine, now you were understandable. The Reds like that.

The Red has a built-in competitive spirit. That means that she or he likes to win a discussion. Also that they can be too eager and say virtually anything at all to come out as winner. They can even behave aggressively since they know that you'll back down. Don't let yourself be fooled, it's just theater. Keep going back to facts; point out the established details you're discussing.

This is really important. Under no circumstances should you allow your staff members to steamroll you. But note this: you should never raise your voice. What you should do is to wait for the storm to blow over and then simply repeat what you said earlier. Again and again. I promise—it isn't personal.

But above all—increase the speed. Your Red staff members will press the accelerator down hard, and if you really want to keep them with you, sometimes you will have to resist your instinct to slow down.

If you do increase your own speed, things will be okay between you. The Reds will respect you—they won't praise you, but their respect is not easy to win. If they do respect you, they might even come to like you.

Your Yellow Staff Members . . . (Match: Good)

. . . also think you're a decent guy. You're a rather inoffensive and unproblematic boss. Since you don't have a particularly high profile and since you allow them to do what they want, they have no problem with you. When they make careless mistakes, you're never going to behead them. Instead, you're going to sneak up beside their desk with furtive hints about how this or that could possibly have been done differently.

The Yellows in your team approve of this sort of thing. They're ridiculously sensitive to criticism. They don't hold a grudge, like you do, but they suffer in the moment. Your soft style works well here. And if you even remember to say happy birthday to them, you'll get lots of bonus points. Since you like talking, and you're a good listener, there are many positive conditions for a really flexible work climate.

You work really well together.

ON THE OTHER HAND . . .

. . . even the Yellows think you can be very timid at times. They don't really know where they stand with you, since you hide your feelings. If they present a wild idea and want to hear how creative they have been, you're going to react by holding up your hands and saying that you don't have any faith in that. You don't particularly like new ideas, and since the Yellows come up with them several times an hour, they're going to feel your annoyance. Since you're the boss, your opinion is important. The problem is that you often keep your opinion to yourself or you dismiss the new idea. That can have a negative effect on the Yellows' good spirits.

This is something of a dilemma. When it comes to changes, you are on different ends of the spectrum. You can pretend to like change, but basically you like the way things work right now. Admit it, and then we can move on. But the Yellows thrive on change. They initiate new practices all the time. There's nothing they like better than novelty. And there are few things you shun more than exactly that.

Here you have a true challenge.

Like the Reds, the Yellows don't want to wait while you sleep on it. They want to get going right away. And when you hesitate, they think you're a bit of a bore.

THESE JACK-IN-THE-BOX TYPES! I COULD TEACH THEM A THING OR TWO ABOUT STABILITY ABOUT CALMNESS, ABOUT . . .

Absolutely. I'm sure you could. But what you say will fall on deaf ears. What you need to do is to listen to the proposals. Put everything else aside. You're a good listener—make use of that in this particular situation.

When the Yellows come up with one crazy idea after the other, you need to take in what they say. There will be endless exposition that sounds like they're going to rebuild the galaxy. You might have the impulse to roll your eyes.

But don't say: *That isn't going to work.*

Don't say: *There's no need for that solution—we don't have any problems in area X.*

When the Yellow stops to get some air—take the chance to stick in a couple of questions instead.

Better to comment: *Interesting idea!* And then ask: *How is that going to work?*

Say things like: *It's great that you have ideas! What are we going to need to carry this out?*

In that way, you help the Yellow sort their thoughts. They can behave like kids on Christmas Eve when they've thought up something new. But let them do their thing. The trick is not to smother their enthusiasm. Are you worried about what this idea might actually result in? All you need do is to ask your Yellow staff member to put everything down on paper. Ask him or her to describe what the purpose of the idea is; what a planned target could look like; what measures would be necessary to get there; and how long it's going to take. If you really want to put an end to it, you can pair up the Yellow with the Blue. The idea might not even make it into writing.

But—and this is important—consider any ideas that seem interesting. Try to ignore your normal instinct to simply dismiss everything new. Sometimes the Yellows are actually right. And then you need to give them a chance.

Your Green Staff Members . . . (Match: Excellent)

. . . do, of course, recognize themselves in you. They understand you very well and they can almost read your thoughts. You have a great deal in common, and they think that you shouldn't be the boss at all, but one of the team. After all—you're on the same wavelength. You are introverted and relationship-oriented; you all like working in a smallish team where everyone has known each other since the 1980s. And you don't stress about things. Together you form the stable security upon which the rest of the organization rests.

They particularly like the way you allow them to work at their usual pace. You don't come along with lots of completely impracticable ideas, and should any changes need to be made, you'll delay the implementation if possible. This suits your Green staff members perfectly.

But also they appreciate that you protect the group, that you always put your staff first before whatever extreme goals top management has come up with.

The odds that you should recruit people like you, other Greens, are rather low. Because it's going to feel best, isn't it?

ON THE OTHER HAND . . .

They would never dream of wanting to become a boss, and the fact that you have taken the job on is impressive but also . . .

a little worrying. Because who are you to raise yourself above everyone else? Green behavior is admittedly relationship-oriented, and they care about the team. But they don't want anybody to stick out too much. If they identify with you and think that you ought to be one of the gang, then there might be signs of envy about your position.

Your Green staff members do appreciate the security you radiate, but they also think that you sometimes show a lack of initiative. Even though they see things that could be improved, they won't do anything unless you point the way. If you're too slow and too kind, they'll wait too. And then, of course, you'll all be left standing on the platform when the train departs.

THESE IRRESPONSIBLE BUMS . . .

Yes, it's a bit like getting a taste of your own medicine, no? But when we shoulder the role of boss, we're no longer one of the gang. You are, despite having worked in the firm for twenty years before becoming a boss, still their boss. You're obliged to deal with these individuals who would prefer to do what they've always done.

Together, you are perhaps the most closely knit group this side of Paris, but that also has its challenges.

You must consider that your Green pals tend to hide themselves among the Yellows and the Blues. You simply need to remind yourself to see all the individuals at the same time, even those who like to maneuver a bit under the radar.

Sometimes you might need the help of an outsider, perhaps your own boss, for a bit of inspiration. Why not talk with somebody who is Yellow-Red, for example? That can complement your deep understanding of your Green staff members.

Your Blue Staff Members . . . (Match: Good)

There's nothing strange about this. Both you and your Blue team are introverts, which means that you recognize the type of energy that you both need. You like to take things calmly and your Blue staff members also like a slower tempo. You want to have time for yourself and you need to have the opportunity to get your bearings in your own head now and then—just like they do. That means that you're going to let each of them work fairly freely at their own pace. And the Blues like the fact that you aren't looking over their shoulder and interfering in what they're doing or not doing. And that you don't just start babbling on. They've made a complete assessment of you, and know that you—just like the Yellow boss in the next corridor—are a true "feelings junkie." They won't give you any bonus points for that, but they'll appreciate the way that you keep most things to yourself.

You're somewhat discreet when you talk, you don't chase them. That's very good. Keep at it. Continue to let your Blue staff members/buddies take the time they need to be able to consider everything really thoroughly.

ON THE OTHER HAND . . .

. . . they aren't actually your buddies. You can't even pretend they are. You'll have to let go of that fantasy. Yet again, there is a whole array of pitfalls when we talk about Blue employees. It would be easy for you to mistake them for

Greens. A big mistake. Even if they're calm, collected, and get through difficult days without grumbling, *they are not Greens*. They're the total opposite of relationship-oriented.

I'm aware of the risk of repeating myself, but the Blues are painfully indifferent to you as an individual. You're just a little square box on the organizational chart. For some reason, you've been given a formal mandate, even though that might surprise them. You are a superior. A function. And at the same time, you're a softie, a "boss" who might wear fuzzy slippers under their desk, whose role they understand in an intellectual sense, but they hardly see you as a strong leader. You're not well enough informed to be that.

Whether or not this is a problem in your particular workplace, I can't say, but it's easy to fall into a special trap here. Because, from the outside, one can mistake a Blue for a Green, so there's an obvious risk of becoming on familiar terms with the wrong person. You might interpret the silence as active listening, which can turn out to be a dreadful error. While you naïvely talk about how you hadn't really wanted your managerial position, under the surface a fierce thought process is analyzing exactly how comprehensive the problem with the "involuntary boss" really is. And the risk-analyst in the Blue comes to life and begins to appraise the potential threat this presents for delivery security.

I'd remind you that Blue individuals aren't interested in your emotions, your experiences, your worries, or your stress. They want to know: Are you well-informed about the details that will make this a perfect job? I'm sorry to say this, but unfortunately you aren't. Your tendency of expressing yourself rather vaguely most definitely doesn't help here. You're too imprecise, too unclear and far too general. And that doesn't work with the Blues.

THOSE ANAL-RETENTIVE STICKLERS FOR DETAILS, THOSE USELESS, ZOMBIE-LIKE . . .

Yes, I know. But together we can deal with this. What you need to do is to continue to stay calm. Don't change the pace at which you work. You have a perfect pace for the job. The Blues are even slower than you, so the fact that you're a couple of notches higher up on the scale of general impatience is actually positive.

But for God's sake: you should immediately stop trying to create a friendly or personal relationship with this gang. You've got the message: all emotions should be removed from your toolbox. Your task is not to make your Blue team more "human." Your task is to ensure that they do their job well and, above all, that they keep to their deadlines. You achieve that by being extremely strict and limiting yourself to only talking about work. You should filter out everything that isn't on the agenda. If you want to confide in somebody, do it somewhere else. You'll only confuse the Blues if you talk about your ill father, or your dog's fleas, or your reluctance to make that unpleasant phone call *to your boss*. Those are things you should only talk about with somebody who doesn't work in the same place as you. Got it?

When you do this, order will establish itself little by little. The Blue team will gradually (but eventually) change their opinion of you, and their faith in you will grow again. Which is good news, because this gang only listen to people that they have confidence in. Let them get on with their work without interruption and ask them to send in all the necessary reports. If you find mistakes—go to the section on feedback to Blue persons. Good luck!

{ 25 }

If You're an Analytical and Objective Blue Boss

Since your strongest color is Blue—possibly in combination with another color—you always know exactly what's going on, what has happened, and what could happen. Nothing misses your eagle eye, and you like to immerse yourself in details. At the same time, some people think you're a stickler for details who always follows the instruction book. This can mean that you're seen as rather conventional.

But not by everybody. Let's look at them via their possible colors and try to figure out the most important differences.

Your Red Staff Members . . . (Match: Bad)

. . . consider your complete control to be admirable. They respect the fact that you don't let a whole lot of unnecessary emotions interfere with work. They like how you keep a cool head and, just like you, they prefer to call bad news by its proper name. Sugarcoating is not for them, and they appreciate that you're outspoken about things that don't work. That is all positive.

Blue bosses most likely choose Red staff members mainly to avoid having to practice so much leadership. The Reds don't want to be directed anyway. They want to be left in peace, and that suits you rather well. You can easily manage your group in detail, but will quite often retain some distance. You're often in your office and let things get on with themselves. And if your Red staff member gets a bit rowdy, you simply shut the door.

ON THE OTHER HAND . . .

. . . your Red staff members will be asking themselves whether you've been drinking brake fluid. Why does everything take such an incredibly long time? Is it really so difficult to get an answer to a simple question? Red staff members want to accelerate and can't understand your reluctance to give a direct answer the very same nanosecond the question was asked.

The way you take the question home, look at it, analyze the situation, and make a logical assessment—that's not their style. You slow them down, and that creates stress and disorder. Red behavior means either getting on with it or getting out of it. If you delay too long, they'll let go of the ball, and it can be difficult to persuade them to pick it up again. Red behavior doesn't include a lot of looking back. Be aware of that. What was, was. Now is now.

THESE HOTHEADS WILL JUST HAVE TO WAIT A BIT. SPEED ISN'T EVERYTHING

It needs to be right and be done right. I realize that. The problem is that for the Reds, speed is more important. If they think that you, as the Blue boss, overdose on circumspection, then they'll stop listening to you. And sometimes you're on the wrong track. The Reds don't have the patience required to persuade you.

The good thing is that none of you suffer if things go a bit sour, and that's a strength. But having continual conflicts does not create the best quality work, and you know that.

The Reds want to see results. Your calm, methodical pace really irks them. When you communicate with them, go straight to the most important data you have. Go to the highlights. To make this clear—read the last line in the annual accounts. Don't bother about how you got there. Just say where you are right now.

Pouring out loads of facts doesn't work at all. Details are poison to Reds. Quoting directly from an Excel spreadsheet is asking for trouble. I know that you would like to give a lot of background on what you have to say. But the Reds don't want to listen to that. They want to know what they should do now. If you fail, they'll pick up their cell phones in the middle of the meeting, and then you've lost them.

Prepare what you are going to say to a Red staff member by writing down three points. Preferably only one line per point. If you manage that, you'll keep her or his attention for more than two minutes. I know, patience is a virtue. But they see action as more important. And sometimes they're right too.

Remind yourself that they have strong egos. If you can satisfy these, you're going to motivate them to stick to the rule book. You do that by asking for input. Ask them if they have ideas and suggestions for how you could move forward. Include their ideas. Show that you value their opinion.

Your Yellow Staff Members . . . (Match: Really Rotten)

. . . think that you're a serious boss. They realize that you have lots of good qualities, and there are days when they wish that they too had more of your instinct for order. They feel that way when they've caused you problems. They would like to buy a car that has been obsessively maintained, but they don't like obsessive maintenance. Do you follow?

That a Blue boss would choose a large number of Yellow staff is of course highly unlikely. It would require quite a lot of personal insight from the boss, but I'm not saying it isn't possible. If you, as a Blue boss, are aware that what you need is an individual with the ability to think outside the box, then you have a winner here. You have somebody who complements you, since you often rely only on well-proven solutions. You could make a brilliant team.

ON THE OTHER HAND . . .

A lively Yellow candidate who hard-sells themselves at the first interview is unfortunately not going to get a second interview. Even though the Yellow's way of communicating is positive, and everything that she or he says sounds great, the Blue boss is going to ask some follow-up questions. That will be the end of it. The Yellow can't give an answer as to how they actually succeeded at their previous job. There's a risk that they haven't read up on the job they're applying for, and they might call the recruiting boss by the wrong first name.

None of that is so serious, but as a boss it tells you something about this individual.

But say that you do have a couple of staff members whose

profile is predominantly Yellow. They're going to want to have fun at work, they want to be inspired. They want to feel and experience things.

How are you going to handle that?

I HAD MY FILL OF JOKERS AT SCHOOL. THESE PEOPLE NEED TO BE MORE SERIOUS

Correct. You will see a very Yellow staff member as nothing short of an administrative meltdown. But the Yellows want to have interesting experiences in their work. How can you arrange for that? You know that they contribute interesting ideas, creative pranks that would never happen without them. You need to give them a lot of room to maneuver.

Yellow staff members in a good mood can achieve miracles, while grumpy and irritable ones can be a nightmare for others. If you can help to create a fun and pleasant environment, then you'll allow them to grow. You don't need to understand why a good atmosphere in the office is so extremely important, you just need to believe me when I say that the Yellows think it is.

You don't need to run around and be amusing yourself; you can let the Yellows take care of that. Just show a little enthusiasm when they shout out joyfully. You don't need to go along with everything, heaven knows it isn't all going to be well-thought-through, but you could at least consider a smile when you listen.

A good tip: if you think your Yellow staff member has completely lost their hold on reality, then you can ask them to write their idea down on a piece of paper. That is better than nixing the idea in the first conversation. Or ask them to send an email. Perhaps that's easier. Say what you want the email to contain. Do *not* assume that you think alike here. Explain that you want to see the purpose of the idea, what the goal could be, and some clear suggestions for measurable goals. If you must, you can also ask what would be improved if the Yellow's recommendations were implemented

It is quite likely that the Yellow won't succeed in putting anything down on paper, and then you won't have to do anything either, will you? If, on the other hand, the Yellow does manage to put together a serious document and sends it to you, then you'll suddenly have something as a starting point. This idea may now be worth taking a closer look at.

Don't forget to focus on the person behind the job title. Stop by the Yellow's desk and ask how they're getting on. Ask personal questions. Listen attentively and ask some follow-up questions. Show that you care. Since this isn't actually one of your own central priorities, you might need to create a routine to start doing it.

I know that you're not the very best source of inspiration. But if you can adopt an easygoing tone at the morning meeting, the Yellows are going to appreciate it. If you've heard a funny joke—tell it. Show that you have a sense of humor. It will only take a minute of your time.

One more thing. What I wrote about the Red staff members and details, applies here too—raised to the fifth power. Yellow staff members abhor details and facts, like vampires shun sunlight. Discussing a particular formula in an Excel spreadsheet is torturous. Don't do it. Pair the Yellow with someone you know keeps track of details, but don't expect the Yellow to have a 100 percent grip on things. That would not be realistic.

Your Green Staff Members . . . (Match: Good)

. . . are satisfied with your calm and considered pace. They like not having to feel the constant stress that Red and Yellow bosses often create. Your patience is appreciated since it gives them the chance to think things over. They know that you'll give them all the time necessary—and even a bit more—when something needs to be done.

They're also impressed by your professional knowledge, and often wish they were just as knowledgeable in your area. The Greens quite often have gaps in their self-confidence, but they feel secure working with a professional boss like you.

I would think that Blue bosses attract Green staff members because of their calm and predictable environments. Even though Green staff members don't actually like all routines, they're going to be good at repeating the same thing time after time. If they know what they're supposed to do, they'll generally do it. There are a lot of positive points in common.

ON THE OTHER HAND . . .

. . . there's a risk that you'll forget to communicate with each other. The Greens will also want to talk feelings; they'll want to know what you think and how you feel about something. I know, it's all a bit tacky. But this is how the Greens function.

The Greens can easily think that you're far too insensitive. That you don't really seem to like people and that you're extremely critical. You see every little fault, and your natural instinct is to point it out. I realize that you would be an excellent quality controller, but the Greens are sensitive to criticism, especially if it's given in front of others. If, at a meeting, you remind Berit that she was really careless the week before in dealing with customer X, she will simply look down at her papers and not answer you. This doesn't mean that she accepts the criticism. It only means that she's not going to publicly express what she really thinks about your anal hair-splitting.

ARE WE GOING TO LOWER OUR STANDARDS HERE, TOO? ISN'T QUALITY IMPORTANT?

Okay, the devil is in the details. But we are talking about people, not industrial robots. You need to realize that they have feelings and are influenced by different things than you are.

The Greens often find it stressful if they don't know where their boss stands. If you rarely show any feelings, it will create uncertainty. One way of building up the trust and faith they need to have in you is to be a bit personal. I don't mean that you have to show them photos of your children's birthday parties, but it might be suitable to say something about what you do in your free time. And just like with your Yellow staff members, you sometimes need to ask the Greens personal questions. Show that you value them.

Your speed is already well adapted for the Greens. Both of you take things easy. Remember that the Greens can find it difficult to give you an answer even when you're ready for it. It doesn't always suffice to have all the facts on the table. Perhaps they haven't thought it over long enough. Give them time to sleep on it.

Continue to deliver concrete background material. It's not

likely that they will read every last page, but they like to have all the material. That also makes for security and stability.

They don't like feeling that they are being controlled. Give them space and time to digest things, and avoid too much passive resistance. Remember that the Greens are extremely loyal and dutiful under the right conditions. Give them guarantees and assurances. Explain that you have a plan and that everything is going to work out.

Focus on reliability and stability. Then you'll get the quality you are looking for.

Your Blue Staff Members . . . (Match: Perfect)

. . . are very satisfied with your nose for quality. If a task is worth doing at all, then it should be done in the correct way. And if there isn't time to do it right, then you can do it yourself. They're safe in the knowledge that you'll never cheat or be careless with important (= all) details. They instinctively know that you have the same discerning criteria.

So is this a *perfect match*?

Perhaps. The Blue boss will undoubtedly be able to see themselves in the Blue staff member. You're recruiting individuals who are just like you. Depending a bit on your driving forces, you're going to understand each other.

ON THE OTHER HAND . . .

. . . there is going to be a rather too homogenous attitude within the group. There is a risk that you'll fall into the same trap as the Yellow boss. People are simply too similar to one another. And it will be a bit like connecting two positive (+) wires together. With a bit of force, it's easy to press them together. But as soon as you let go, they'll separate.

The challenges are of another type. If you're too similar, there's a different sort of friction than if you are too dissimilar. I have been to some group meetings with technical departments where everyone, including the boss, has been deepest Blue. They are the most depressing meetings I've ever attended. Like being at a funeral service. Nobody really needs to discuss anything. They all think they know best and they see the meeting as an inexcusable waste of time. They just want to get back to their desks.

THEY READ THE WRONG BOOKS. THEIR PROBLEM.

Your Blue staff members want the facts. But did you know that they might have other gods before you? If your Blue staff member has a guru from this branch and you have another one, there can be one hell of a lot of friction between you. Your "facts" don't match, and neither of you is going to back down unless exceptionally reliable evidence is presented. Then that must, of course, be examined and double-checked. There's a risk that the machinery will grind to a total halt before everything has been satisfactorily sorted out.

What's important for you is to actually retain control over what's happening. Blue staff members like to make their own tracks down dead ends. You only have to look at yourself. Occasionally you stumble across something extremely fascinating. You start looking into it and at some point you suddenly realize that the sun has set while you've been delving into something that might—or might not—be relevant to what you were originally looking for. Make sure your Blue staff members stick to the path. Their instinct is to dig right down to groundwater, but the group won't get anywhere at all if the boss allows too much of that sort of thing.

When you set the tone, be very careful. Together with the Blues, go through all the advantages and disadvantages of method X. Give them the proof neatly packaged in a logical form. Allow some discussion, but don't let it get out of hand. Don't accept any more postponements for further investigation.

It's time to act. Make sure you do.

Bear this in mind too: everything you say and everything you do will be noted. Be on your guard and make sure that you always—no exceptions—follow up on your own commitments. If you've promised a particular thing, the Blues will have made a note. They might not confront you if you don't ask a direct question, but they keep track of what you've done or haven't done.

And don't forget that they find it disturbing that you're always right. Sometimes you'll be wrong, and it can irritate the Blues among your staff. As usual, you might not find out about this. Their stone faces don't reveal anything. But if you never give way, they will eventually stop listening to you.

Summary

As you can see, this is not just about you. You need to know *both* how you yourself function *and* keep track of your staff members. As you get to know them better, your dialogue and everyday communication will work better too. But this isn't going to be free. You'll have to work to get there.

Do it. It's worth the effort. I guarantee it.

{ 26 }

The Best Way to Put a Team Together

As the boss and leader, you also need to look beyond the usual qualifications. Having a formal education is probably never going to be negative, it shows that the person concerned has the capacity to learn things. Even though it's difficult to recruit good people when this chapter is being written [in Sweden, 2018], I can guarantee that you'll avoid a lot of headaches if you also think about how the new man or woman is going to work in the group.

It is, of course, controversial to claim that a specific educational background is not the only thing that counts in a recruiting context, but the fact is that with the wrong people on the team, you're not going to achieve anything at all—regardless of how many university courses and degrees they have. If the group is ripped apart by conflict, then it doesn't matter how skillful the individuals are. If cooperation is necessary, you need to consider how you think the different people would function together. What does it help with individuals who are stars in their respective areas, if they refuse to talk with one another?

If you ask some members of the group to form a mini-team for a particular task—which staff members will you let work together? There's an obvious risk that they'll form teams according to whether they like each other or not, instead of thinking about what would create the best group.

As boss, you can't sit by and let it happen. You need to be alert.

Should They Be Similar or Dissimilar?

In theory, the best team is the one with the greatest spread in regard to colors and driving forces. Then you get the best mix of ideas, abilities, and all different approaches. It will be a dynamic group.

Somewhat simplified, you could say that the Yellow team member gets an idea, the Red member says *Go*, the Green member does the actual job, and the Blue member does a final appraisal to see if it turned out like it was meant to.

Yes, that is a very rough simplification. In real life, it isn't so simple. Let's say that you really do have a perfect balance within the group. You have approximately the same amount of each color among the staff members. Perfect! Now, a considerable responsibility rests on your shoulders. As the leader for the group, you need to deal with all four colors. And all six driving forces. Not to mention the journey through the four development phases. More on that soon.

When it comes to driving forces, it's definitely simpler if

everyone is there for the same reason. You go to your job to achieve the same thing and it's fairly easy to understand the motives of your work colleagues. Unless they're all individualists, of course. Then each of them will want to make decisions, and you can guess how that will end. They can't all hold the rudder, not at the same time anyway.

It's complicated.

If we're only talking colors, then my advice is still that you try to get a good mix in the group, and it's going to work better if you spread this knowledge you've learned in this book. If they all have a good understanding of each other, it will help to reduce any friction.

There are natural points of contact between certain colors, just like there are natural challenges between others. Some of them are really tricky to deal with.

Let's take a closer look at what it can look like.

Red Battering Rams

A team of only Red people might not sound like a dream, at any rate not if we're talking about teamwork and consensus. There's going to be a whole lot of shouting and ordering about, but it's not certain that any of them will feel any exceptional desire to listen to the others. They'll often end up struggling with each other and everyone outside the group is going to have to duck to avoid being hit.

On the other hand, the Reds are going to understand each other very well. They're all in agreement that everybody should limit their talking and go full speed. The need to sit with a cup of coffee and have a nice time is nonexistent, and they don't care what everyone is doing on the weekends. Here, it's the job that counts.

None of them particularly care if there is conflict within the group. For god's sake, conflict is simply another way of communicating. The fact that a Red person can argue with their poor colleague but still be friends is not seen as being the slightest bit odd. It was only a factual matter after all. That doesn't affect the rest of their relationship to any extent.

But sure. It probably isn't the smoothest solution to just have Reds in a group. Unless you want this group to be finished before all the others, of course. Then all the Reds are really going to go full speed. They intend to win this.

Yellows Who Enjoy Life

An all-Yellow team—what do you say about that? Can it possibly be more entertaining than that? Put five entirely Yellow people in a room and slam the door shut. Look in after a couple of hours and ask them how they're getting on. Their answer?

It's going really great! We are so inspired and we're having one hell of a good time!

They are going to understand each other in all respects, you can be sure of that. Everyone in the room realizes the value of building relationships and creating a congenial and relaxed atmosphere. If you ask them who is making notes and in charge of the minutes, you'll be met with blank looks. *Write things down? No, no, we don't work like that.*

But only Yellow people is probably not an especially optimal solution either. They would, of course, create ideas that would impress everybody, but they won't be able to find their papers. And forget any idea of a risk analysis. We're talking about visionary creativity on an atmospheric level, and nothing is going to stand in its way. Who is actually going to carry out all these plans? That remains a mystery.

No, with only Yellow in the team, there would be a world record for best work environment, but add to that a lot of talk and surprisingly little action. These people are good at starting things, but they find it alarmingly arduous to bring themselves to actually do them. For that, something else is necessary.

Cozy Green Friends

I have always said that the Greens are built for cooperation. It's where they always begin. So the best team should be made up of only Green individuals, right? They look for cooperation and consensus; they want nothing more than for everybody to agree and think the same. This is probably your dream team.

But think again.

If everybody agreed about everything all the time—what is going to happen to the group dynamic? And who is going to kick start the whole thing? These cozy Green folks will only be thinking one thing: *who am I to tell the others what they ought to do? I hope that somebody else takes charge so that I don't have to.* If everybody thinks the same way . . . well, you realize what's going to happen—absolutely nothing.

The risk is that in the light of all the potential differences of opinion, the group never gets going. And you are going to wonder what's actually happening. But, yes, the Greens are going to understand each other very well. They're going to like each other's company and that no demands are made. This team will sail nicely along, right over the edge of the waterfall.

Blue Sticklers for Details

Well, that leaves the Blue group. Here there is deafening silence. Everything is going to be extremely well sorted and documented, nothing is going to be left to chance. No mistakes will be tolerated, and perfection lies just around the corner.

Perhaps this is the best grouping—you can expect a perfect result every time.

Except for one detail: they never finish anything. This gang will never stop planning. There will always be further details to consider, more risks to appraise; yet another document to put together before they start work.

Even though the Blues understand their colleagues' need for pedantry, and even though they all like details more than anything else, and despite the fact that none of them is going to involve anybody else in any sticky sentimental nonsense, it isn't going to work out well. This gang will never leave the starting gate.

Wrong: they won't even get their running shoes on.

Ok, I Get it. Diversity Is a Good Thing

It is *indeed* good. The team gains so many more dimensions and so many more approaches than it otherwise would. I really do recommend that you consider what the mix should be like in your particular group. The greatest mistake you make is to rely on your gut feeling. There are a lot of methods to complicate the recruitment process, and not all of them are good. But you need to be attentive when you consider who you pick for your team.

One of the most common mistakes that inexperienced bosses make is to employ people they like. Because what sort of people do you instinctively like? Exactly—people who are similar to you. She must be a good person—she's exactly like me! The risk is that the group will gradually be dangerously homogenous.

Having said this, I want to show that different colors work well together in different degrees.

This picture actually explains it quite simply:

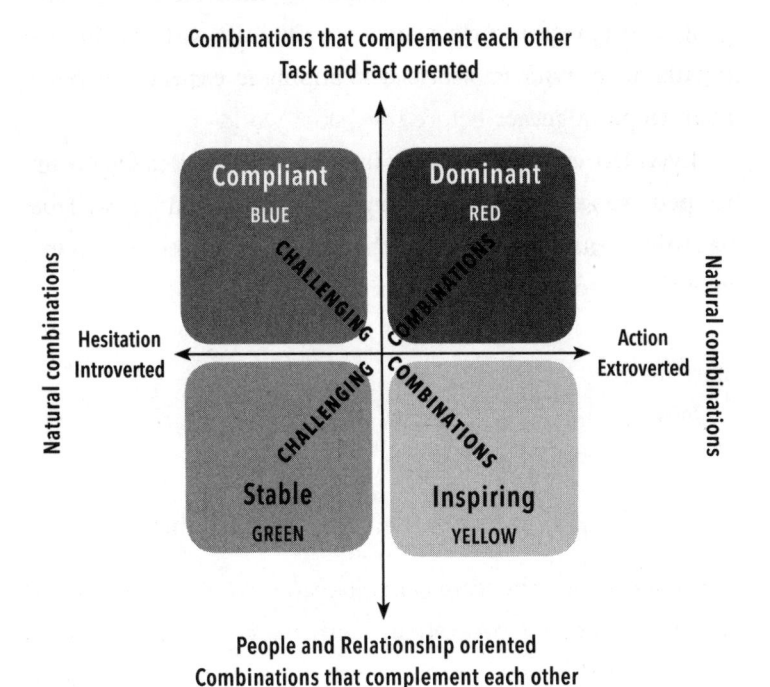

Combinations that complement each other
Task and Fact oriented

Compliant BLUE	**Dominant** RED
Stable GREEN	**Inspiring** YELLOW

Natural combinations (left side)
Natural combinations (right side)

Hesitation / Introverted ← → Action / Extroverted

CHALLENGING COMBINATIONS (diagonals)

People and Relationship oriented
Combinations that complement each other

My own experience is that it's easier to reach each other on the vertical axis than on the horizontal one. It seems as if people feel more comfortable within extrovert and introvert behavior respectively, than within task- and person-oriented behavior. Why exactly this is can be a point of discussion. It's probably connected with energy. The Greens and the Blues prefer a calmer pace that gives energy to their everyday life, while the Yellows and the Reds appreciate more activity.

And as you'll already have worked out, there are a couple of problematic combinations, and those are the diagonal connections. Blue–Yellow and Red–Green. So far there's nothing weird about this.

My basic tip is that if you really want a good balance in the group and really sharp dynamics—then make sure you get a good spread of colors among your staff, without lowering standards with regard to education and experience. It's a question of balance.

But when you do this, bear in mind that even if the group becomes more varied and complete, more demands will be made on you as the leader of the group. You'll need to hone your ability to deal with different colors.

{ 27 }

Helping Your Team Become Active Participants

Okay. Let's assume that from now on you adapt your communication to your various staff members. It is, of course, a challenge to talk to people with different colors at the same time, I can't deny that. But there are nevertheless approaches that are better than just doing what you always have done.

Let's take a look at what further pitfalls you might encounter. Sometimes, what's crystal clear inside your own head isn't equally apparent for others around you.

Yes, but . . . you might be thinking now, we've already established important basic values within the organization! We've discussed our guiding lights, our visions, our mission statement, our task, etc.

We've agreed on this—everybody approved—agreed that what is the most important is to stand for honesty, cooperation, respect, and responsibility. We even agreed on what these words mean. The consultant who helped us with that explained that the words were useless unless we could describe the behaviors they led to. But we did that! We even hung up everything on the office walls. Everyone can read the whole spiel every single day.

I understand your reaction. So why do your staff members not do what they promised and what they agreed to? Why didn't it work? Why do they, for example, not take full responsibility—you've talked about how important it is and how you should do it. You even made plans for what you should do if you see behaviors that don't agree with these goals.

In short: what's actually the problem?

There *are* workplaces where this works well. Where all the staff members know what they should do, the majority take full responsibility, and cooperation is painless from morning to night. Conflict is rare, and those that do occur lead to fruitful new lessons. They all feel that they're active participants; the bosses don't interfere in details, nor do they leave the beginners all alone. Profitability is good, staff like their work very much, customers are satisfied. Everything is—more or less—lovely.

These organizations do indeed exist. I've seen them. But to be perfectly honest—they're rather rare.

Getting everything in place requires an enormous amount of work, much more than you can imagine. Quite often it takes ten times more work than the leadership first thinks it will. One of the problems is actually that they bring in consultants to help them too often. Don't get me wrong, it's fine to use consultants to get things started. But they can only point in the right direction—they can't do the actual job and get everything to work. It's the organization itself that must implement all the new elements.

Also, there are consultants who don't know what they're doing. The most common mistake is that a consultant convinces decision-makers that new ideas in leadership will be simple to implement.

They are not.

It's difficult.

And sometimes it's an impossible task.

Creating real change is tricky. Everybody in the firm has inherited a history, and they bring their own experiences and understandings with them when they come to a new job. If you've been there a long time, you might well be a part of the problem. Things are the way they are, because they've always been like that.

The purpose of this book is not to teach you how you should establish a new ethical framework or how you should start new routines in your business and activities. I aspire to give you thoughts and ideas about how you can communicate with your staff in an effective manner. So I'm taking some shortcuts. Perhaps you are thinking: *What an idiot—he doesn't understand anything. What does he know about the problems I wrestle with every day?*

But I do know. I'm simply choosing to jump directly to communication.

You—and your bosses—need to act as role models and stand up for everything you've agreed upon. Leadership is, in its essence, painfully similar to parenthood: your children don't do what you say, they do what you do. And sometimes the similarities between the team and your own children are striking.

Let's say that you have some new ideas that you want to put into practice. Perhaps you've acquired the help of some smart consultants, and you've put together a plan that you and your immediate bosses really believe in. What's going to happen how?

Why the Fancy Words in Your Ethical Policy Don't Work

We need to talk about how you make your staff active participants in what is happening. People want to participate. We know that now. Most people want to feel that they're a part of the whole. It can take time to build up that commitment, but I can confirm that once you've managed to get everyone interested in the group's development, you're not going to want to return to how it was before.

You don't like it when your boss gives you orders without context. You want to have a certain degree of understanding about what you're expected to be doing.

So how can you manage this? Everybody seems to listen in different ways, and they're interested in different things. So if all workplaces consist of a mix of Red, Yellow, Green, and Blue—is it doomed from the start? Should we just give up? Sometimes I get the feeling that certain bosses behave like people following an unsuccessful diet. It didn't work, so they might just as well go back to gorging themselves on peanuts and beer. They give up, go back to their old selves, and hope that everybody else will adapt to them.

That's perhaps the very worst method.

But there is a way out.

Why Does the Flow of Information Never Work?

This has become something of a bad joke.

We don't get any information here. Roughly like that old cliché about rowdy teenagers causing trouble out in town because they don't have a place to be. I can't even smile at that excuse any longer.

Today, of course, the exact opposite applies. We find ourselves in a sort of permanent nirvana for information lovers. It's become so easy to reach out. All the digital aids mean that anybody can send out anything at all by just pressing a few keys on their keyboard. The intranets in most organizations overflow with valuable information.

But who's going to read all that? People have a job to do.

A couple of years ago, I coached the managing director in a fairly large company. He was Blue-Red and took care to see that everything was done properly. The problem was that instead of learning how people functioned, he simply ticked off logical activities on a checklist. He didn't think it was his problem how these actions were received.

He was, for example, confounded as to why the staff hadn't embraced the company's new vision. Nobody seemed to understand it, which he found extremely strange. He'd made use of some fantastically expensive management consultants who had shown him how the vision should be developed. And now there wasn't anybody who understood it or worked to make it a reality. When he talked about it at meetings, he was met with blank stares.

"I don't understand," he said, "I've gone through and explained the vision at a meeting. I've even emailed a summary of it to everyone."

He showed me the email. A nice layout and well formulated. I couldn't have done it better myself.

"Umm," I tried, "how many people opened that email?"

"How should I know?" he answered, unable to grasp what I was getting at.

I said, "Well, how many people read that email then? The *whole* email?"

He shook his head. "That's impossible to know."

"Okay, of those who really did read the *whole* email—and there is quite a lot of text there—how many actually understood the content?"

"I don't know that either," said the man with a furrowed brow.

"Of those who read and understood the content—how many *believed* what they read?"

"I have no idea."

"Of this rapidly shrinking group who believed what they read—how many actually *remembered* what they had read?"

Somewhere here, the director started to scratch his nose, and who am I to blame him?

"Okay," I summarized, "there are rather a lot of 'don't knows' around a number of vital points about this vision which is meant to be important for the company's survival.

Don't misunderstand me," I said, "I think this is a really excellent vision. But if we eliminate everyone who didn't open the email, everyone who didn't manage to read it, everyone who didn't understand the contents, and everyone who didn't believe it; we can also eliminate everyone forgot what the email said. There's basically nobody left—are you really surprised that nobody seems to live your vision?"

The managing director's answer? "Hmm."

Sometimes you don't need to punish people more than necessary.

Most people don't send out information in order to deliberately confuse their team, but that's often what they succeed in doing.

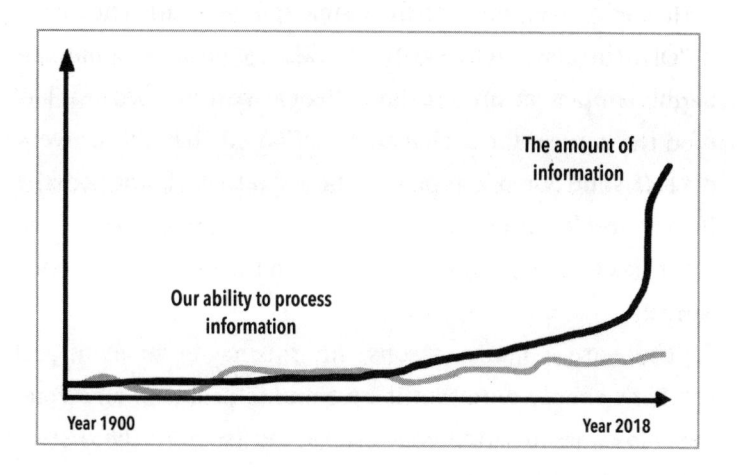

SPSS

Nowadays, there's so much information to take in that our poor brains threaten to boil over. Sometimes it feels like we've completely lost control. There are too many channels, too many digital tools, too much information to take in, and too many interesting feeds to follow. We basically sleep holding our cell phones. I'm just waiting for somebody to establish the abbreviation SPSS—*SmartPhone Stress Syndrome*. Perhaps it already exists.

Of course, you don't struggle with this, but many of us find it hard to tear our eyes away from our cell phone. It holds the whole world. According to the latest study I read (on the internet, where else?), we look at our smartphones every three minutes on average. On average.

Since there are presumably many people like myself who are nowhere near that average, there must be lots and lots of people who do it much more often. I see a lot of people who hardly ever let go of their smartphone at all. They carry it with them wherever they're walking because something might happen at any second. People search—with a look of utter panic—for a charging station so that the universe doesn't shut down completely. Perhaps they'll stop existing if they aren't online for a critical fifteen minutes? This neediness has exploded in our faces. I don't know how it's going to end.

There are so many reasons why this has become our reality. Let's simply note that it's a genuine problem, and you'll never be able to guide your staff away from all the distractions that technology has given us. I'm not saying that you should give up. It's not acceptable to be on Facebook during paid working hours, any more than it is to phone an old friend from your desk and waste an hour and then not have time to finish your work for the day. But we have a challenge here, and we know what it is. There's no point in refusing to see that reality.

Who Is the Information for, Anyway?

But, if you as the boss want to be heard over what has become the deafening roar of technological distraction, how can you go about that? To start with, think about who really needs to know what you're going to say.

A couple of common mistakes I frequently see in my work:

On the one hand, the boss sends information to everybody. They copy everyone to be on the safe side. Why? Sometimes just so they can say: *I did actually send this to you.* You did your job, the bases are covered. Now it's up to your staff to take in the information. On the other hand, you can load things up to the intranet, your internal digital library. And that must be good, right? There, you can sort various types of information into different areas of interest. It's easier for anyone who wants to find things. It's no longer like looking for the single email in a haystack. Or . . . how does this work?

You need to remember that many people *never* look at the intranet. The reason is simple: the intranet—which started as a simple tool with just a few headings like "Sales," "Marketing," "Production," and "Personnel"—has developed into a digital monster that nobody has any proper control of. Some organizations have let their intranet go completely wild. It now contains so much information that nobody actually knows what's there.

And guess what? Your staff has no idea what's there either. They won't be bothered to go looking. And different behavior types have different levels of patience with this. There is no point exclaiming that it's highly irresponsible to not use the intranet and having a stern discussion tomorrow. You need a plan.

How Do You Reach Each Color, Respectively?

Think in terms of how you can get the needed information to each specific individual. And think, above all, about how to express yourself. Bureaucratic declarations that are reminiscent of proclamations from the Soviet Union aren't going to work. It's possible that your really Blue staff members might struggle through such a mess and get the message. But the rest of the group? They're going to let that email molder in their inbox and claim that they haven't been told a thing. Remember the managing director earlier in this chapter?

What you need is a certain amount of imagination and a bit of time. And don't forget: if you've followed my earlier advice about how you to handle your time, there's going to be time for this. This is something you do when you're in the leader-box, not in the specialist-box.

The Information Pyramid

Imagine that you're writing a newspaper article. You structure it thoughtfully. Different profiles take in the various parts of the article in different ways. We can discuss for hours how each person has the responsibility to read and absorb what you—their *boss*—send out.

Yeah, sure. That's absolutely correct. But now keep reading!

RED
Brief facts — Get to the point

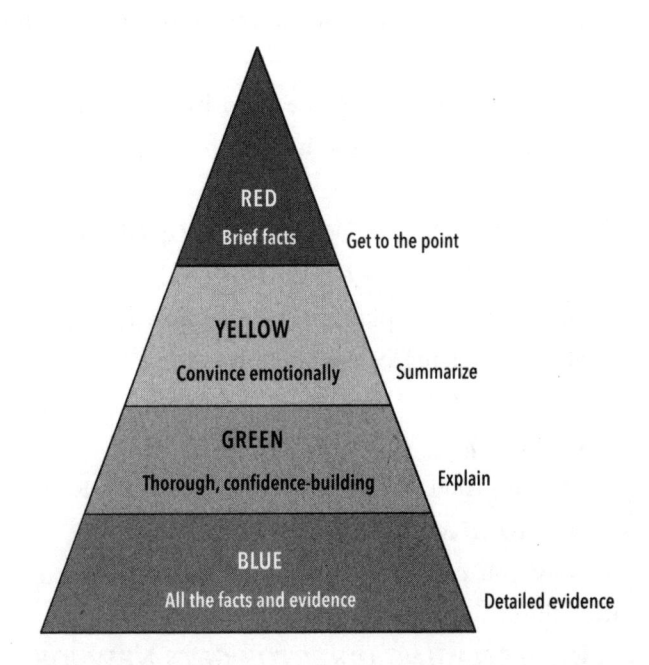

YELLOW
Convince emotionally — Summarize

GREEN
Thorough, confidence-building — Explain

BLUE
All the facts and evidence — Detailed evidence

The Heading

Your Red staff members think there's too much information and that it's far too long-winded. If they don't immediately grasp what the email, or the information sheet, is about, they'll put it aside. Not with the intention of reading it later—you can forget that idea right now! The Reds put it aside because it wasn't interesting. If it isn't interesting now, then it won't be interesting later either. Away with it!

You need to create a heading that tempts them to at least keep on reading. The heading *Decision regarding case 12:54* is painfully boring and will end up in the Trash before you can say *Taxation Authority*.

Sorry. Your Red staff members simply aren't going to read any further.

The heading needs to be hard-hitting; it needs to imply that this is important, and it needs to tempt the reader to keep on reading.

Try: *THE PROBLEM WITH THE OFFICE VENTILATION IS NOW SOLVED!*

Now you can explain in the text how the ventilation firm went about getting better air in the office.

Or: *DOES NO ONE WANT TO COME TO THE CHRISTMAS PARTY?*

Then it's time to urge your staff to actually RSVP right way

Or: *MORE MONEY FOR EVERYBODY!*

Now you can tell them about the latest union agreement after the long negotiations.

Or: *MANAGING DIRECTOR GETS NEW JOB!*

I promise you that even the Reds will want to know exactly which managing director this is about. And who the new one is.

The Introduction

Your Yellow staff members like informal and pleasant information. Naturally, not all news is good news—for example, it's hard to describe the impending layoffs in positive terms. But that doesn't alter the fact that the Yellows also have a rather narrow window of attention. Nor do they have much patience with long-winded, uninteresting manifestos that they don't think involve them.

Say that you succeeded with the heading. You got the attention of the Reds, and you probably got all the others on board too. Now you want to get both the Reds and the Yellows to delve deeper into your extremely well thought out and important document.

The introduction is now your best friend. Newspaper editors are good at this. A newspaper article is, of course, structured precisely in this way. A heading that will interest and perhaps shock the prospective reader. An introduction which gives a short summary of what the article itself contains.

Your Yellow staff members want to be *moved*. They want the text to reach them and persuade them to continue to read. To a certain extent, they want to be entertained and they want to *experience* something.

A good introduction summarizes the whole page in four concise but pithy lines. Look at an evening paper and you'll see what I mean. There's always a risk that the Yellows won't read on after the introduction, that they think they've already understood everything. And perhaps that might even be the case. Sometimes you might not even need to waste more ink on something that could be described in only four lines.

You don't need to contact the communication department every time there is a blockage in the gents' toilet on floor two. But avoid depressing bureaucratese. It doesn't work on the Yellows.

So now I need to be a copywriter too? I do actually have a job to do.

It's up to you. You're the boss. Your job is to reach your staff.

The Actual Article

If you've caught the attention of the Reds with your heading, I can promise you that you'll have reached all the others. If you got the Yellows to keep their eyes on the screen or paper with a pithy introduction, I guarantee that you also kept the Greens and the Blues in the loop.

There's a challenge here.

The Greens want to be convinced on a more basic level. Remember that they intensely dislike changes, especially quick ones. If they suspect that you're trying to get them to follow a new routine, or anything that doesn't sound familiar, they're going to be suspicious and will read with narrowed eyes. You don't want that to happen.

The key word here is *faith*.

If the Green staff have faith in you as the boss, they'll be more likely to take in the message or information. If they really trust you, you'll find it much easier to reach them.

The problem is that you can't build up that sort of faith on a piece of paper. If you want to be certain that you've reached the Greens, you need to have built up their trust in you over a long period. If you're new in your position, they'll certainly read what you write, but it will take a while to win that faith. If they do trust you as a sender of the message, it doesn't really matter whether what you say is correct or not. That isn't what this is about. You need to get them to *feel* that this is good.

On the other hand—if they do have faith in you, you can write almost anything at all. They'll take it in. That's why Green employees tend to listen more to each other than to what the management has to say. If one person in the group—perhaps a Green person—says that the new business system is no good, then it doesn't make any difference if a boss—who may, or may not, be trustworthy—claims the opposite.

The good news is that the Greens have the patience to read

through what you have to say. A lot more than the Reds and the Yellows.

But Where Is the Evidence . . . ?

Your Blue employee won't have any difficulty in progressing from the heading to the introduction and then on through the main text. His or her patience and concentration are nothing to worry about. They can fiddle around with the same Excel spreadsheet for weeks.

The challenge here is that the Blues have one question in their heads all the time: How do you know this? Is there any proof for what you claim in this email? Or is it just the usual nonsense from the management about visions and other nonsense stuff? Where is the concrete evidence?

The simplest thing you can do is to add some data at the end. It can be a graph of some kind. Figures are great. Details from a spreadsheet could be incredibly useful. The Blue person wants to know—is this correct?

Don't misunderstand me, they won't necessarily think that you're trying to con them. But they'll wonder whether you really know what's what.

Many bosses without Blue in their profile are almost scared by their Blue staff. They're the ones who always ask questions on a molecular level, and it can be hard to know what to answer.

I don't mean that you must quote a research report as a reference if you say that the folks working outside today should wear some winter boots. Most people are aware that it's colder in winter than in the summer. But if you can quote the national weather service when you say that the temperature will probably be below freezing this morning, then you've done a good job. It simply shows that you're diligent and that you take the task seriously. The fact that your really Blue staff member has already checked the weather forecast doesn't matter. You've been thorough and reliable and they appreciate that. The more exact data you provide, the more credible you will be in the eyes of the Blues.

Well, Then, How Do We Summarize This?

It's hard to reach everybody with new information. But you already knew that, and this is part of the explanation. If you've caught the attention of the Reds, used a powerful introduction that attracted the Yellows, created a main section that was so nice and thorough that you even won the Greens over to your side, and now you've also added some evidence for the Blues—then you really have made a good impression on most of your staff.

Well done!

And you can also use this method at the next group meeting. Do you usually show pictures? Fine. Make sure that the first pictures follow the flow that I've just described. And end with a nice summary that ties it all together. If possible—hand out some documentation to anyone who wants it (the Blues).

If you only present your material verbally, you can still structure it in the same way. Begin with something that catches everybody's attention.

It works. And your staff members are going to think you're a damned good and articulate boss.

Communication takes place on the terms of the listener. People hear what they want to hear. By adapting your message or information, you increase the likelihood that you'll reach them. By just doing what you have always done, you limit your chances of getting anyone to listen at all.

Now it's up to you.

{ 28 }

When Everyone Agrees but Still Doesn't Do Anything . . .

You know what it's like. In the meeting—where you've just announced the new direction or the new IT system or simply established the fact that the old workflow didn't work, and now we are going to change it—everyone agreed that it was a good idea. Now everybody has promised to give this new method a go. But as soon as you leave the meeting, the majority go off and keep right on doing things the same way.

Are they just lazy? The kind of people who refuse to do the job properly, and who—from pure indolence—stick to their old ways? Perhaps you can identify those who are too comfortable to be able to accept changes or to simply work a bit harder.

A good way to check whether what you've said is actually being absorbed is to ask for confirmation. If you know that a particular member of staff usually listens with their ears closed, can you ask him or her to say whether they've understood what you've laid out? Ask questions during the meeting. Ask the person concerned to summarize what you just said.

In many meetings, hardly anyone speaks besides the boss. This is partly a cultural issue, but it also depends on which type of staff members you have. If they are predominantly introverted—that is Green and Blue—they're going to be quieter than usual. It's only the young Yellow woman over on the left who talks during every meeting. But the others are tired of her, so she's also become quieter than usual.

If the people you have in front of you are predominantly extroverted—Red and Yellow—things become more lively. Then you may likely be interrupted. I don't think that matters so much as long as the interruptions are relevant and you have a plan of what you want to say—perhaps in the form of a simple outline on a piece of paper so that you can always find your way back to the central issue.

If your group is mainly Blue and Red, you can keep your message or information more strictly factual. If the opposite applies—your group is Green and Yellow—you need to consider the relationship issue. You'll have to soften some things and think about the tone of your voice. None of this is right or wrong, it's simply about a wise adaptation to the people in front of you. But don't forget that not all people listen the same way.

Is Anything Going to Happen At All?

Whatever you talked about probably contained an exhortation that somebody should do something. You want your group to start working according to a new routine, to make a change to something, shift their focus to a certain question. Even if you've asked your gang questions on an individual level during your presentation, the job isn't done yet. You'll have to follow up on certain things. Life is full of distractions.

The reason it's so difficult to implement changes within an organization is due to the same psychological causes that make it hard to improve your physique . . . i.e., to get fit. Abruptly starting on a diet or an exercise program is just as challenging as establishing a new vision or getting staff to embrace new ethics codes. This isn't necessarily about your staff being slow or lazy.

The problem is that it takes time to see any real result. If you start exercising, you might do so really intensively for one month. You might feel that you are doing something good for your health, but you won't really see how the muscles start to spread over your body. If you want a stomach bulging with muscles, go for it. But just remember that the late-night advertisement is wrong. It isn't enough to think intensively about your new stomach muscles and then devour a bar of chocolate. You must work hard to get anywhere. You must do at least one million sit-ups and strictly follow your diet for six months.

Since it takes a lot of time, the majority of aspiring fitness buffs give up. It takes too long to achieve the results and there's no point in trying. It's not even necessarily about laziness.

The same thing applies to changes you want to introduce in your organization. Especially in the case of major changes, such as company vision and ethical policy, or implementing a new mission statement, the visible results will be a long time coming. And if you ask your staff if they've noticed any changes in leadership—after all the bosses took that expensive leadership course—the answers will often be somewhat hesitant.

They don't know. They haven't thought about it. They don't see any real changes. In the worst case, you yourself won't have incorporated what you learned on the course. So how are they going to be able to see any difference?

The 3-Step Model

I have a favorite method for implementing any kind of change. I call it the 3-step model.

What does that mean?

1. Follow up
2. Follow up
3. Follow up

The path to hell is paved with good intentions. How many times have you thought, *I'm going to follow up on this so that I know it gets done? This is so important that it can't get lost in the shuffle. I'm going to take my responsibility as boss seriously and always get back to my staff and help them in their development.*

Good. Then you know that follow-up is important.

Sometimes it's absolutely critical. Rarely is it sufficient to say something only once. Sometimes once just doesn't count. Sometimes everyone agrees at the meeting. Let's do it!

Good. Fine. We'll get going.

But then unfortunately, something else comes up.

Quite often you found some new task on your desk and suddenly the focus was somewhere else. But if you devoted so much time to area X last fall, why not make sure that something really happens? That people follow the new guidelines or whatever it was?

When the boss drops the ball, it's often about her or his ability to balance between being a leader and being a specialist. It's often an activity that requires leadership, and what halts the process is related to the specialist side of the managerial role.

Time for a confession. The 3-step model isn't what I wrote above. The correct description of the 3 steps is:

1. Follow up
2. Assess
3. Persevere

Follow Up

To follow up with your staff isn't really that difficult. You just have to keep track—are they doing what we agreed they should do? As usual, this looks a little different depending on color.

The **Reds**—you need to go to them directly. Either the job has already been done, or it ended up on the backburner. It depends on whether the Red thought it was important, or not. If it wasn't important, it was set aside. There's a risk that your Red member of staff will never return to the question. You need to check in and make sure they actually deal with it.

Your **Yellow** staff member has already managed to tell everyone what a fascinating task they've been given. It's going to be really interesting and the future looks bright. However, sometimes the Yellow has started off with tons of enthusiasm but come across a little problem. It derailed the project, and it's not going to get anywhere until inspiration returns. Help the person concerned get back onto the right track, otherwise something new is going to take all their focus.

Your **Green** staff member hasn't necessarily started on the task. Perhaps it simply didn't feel like the right sort of day to start. Help the Green onto the track so they can get started. It might also be the case that the Green hasn't entirely accepted what you've told them. That, however, is a minor problem. Loyal as they are, the Greens will try to get the job done.

Your **Blue** staff members . . . yes, well. It's fairly likely that they've already started planning to do the task. They've noted it in their calendar—the first step, however, is not to do what you asked them to do. The first thing they do is to plan to start. The Blues won't forget what needs to be done, but they may need your help to actually start digging. Help them get started, listen to the arguments about why you should think it all through again; then make sure that they get going with what you asked them to do.

Assess

You need to keep track of how the task is going. Even though the idea of assessing somebody's work makes you feel a little uneasy, this is nevertheless something you need to do. I don't mean that you should give your staff member a grade. What I am saying is: check that they do what you asked them to do, in the way you wanted, and at the speed you wanted. Or are they suddenly busy with something completely different?

Sometimes that happens, and your job is then to rearrange this and that back to the scenario you agreed on. If somebody has some good ideas and sensible suggestions in the midst of all this, you of course listen, but sometimes it's simply about making sure the job gets done as it was intended.

Then you need to give feedback, and I will return to that under the heading Feedback. Sometimes everything works exactly as intended; other times you have to go in and adjust things. Do it. Take responsibility. Don't just "hope" that everything will sort itself out.

But the most important thing to remember is the next heading:

Persevere

Have you got what it takes? To go back time after time after time after time . . .

Here, your own color can be key in determining how many times you manage to follow up with staff member Y. There are lots of reasons why things sometimes don't turn out as you intended. You usually knew what you were doing when you delegated a particular task. And if you said in August that the task was important, it's likely still important in October.

I explained the situation at the monthly meeting. They said they understood; my job is done.

No, actually, it isn't. Your job is to be able to give all the support and the instructions necessary so that your staff members do whatever it was you talked about. If they have lots of experience, this is a minor problem, but if this involves some new tasks for them, you can't simply assume that it will suffice to just ask them a single time, or even ten times. Sometimes you need to follow up umpteen times before everything clicks.

The Red Boss

If you're Red, you might find this irritating. *What don't they understand? Nobody spoke up against this.*

My tip for you is to drop that attitude and finish the job. Get back to them as often as necessary until you begin to see results you want to see. Remind the employee in question that you'd agreed on this. Offer to explain it again when you say this. This will help you all reach the goal much faster.

The Yellow Boss

If you're a predominantly Yellow boss, then follow-up quite likely bores you; having to go back is like looking at history, and who likes that? But think about it. Just looking forward doesn't work. The rear-view mirror is there for a reason. Sometimes you need to look at that too.

The job will be so much more fun if you actually get what you want. And you'll win enormous respect from your staff if you show that you care about them so much that you persist in following up once a week for four months in order to get the job done. Mark the times in your calendar now. Make sure that your digital calendar regularly reminds you with an alarm function.

And don't just turn the alarm off when it comes on. You can't allow other things to take priority: don't book any meetings in the same time slot unless you move the follow-up to another time the same day. Go to your staff member and follow up no matter what.

The Green Boss

If your own profile is predominantly Green, you have a challenge here, and you know what it is. To need to follow up with another person can be considered criticism. And who are you to criticize another person? I must at this point, and in all humility, remind you that it is your job. By all means do it in your usual, friendly manner, but make sure it happens. You're the boss.

One way to reduce any friction between you and your staff is to warn them in advance that you're actually going to follow up—with the intention of giving them the support they need to fulfill their task. Explain that you're following up for their sake. But resist the instinct to "forget" the follow-up. That only results in lots of headaches. If you're not accustomed to following up with your staff, then you'll have a natural resistance to doing it. You need to build a new routine that feels sensible. Mark the times in your calendar for each week's follow-ups. Your staff will soon come to understand that you really do care about them, and they will feel confidence in you as their boss.

The Blue Boss

Let's say that you're Blue. In that case I've just wasted lots of time. Going back to a task never scared you before, so why would it this time? Following up on things and having a regular routine for the process isn't a problem for you. You understood exactly what I wrote to the Green boss above. You probably have the greatest perseverance of all the colors. You can repeat the same thing over and over again, as long as you see the purpose.

So what is the point?

What you need to remind yourself is that your staff members aren't robots. They're human beings of flesh and blood, and they think, feel, and experience things. They don't function like logical machines. Things happen en route. Just because you have said one thing on one occasion doesn't mean that it's going to be exactly how you said. You need to come back and check that all is going well. Assessment isn't a problem either, although it might be a problem to talk regularly with your staff. They need you. And you want to follow up with them as well because when you do the quality of what they deliver will be much higher.

What do you think? How good are you at following up with your staff? Do you know, or do you have certain gaps in your awareness? The simplest way you can do it is to just walk past the person's desk a couple of times a week and ask how things are going.

Good luck with the 3-step model.

{ 29 }

Where the Real Slackers Come From

However well you carry out your managerial role, sometimes situations can arise that are outside your control. My tip is that you don't blame yourself too much when it happens. Remember that no system is perfect. Accept that however well you do your job, you can't control everything. The unexpected can always happen.

Imagine a farmer who does everything exactly how it should be done. He spreads fertilizer on his fields, he sows, he regularly checks for weeds. He gets up at the crack of dawn and doesn't go to bed until a few hours before it's time to get up again (in Sweden the summer days are very long). He tries to prevent damage from birds, insects, and vermin of all sorts. He sees his crops grow, and he starts to plan the harvest.

Then along comes a hailstorm and destroys everything.

Why?

Because that's how our planet is. Sometimes things go totally wrong.

When your staff are affected by something similar, they'll

lose their balance. They might try to focus, but they'll be affected by the situation. When this happens, you need to know how you can deal with them.

If you've been a boss for a while, you already know this: leading people is a complicated task. It might look simple on paper, but in real life it's not a cakewalk.

If you're seriously considering applying for a managerial position, then you might already suspect that there may be more challenges than you thought.

If you're an employee without any managerial or personnel responsibility, and you've had good reason to doubt the intellectual faculties of your boss, I hope that you'll now begin to realize why things sometimes don't look like you want them to look. There are simply too many things that can go totally wrong.

Let's be honest. There are reasons why many people want a managerial position anyway. The status it gives you (despite everything); the freedom you imagine it will give you; the power, of course; and the salary, to mention just a few examples. But anyone who applies for their first managerial position ought to seriously think about whether they really understand what it is they're taking on.

I'm not trying to scare you off. Leadership is difficult, but I welcome all who keenly aspire to the job to go for it. It's an overwhelming experience, and it doesn't have to go as badly for you as it did for me more than twenty-five years ago.

Those of you who recruit managers: pay less attention to formal education and exams, and more to whether this person really has what it takes to lead others. Since there's no formal educational course to become a boss, it's important to ask the right questions. It's easy to be fooled by a fancy-looking résumé.

But I've Understood This Stuff with the Colors, So I'm Set Now Right?

I wish it were that simple. But the colors, the behavior profiles, are just one of several dimensions. It's also important to understand driving forces. Experience, motivation, general background, culture, and a whole slew of other factors also play a role. There are loads of things to take into consideration if you are going to call yourself an efficient boss.

And, naturally, the development levels.

Don't Rake Up Even More Things to Mess Up My Job

The development levels are what determine how ready somebody is to take on a certain task. You'll have noticed that sometimes your staff solves a problem in five minutes, while on other occasions it can take five hours for them to do something that really shouldn't be very complicated. Sometimes they sit and stare at the screen with a task they know perfectly well how to handle—but they can't seem to get started

I described this in the first part of the book.

Do you remember the story from the first part of the book about my old friend George who drove into a ditch with his far-too-big SUV? The reason he got stuck in the first place was that he misjudged the task and that his own competence was not as strong as his commitment. So he ended up stuck

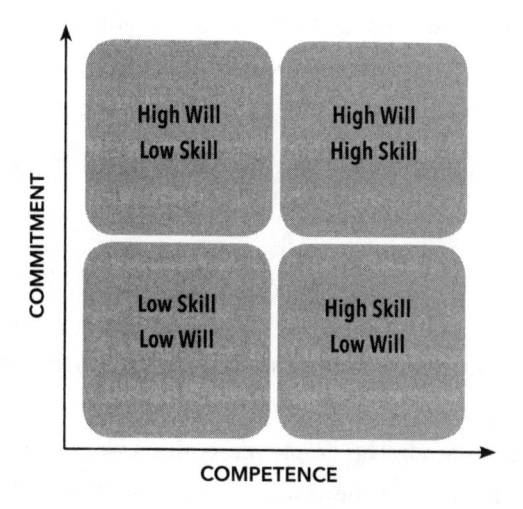

```
                    ↑
        ┌─────────────┬─────────────┐
        │  High Will  │  High Will  │
        │  Low Skill  │  High Skill │
COMMITMENT
        │  Low Skill  │  High Skill │
        │  Low Will   │  Low Will   │
        └─────────────┴─────────────┘
                                    →
              COMPETENCE
```

in a ditch. The only way he got out of that ditch was because a farmer happened to come along and could tow him out. He got help.

What's This Got to Do with Leadership?

Everything! Your task is not to do the work of your staff. Your job is to make sure that your employees know how they should carry out their work. *That* is your job. Your staff are your most important asset.

Not your own boss, not your customers.

Your staff.

Hang on there, smarty-pants, the customers are the most important. Without them we wouldn't earn any money.

Perfectly correct. For your staff, yes. They should serve the customers. But you should make sure that your staff have the best possible conditions to do just that. If you don't, then you're a completely superfluous boss. If you don't handle your staff, you're simply not needed. If they're forced to rely on one another while you devote your time to handling customers, you're simply an overpaid customer service assistant/salesman/whatever. Not a leader.

1. What Is the Task?

What have you actually asked this person to do? Do you remember the example with Jonas and Kenneth on page 222? Neither the boss nor the employee really knew what it was that Kenneth ought to be doing every day. This led to the whole thing capsizing and everybody feeling bad. It doesn't have to end up like that for you. But do make sure that you and your staff are agreed on what you need them to do.

You should be quite specific. I definitely recommend crystal clarity rather than vagueness. If you're crystal clear, your member of staff can always say: *Got it! I understand*. If you're incomprehensible and rambling, your staff member might not even know what needs to be clarified.

Don't say: *Can you check this contract?*

This might be crystal clear in your head. There's a risk, however, that your head is the only place where it's clear. It's possible not even you really know what you're asking.

Check the contract? Can it get any vaguer than that?

Try saying: *I want you to call the customer and ask them to read the contract thoroughly. I need to have it signed on my desk before 5 p.m. today. Okay?*

This is considerably better. It explains exactly what you

need from them. You tell them what is involved and you ask for their approval by ending with *Okay?*

As you can guess, these two alternatives will lead to totally different outcomes. Different staff members in different phases will interpret Option 1 totally differently. Option 2, however, gives much less room for interpretation.

Before you think: *I want to give my staff the freedom to think for themselves*, I will point out that you must make sure you're in agreement about what they're going to think independently about. If you need the contract signed by five o'clock today, at the latest, that can't be changed just because your staff wants to retain their independence.

In summary: make sure you know what needs to be done.

2. Assess the Competence of Your Staff Member in the Face of the Specific Task.

Okay. You know what needs to be done, and you have no problem communicating that. You plan to delegate the task to a particular member of staff, Karin. What you now need to ask yourself is whether Karin knows how to do the job. If it's a simple task, the answer is probably just as simple. If it's a more complex task that involves different parts, perhaps the answer is not quite so simple.

Some clues might be to consider if Karin has managed to do this type of task before. If the answer is *yes, she does it every week*, then that's clear. Or is it? If she does the job regularly, does she do it the best way? If only you realized how many people struggle along in their everyday work doing things they've barely mastered! So the question is, in fact, relevant: *does she do it the best way possible?*

If the answer is still *yes*, then it's a straightforward decision to delegate. If the answer is *no, she often ends up having difficulties*, well, then *you* have a job to do. You need to find out what's missing. Perhaps she simply doesn't know the right way to do the task.

A tip on how to discover what Karin knows about this particular task: ask Karin!!

Before you do that, you need to think about how she's going to answer. This is connected to a whole lot of things: her motivation, her self-confidence, her DISC color, and even her driving forces. Also, the depressing fact that extremely few people will actively admit to limitations in their competence around things they ought to have fully understood five years ago. I would squirm around for quite a while before I admitted that I haven't had a clue what I've been doing at work the last few years.

The best way to assess Karin's ability is to look at what she actually delivers. You can simply examine the quality of her work.

Yes, you *can* do that, you're her boss. Do it in a polite and correct manner, but do it. You can't avoid this by telling yourself that Karin wouldn't like it, or would be angry if you double checked her work. You're her boss and your task includes that sort of check.

Think about it: if you don't know how well she does the job, and Karin doesn't know either—who else is going to?

People talk too much, and some people are very arrogant. But only *exhibited* competence counts. Imagine that you ask Karin if she can ride a bike. *Of course I can*, she answers. In my view, you need to ask her to ride round the yard so you can see how well she can handle a bike. If she replies: *nope, just not feeling it today*, well, then you have cause to wonder just how good her skills are.

3. Try to Assess Your Staff Member's Commitment to the Task.

This can be hard to measure. The simplest way is to divide commitment into two parts: motivation and self-confidence.

Motivation

Does Karin want to take on this task?

Does Karin seem enthusiastic, does she have the energy, is there a glow in her eye when you ask her to take care of area Z? She doesn't have to jump for joy, but it's a good sign if you get some kind of reaction when you delegate the job. If you're met with a smile and the comment: *It'll be fun to sort that out!*, then you are on to a winner!

If, however, you meet with a deep sigh and some doomsday-like comment about how she's *going to die at [her] desk buried under work anyway so, sure, why not add a little bit more?* Well, then you need to pull up a chair and sit down with Karin for a while.

I realize that it's rarely as clear-cut as that, but you need to look for these signals. Think about how each color would express themselves.

Note: don't confuse a generally positive attitude with motivation for this particular task. For example, Yellow staff members can sound positive about almost anything, even if they're not motivated. Being an optimist is not the same as loving the idea of cleaning out the cellar storeroom on a Saturday.

Self-Confidence

This one is a bit trickier. Does Karin trust her own ability? There's a lot of self-confidence in two of the phases (see Chapter 16 about development levels), the first and the fourth. In the first, the strong self-confidence is because the person doesn't have proper insight into the task. It feels good, because they don't know what they're taking on. In Part One of this book, I called that phase *unconsciously incompetent*.

In the fourth phase, self-confidence is based on the awareness that she really can master the task, regardless of how complex it is. She's seen herself succeed several times and dares to trust her own ability. She is *consciously competent*.

In the second phase, Karin is *consciously incompetent*, and it's wounded her self-confidence. She's already driven into the ditch—if you can put up with that metaphor yet again—and is now painfully aware that she can't do it all. Her confidence in her own ability is simply low. Sometimes it's nonexistent. She has given up.

Phases one, two, and four are actually fairly simple to identify. By asking a few control questions, you can quickly find out where Karin is between these development levels.

But the third phase is trickier. Here Karin is *unconsciously competent*, that is: she actually knows the job well, but she

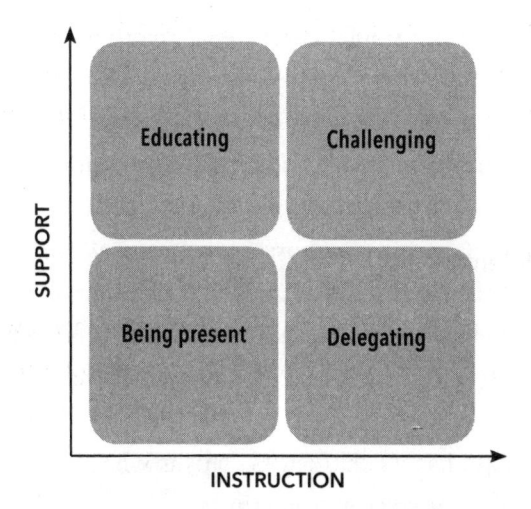

```
         ↑
    ┌─────────┬──────────┐
    │Educating│Challenging│
SUPPORT─────┼──────────┤
    │Being    │Delegating│
    │present  │          │
    └─────────┴──────────┘→
           INSTRUCTION
```

hasn't realized it herself. She hesitates despite the fact that you, her boss, perhaps think she ought to put on her running shoes and leave the starting line. But Karin hasn't realized this herself. She has no success to lean against, so she feels uncertain.

What's the conclusion?

You need to evaluate Karin's self-confidence. This isn't about competence. Nor is it about whether she has the energy to carry out the task or wants to do so. What you're looking for is whether she has the confidence that she *believes* she can do it.

You have only got to look at yourself. Or myself. There are lots of things I would like to do but that I would never attempt. And the same applies to Karin. The challenge in the third phase is that it can vary rather a lot. It's often a person's mood on a particular day that governs self-confidence. Good days mean it can be quite good; other days it can be back at rock bottom again. She isn't in the fourth phase until all three factors are stable: competence, motivation, and self-confidence.

This is a natural process . . . so why are you needed in that case?

Sometimes I come across bosses who make all sorts of comments about this, and some of them make a point of how their staff needs to manage themselves since the boss is crazy busy. But then they miss the whole point, or they've consciously chosen to ignore it.

Every phase has its challenges. This is what I want you to do every time you delegate something:

1. Describe the task clearly and distinctly
2. Assess your staff member's development phase
3. Decide upon your staff member's need of leadership
4. Give the person what is necessary

Simple, isn't it?

As some wise person has said: *In theory there is no difference between theory and practice. But in practice there is.*

On the top of the next page is a checklist of what you need to bear in mind:

As usual, you can do exactly what you want. But you ought to be able to translate this to fit your particular situation.

One way of becoming good at analyzing your employees is to test yourself. If you can do that without embellishing the truth, then you can probably manage your staff member's needs.

I do this with myself when I'm going to take on a new task. Now I'm talking about bigger things than day to day work; in

PHASES	WHAT THEY DO	WHAT THEY NEED	WHAT YOU OUGHT TO GIVE THEM
1st Phase	Can do it themselves, optimistic, keen – attempt everything, curious, ignorant, want to know, ask, often make mistakes, poor results	Praise for enthusiasm, clear goals, instruction on what, when, how, clear action plans, a lot of facts, time-frames, close follow-up, feedback often, limitation of responsibilities	Praise their enthusiasm, set goals, talk about desired results, give clear instructions on when, what, how and with whom, most decisions already made, decide what, when and together with whom
2nd Phase	Are stressed/tense, unmotivated, frustrated, disappointed, don't listen, questioning, complain a lot, slow pace, no results	Praise for attempting, clear goals, explanation why, total picture. OK to make mistakes, somebody who believes in them, somebody who listens, close follow-up, feedback often, repeated pep-talks	Praise the attempt, let staff-member discuss their problems, explain why, give big picture, make staff-member involved in problem-solving, make the final decision after listening to staff-member, encourage continually–give feedback
3rd Phase	Self-critical, cautious, hesitant, ask even when they know the answer, has the competence but won't act, uncertain, variable mood, rollercoaster ride, variable result. Making progress	Praise for competence, possibility to talk about their worry, support and encouragement to solve own problems, access to mentor, help to remove obstacles, own success, greater freedom, a pat on the back	Praise their competence, remove obstacles, ask staff-member to take initiative for plan of action and problem-solving, be a sounding board and encourage discussion, share responsibility with staff-member to identify problems and set goals, point out earlier successes and knowledge to build up self confidence
4th Phase	Independent, full of confidence, thoroughly competent, inspires others, self-disciplined, fast pace, good results, ideas	Praise for results, to be seen, independence, own responsibility, a leader who behaves more as a sounding board than a boss, variation, challenges, feeling of growing and developing	Praise the result, define problems and desired result together with staff-member, let staff-member act as mentor for others in the organization, urge staff-member to do even better, allow staff-member to take over

those situations I most often feel I'm in the fourth phase. But I want to be honest and not be too conceited.

My claim that I'm in the fourth phase for all tasks could be due to three things:

I'm also good at self-deception
My personal insight is negligible
It's been a long time since I tried anything new

Thomas, Lecturer—An Example

I give a lot of lectures. An awful lot. When you hold this book in your hand I will probably be on my way to a lecture, in the midst of giving a lecture, or on my way home from one. The audience may vary, but we'll take this from the beginning and follow Hersey and Blanchard's idea:

Step 1: Define the Task

To lecture to an unknown audience on the theme of effective communication.

Step 2: Assess Own Competence for the Specific Task

After having worked with the subject for more than twenty years, I consider myself to be very good at it. I know the topic very well. I know how to present the information, I can create material in PowerPoint, and I'm a good entertainer. My competence is *high*.

Step 3: Assess Commitment for the Specific Task

Being a bit of a theater geek, I like standing on a stage and talking to people who really want to listen to what I have to say. My motivation is thus very high. Since I've talked about the very subject of communication based on the DISC tool at least several thousand times, my self-confidence is high. My commitment can thus be summarized as *high*.

What's the Analysis?

That I am in the fourth phase in regard to giving a lecture on effective communication. My coach only needs to ensure that I get new stimulation and new challenges. And give me the room to maneuver that I need.

Okay, I'm a competent and skilled lecturer. I can talk about anything whatsoever from a stage. Book me every time!

But hang on a moment. Is that really true?

Imagine this: if the organizer of the lecture comes up on to the stage two minutes before I start and whispers in my ear that I shouldn't worry too much about the grumpy crowd—*they really do hate going to lectures and they think that all this communication stuff is nonsense*—it would undoubtedly affect my self-confidence.

I still want to be there, and I've still mastered the subject, but what if they hate what I say and start booing? I've experienced that too, and it's no fun at all. So for this lecture I find myself in the third phase. High competence but uncertain commitment. The situation has changed. Nevertheless, I still know exactly what I'm going to do.

What if somebody asks me if I can give a lecture about something I'm not familiar with? Perhaps they want me to talk about children with psychiatric diagnoses? Then I would find myself in the second phase, since I'm neither capable of talking about psychiatric diagnoses—because I know nothing about it—nor do I want to talk about it.

Low commitment because of low motivation and low self-confidence—I know that there must be ten thousand people in this country who know the subject better than I do. And my *low competence* wouldn't even get me through the first fifteen minutes. The experienced lecturer's façade has crumbled to nothing. This isn't just about me, but about me in relation to a particular task.

The Situation Is the Deciding Factor Every Time

This is what makes everyday leadership a little trickier than you might have thought. In my case, I'm not a sharp lecturer in general, but I am on specific subjects that I know and want to talk about. But you couldn't claim that I'm always a skilled lecturer. It simply depends quite on the situation.

Different people should be treated differently. Remember everything I have written about DISC colors and driving forces.

But even the *same* people should be treated *differently*. Even though colors and driving forces are constant, development levels change all the time.

So what should we conclude from all this?

That there isn't just one way to lead people. It depends on lots of factors. Anyone who claims that this is what you do when you lead people is often wrong for that very reason.

This is what Hersey and Blanchard found in their studies. And I think we can calmly assume that it's an appropriate model for most of us. Now, the only thing you need to do is to start seeing your staff in light of the four development levels. You're going to work miracles in the group with your newfound insights.

{ 30 }

Feedback...
the Hardest Part...

Feedback is a tricky area in general. It's rarely simple and many bosses avoid the area since they don't know how you go about it. That is, of course, not the right solution. The right solution is to find out how it works and get out in the world and practice what you've learned

Elizabeth Kuylenstierna, in her excellent book *Success with Feedback,* writes that we get about 90 percent or more of the total amount of feedback we will receive in our life during our first six years. And it's good that we acknowledge our children. But later on, then what? Should the remaining 10 percent be spread over the last eighty or so years?

Let's be honest: we're utterly useless when it comes to acknowledging each other in a good way. And not only that: we're also hopeless at receiving feedback. Proper feedback that really takes hold and creates change requires a very specific sort of communication. You can't express yourself vaguely, and you need to have decided what you want to convey.

The Two Challenges with Feedback

To solve a problem, you first need to be aware of what the problem is. So I've divided the question of effective feedback into two main challenges:

1. Nobody wants to give feedback
2. Nobody wants to receive it

Far too few people are genuinely interested in giving good feedback, and hardly anyone at all wants to hear it. If we can solve these two minor details, you'll probably manage very well in your role as leader.

Good feedback is also about communication. And, as usual, the problem with communication is that you think that it's taken place. Sometimes a little nod and a positive grunt from you are sufficient to indicate that you liked what your staff member has done. But often you'll have to make more of an effort than that.

Since feedback can also be positive or negative, a raised eyebrow at the wrong moment can be interpreted as being totally negative. It depends on who raised their eyebrow, but also on who saw it.

Some Things to Keep in Mind as a Boss

RED BOSSES tend to fail to give feedback since they don't understand the point of lots of sweet-talking. *People do actually get paid to do their job. So don't come to me looking for praise.* If they do give any real feedback, it's often negative.

Something has gone seriously wrong and now we need to find who is to blame.

YELLOW BOSSES often fail to give functional feedback because they're rather self-centered. They often forget that other people want some praise too, for example. Often, when they do actually give feedback it's positive, but so longwinded and exaggerated that the receiver finds it embarrassing. Negative feedback is completely avoided if possible. It's difficult to handle, and perhaps the problem will disappear on its own anyway.

GREEN BOSSES avoid giving negative feedback since it might lead to conflict. Perhaps somebody will get angry, or even very upset, which is of course just as bad. Positive feedback can be given face-to-face, which is fairly risk-free.

BLUE BOSSES are clever at giving negative feedback. They make a note of all the errors that arise, and in their striving for heavenly perfection they conscientiously point out every single mistake their staff member makes. They aren't so good at giving positive feedback. What applies here is: *no* news is *good* news.

The problem is that many bosses base their feedback strategy on their own attitude. Some of them, in all seriousness, claim that they don't need any praise. They already know what they're good at, and don't even want to be acknowledged.

I must express myself extremely clearly here: *that's just nonsense.* It's an immature macho-thing that has no credibility whatsoever. Everybody enjoys being praised, but it must be the right sort of praise at the right time, and the praise must also be about something that the recipient actually cares about.

If we start from the four development levels, you can see

to which areas you should direct your praise and feedback. Below is a sort of key for how to go about it. But remember: this is *what* you need to keep track of. But *how* you do it, that is connected to the DISC colors. Okay?

The First Phase—High Will, Low Skill

What are we praising here? In this stage they want to be acknowledged for their enthusiasm. They want to hear that they're full of energy and that it's great to see that they give 100 percent all the time. That is a very different thing than hearing that you're fantastically good at your job.

You should *not* say to a happy beginner that they're good at their job. Reason: it isn't true. What qualities mark the first phase? High commitment and *low* competence. It's simply wrong to say that somebody with low competence for a task is great at their job. It would be a lie, and you should avoid lies.

And, besides, you need to add energy in this phase. What you, as boss, want to do here is to steer the energy in the right direction. You do that by giving instructions, not by further inflating the person's ego.

It's great to see that you're eager to get started. Now, this is what you should do . . .

The Second Phase—Low Will, Low Skill

How do you praise the person who has ended up in a minefield of problems? Here they need to be acknowledged for the *attempt*. It's a challenge to even manage to work at all when everything goes totally wrong. They want praise for not having given up. This person has low competence but also low commitment. The little they get done, goes wrong.

Giving pep talks and cheering them along with *you can do it!* is condescending and does more damage than good. The roof is falling in on the poor guy. Instead, acknowledge the feelings of difficulty and give positive feedback so that they *don't* give up. Sometimes you might need to say this every single day for several months.

I know it's tough going, but I'm going to help you along.

The Third Phase—Low Will, High Skill

These are the people who need to hear that they can do it. They need praise for their competence. They have quite a high competence but often weak self-confidence. Now is the right time to say: *You can do it! I believe in you!*

Your employee doesn't believe in themselves. He or she has no *success stories* to fall back upon. They haven't seen themselves succeed. They need this pep talk.

I know that you feel uncertain, but you've got what it takes. You've done it before.

The Fourth Phase—High Will, High Skill

It is easy to get the impression that your independent staff members don't need anything at all. But that's not the case. It's entirely wrong to praise them for their enthusiasm. To acknowledge them because they work hard is almost insulting. To claim that they're clever isn't quite right either—they already know that.

They have high competence and high commitment. They need to be acknowledged for the results they achieve. If you say to a staff member who has done a top job for a long time that you think she's clever, she'll simply give you a weird look. It's almost ridiculous. The only thing she is going to think is: *I know that.*

The result is what you emphasize.

I'm really pleased with what you contribute to our work.

The Discordant Bank Manager

Different development phases need a different focus on the praise you emphasize. Many bosses don't succeed particularly well with their praise, and sometimes I think it's because they give the wrong praise at the wrong time. But there are also bosses who take their staff for granted. Or they're so absorbed in their job that the idea doesn't even occur to them. You need a plan for this. But make sure it's a good plan, one that works.

Many years ago I worked, as I've mentioned several times, at a bank. It was in the days when we still had branch offices. We worked away out on the floor and Ulf, the manager, would frequently look out from his office at the end of the hall. He'd come up to Customer Service and say that he was satisfied with the week's work. We naturally lapped up the praise.

That was repeated now and then. He came out and praised us, said that we all did a good job. Great. But after a while somebody in the group started to wonder what exactly he was so satisfied with. So next time he came to the group somebody asked him: *It's great that you're pleased, Ulf, but is there anything in particular you would like to emphasize so we can do more of it?*

Ulf said that he thought that we looked *strong. Keep at it!* Then he went off.

He had no idea what we'd actually done that week. Besides, we'd begun to notice a certain pattern. Somebody realized that he usually came at about the same time every week. Friday after three o'clock.

One afternoon when he wasn't in the office, we snuck in to his office and had a peep at his calendar. In those days it was an analog arrangement. What we found when we looked back over a few weeks was a dreadful eye-opener.

At three o'clock every Friday he'd written: *Praise the staff.*

It was a depressing insight. He was obliged to write it down to even remember to acknowledge us. The next time he came out to cheer us on before the weekend, nobody could even be bothered to turn around and thank him. We had completely lost faith in him and his intentions.

Don't be like Ulf. Notice what your staff are good at, so that you can give them praise that is meaningful.

But What About Bad News?

I've lost track of how many times I've had the following conversation with some boss or other whom I've been coaching in leadership. We've presumably talked about how you follow up with staff, and we've certainly talked about feedback. It often goes something like this:

> **Me:** *I had a short meeting with Martin this morning. He behaved in his usual manner. Weren't you going to address that bad behavior with him last week?*

The boss: *Yes, I was, but you know how it is.*
Me: *I'm not sure I do. How is it?*
The boss: *I'm waiting for the right moment.*
Me: *The right moment? When is that?*
The boss: (quite often with expressive body language) *Exactly!*

At around this point I'm expected to agree on how difficult it is to find the right moment to inform poor Martin that his behavior has caused half the staff to hand in their notice.

But I don't buy that. The *right* moment to give negative feedback *never* comes along.

Think about yourself. There's somebody in your immediate proximity—it could be your boss, but it could just as well be your husband or wife—who has some views on your behavior. Can you tell me when the right moment would be for you to receive a bit of negative feedback?

When you've finished eating? When you're just about to eat? In the morning, so that the whole day is ruined? Perhaps in the evening, so that your night's sleep is guaranteed to be wrecked. At the beginning of the week or at the end? Should the sun be shining, or is it okay to hear some hard truths even when it's raining outside?

And think what it would be like if you've already had some negative criticism from somebody else that day. Do you want some more straightaway, or do you want to spread the bad news more evenly over the week? Perhaps with a cup of freshly brewed coffee, a warm afternoon when you've just broken a new sales record—is that a good moment to hear that you're a total idiot?

However you look at this, there simply isn't a perfect moment.

Accept that and pencil in that unpleasant conversation. If you can't make yourself do it, it's probably because you feel uncertain or you don't know how it is going to be received; perhaps you don't want to hurt this person or it could be that you don't even know what you want to say.

You have a heart. I respect you for that.

Bacon in His Beard

Imagine this: you're sitting at a morning meeting and one of the participants has a tiny bit of his breakfast left in his beard. You can't see exactly what it is, but it looks particularly unappealing. What do you do?

Answer: *nothing*.

You don't want to embarrass him in front of everyone else. Everybody, of course, sees the bits of food, but they think the same as you. You suffer through the entire meeting and every time the guy opens his mouth you try to look at him without thinking that he has some bits of bacon on his face. It doesn't work.

At four o'clock in the afternoon, you meet the same guy in the corridor. He still has those little bits of bacon in his beard. It looks even worse than in the morning, and you can't help thinking: *Has he gone around with that all day long? Why hasn't anybody said anything?*

So what do you do now?

Answer: *nothing*. You still don't want to embarrass him. Apart from the obvious: if you tell him now, he'll realize that the bacon is from his breakfast, and then he will know that you must have seen it at the morning meeting. You're trapped by your own passivity.

Swap the man for a woman, and the bacon for a leaf in her hair. You see the problem.

What would you prefer personally? To go around with food on your face all day long, or that somebody discreetly says *I think you have something there . . . ?*

Feedback Is Not Dangerous

Everyone who makes mistakes needs to hear about them, which is to say they must simply accept some negative feedback. Nobody is without fault. Every single little misstep by a particular staff member is not necessarily worth commenting on, but if you have an opinion on something, then you actually ought to address it with the person concerned.

People making mistakes at work is not the end of the world. It simply shows that they still have something to learn. And if it reflects shortcomings in their competence, then you have a clear mission: make sure that they learn better how the job should be carried out. On the one hand, that's the simple solution.

It is, however, harder to adjust crazy behavior that's connected to a lack of commitment, or things that go wrong on account of somebody's personal qualities. The longer an individual has worked in the same position, the less likely it is that competence is the issue. The same with bosses: the higher up they are, the rarer it is that competence is the problem. It's usually about behavior. As I mentioned earlier, it's your job as the boss to adjust what they do if they don't follow the rule book or if they're careless or forget details.

So you must give negative feedback—or criticism—in your role as leader.

As I've shown above, different types of feedback are needed in different development phases. I would like to remind you that this informs what you should emphasize. Now we can look at how you should go about it. We need to think about the DISC colors again.

How you communicate will determine if the feedback has any effect.

Your Red Staff Member

The Reds are careless with details and take short cuts to save time. If things go wrong en route, they have a tendency to blame others. The simplest thing you can do is to say it straight. Don't sugarcoat.

Say: *What you did on project X was not what we agreed on.*

When the Red sounds the war trumpet and starts blustering, you should be very concrete.

You say: *You promised me you'd finish before Friday and you were also going to tell the customer that everything was ready. Instead you went directly home and started your weekend, even though you'd deviated from the plan on points two and three. Do it again, and do it correctly.*

That is extremely concrete. Your Red staff member might very well get angry, so make sure you know what you're talking about. The atmosphere can become very unpleasant.

Stay calm, don't fall into that trap. Show that you're not going to give in. You have no reason to back down.

When things have cooled down a little and the Red realizes that you aren't going to let go, calm might suddenly return. You might even be surprised by how quickly their anger dries up. Then ask her or him to repeat what you've just told them. Make sure that they get it all right.

Then ask if you need to follow up on what you've agreed upon. If it was a major issue and it's important that it's made right, I assume you'll keep an eye of the whole thing anyway. But if the Red has understood and accepted that they've made a major mess, they'll get it right.

Your Yellow Staff Member

Yellow staff members miss details, they don't remember what they promised, and they have difficulty finding their files and papers. When you come with criticism, it can be a bit like pulling the rug out from under their feet.

It's a good idea to write down everything with bullets for your own sake. The list may look like this:

- Say that project X is past the deadline as well as over budget
- Give concrete examples
- Ask them to confirm every part
- Ask for a plan of action
- Remember to emphasize that Henrik is liked by everyone in the project

Don't say that Henrik has been careless, say that he neglected to document everything according to the plan. Don't say that he always comes late; say that he came late to two of the project meetings he was supposed to lead.

Henrik would rather talk about nice things, so you want to make sure he confirms what you're telling him throughout the meeting. And afterwards, check that he actually heard what you said.

He's going to change the subject all the time.

You should also expect defense mechanisms. Henrik might say it isn't his fault and project the problem on somebody else. There's a risk that you'll change your standpoint since Henrik is very convincing. Go back to your checklist and make sure you've dealt with everything.

Emphasize that you're talking about what Henrik has (or hasn't) *done*, not about who he *is*. Make it clear that certain types of behavior need to be improved. Be tough about the things you're discussing but gentle on the relationship issue. Don't let Henrik break out into a long tirade about how you don't like him anymore. And ask him to repeat what you've said. Continue to do that until Henrik has taken in everything.

And bear in mind that when Henrik returns to his desk, something much more pleasant might catch his eye. Make sure that the whole thing isn't forgotten. Be sure to follow up—fairly soon.

Your Green Staff Member

The Green staff members' mistakes are often about passivity. They wait too long because something doesn't feel right; they'll disregard unpleasant tasks and they tend to duck away from problems. They're too vague about what they want from others—customers, colleagues, their own staff (if we're talking about an intermediate manager), or perhaps even you—which means that they're sometimes obliged to work without things functioning properly.

You should start this conversation with gentle and friendly words. Take care of your relationship. However, what you have to say must be understood.

Be tough when it comes to the point at hand, but be careful not to spoil the relationship.

Just like before, you should give concrete examples. (No, I don't know any color who needs vague, abstract examples.) Try to differentiate between a gentle choice of words and exaggeratedly sugarcoating. The former is good, the latter can be catastrophic.

And don't let Jennifer just sit there in silence. She might not try to shift the blame, but Green Jennifer can collapse into total compliancy. She might capitulate totally and accuse herself of being responsible for every mistake since the dawn of mankind.

I'm so stupid!

Here, you run the risk of being confronted by a well-developed martyrdom. The pitiful victim makes an appearance, and if you're not very careful, you're going to start feeling sorry for her.

Stick to your plan.

Say things like: *I realize that this is difficult for you, Jennifer, but I can help you to sort it out.*

Confirm that Jennifer is appreciated. Not popular, like the Yellow, but appreciated.

Ask her to repeat what you've agreed upon. Correct her as soon as something doesn't sound like you expect it to.

And make sure you follow up on this pretty soon. She won't want to change her routine just because she's promised her boss she would. Your job is to ensure that it happens regardless.

Your Blue Staff Member

The Blue staff members also make mistakes, even though they're perfectionists. They dig too deep into certain questions and simply don't finish on time. They tend to ignore any given deadline.

Really Blue people can become extremely upset over a tiny little mistake. They have unnatural demands for perfection and find it hard to accept any deviations at all. And that applies to themselves too.

However, they certainly don't like anybody else discovering that they've made a mistake; if you comment on their behavior, they'll find it unpleasant. If you can provide written documentation, that would be preferable.

Do your best to avoid being personal. Don't gloss over anything, and if they are looking dejected—don't touch them. They don't want to be consoled. Stick to the factual matters only.

Then come the detailed questions. Who said what? What did he mean by it? How do you know this? Are you really sure? There is no end to them, and if you really want to see a change, it's best that you attempt to answer them.

As usual, you want your Blue staff member to confirm that

he's understood what you've said and whatever it is you've now agreed upon. If you have jointly decided on a deadline, you must make sure your staff member accepts it. And follow up after a while.

In Summary

You can, of course, calibrate your feedback even more finely than this. The situation determines your strategy, but what I've focused on here is how you can lead the dialogue depending on color. Knowing what you need to do is good, but you also need to know *how* to do it.

{31}

Why "Why" Is the Most Important Question

I talked about people's driving forces in the first part of this book. They're important to consider if you want to create the best possible team, get the best from every given staff member, have the most congenial atmosphere possible in a workplace—and get the results I know you want to achieve. Regardless of whether this is about profitability, customer satisfaction, staff satisfaction, or quality—if you understand the driving forces of the group, you'll soon know which buttons to press.

If, for example, you want to implement a change—how do you go about it? You can, of course, look at which DISC colors the group has. If you have Yellow people, they'll love you for finally proposing something new. The Reds will want to know why it took you so long, the Greens will very likely become a bit stressed, and the Blues will want to know why this particular change is a good idea. So that's how you prepare your arguments in favor of the change.

You say it straight to the Reds and send them off to get started.

You inspire the Yellows so that they cheer and jump for joy upon hearing your ideas. With the Greens, you step carefully and drag out the process over three separate meetings.

And with the Blues you book a rather long meeting where you share all the phenomenal documentation you've put together to show that you've come to the right decision.

But—this is only *how* you communicate your ideas and proposals.

It just means that the members of your group understand you in their own way. That isn't the same thing as saying that they'll actually start working according to the new routine or that they're going to follow the new instructions or whatever it is you've thought up.

What you need to do is to alter the habits that make them continue doing what they've always done. Altering habits is the key to change. It's not enough to inform people how things are going to be; it's far from sufficient to just have some courses on the new tool. Knowledge alone will not get you the whole way.

How many in-house courses have you personally attended over the years, without really taking anything back to the office?

Be honest, at least with yourself.

And why don't we change? Because we're complex beings. Why don't we do this simple thing? Answer: it's even simpler not to do it.

How do you change people's habits? You do it by looking at their driving forces.

It's necessary to appeal to someone's driving forces to get him or her to really come on board.

The Reason Why Lights Should Be Turned Off

I grew up during the first oil crisis. In the early 1970s, people realized that oil supplies would not last forever. The question of how we use our energy became highly relevant, and society started to talk about how people should limit their use in some ways. Gas prices skyrocketed, and the public marched in the streets in protest. The question of our not-so-everlasting resources came under discussion. It became popular to save energy. To the best of my knowledge, this was the first time in history people did that.

My parents told me to turn off the lights when I left the room. Not because our light bulbs ran on oil, but because the cost of energy was of immediate interest. Perhaps this was connected to the fact that heating up here in the cold north became so expensive that we had to cut back on other things. I don't know.

But they told me to turn off the light if I wasn't going to stay in the room.

And however logical that is, there are many people reading this book who don't think it matters in the slightest. What difference does it make if I leave a light switched on for a few hours? I'll be returning to the room later on anyway.

Why Do We Actually Do It?

Different people with different driving forces will contemplate saving electricity only if there is a sensible reason to do so.

That's what the environmental movement is still fighting against. Humanity still wastes energy in our part of the world. Why? Well, we can afford to. If it didn't look so stupid, we'd probably also let the kitchen faucet run while we did something else. After all, I'm going to get some more water in an hour or two. What does it matter?

Or we don't believe in climate change and we think that the greenhouse effect sounds exaggerated. Perhaps we simply ignore the issue. Other things are more important.

But here is the key: when there is a genuine motivator behind a change, most people will embrace that change. The crunch is that different people embrace the same change—but for completely different reasons.

Somebody with a **high utilitarian driving force** appreciates efficiency. Leaving lights turned on is evidence of inefficiency. It's quite simply a waste of resources. Even if I can afford it, I could use the money for something smarter.

If, instead, I have a **low utilitarian driving force**, I might not care so much. Saving a few cents here, a few cents there—what difference does it make?

A theoretician might see the concrete benefit from turning off the lights if he understands how this would affect total energy use.

An aesthete would need to connect energy waste with the realization that it uses up the resources of Mother Earth, and that soon we might not have any planet to use as we want.

An individualist would most likely do whatever he or she wants. If that person is appointed an energy policeman, then they'll make sure that all the lights are turned off in every house on the block.

And **the traditionalist** considers that it's simply wrong to leave the lights turned on if nobody is there to see it. It might not even need to be explained. Or it could be a human right to leave the lights on. It's all about which ethical values are important.

The point of this very simplified example is just to explain one thing: if you want to get people to embrace a change of some sort, think about their driving forces and adapt your arguments accordingly.

Different people embrace the *same* change for *different* reasons.

Personally, I still turn lights off when I leave a room. My parents went on about this so much when I grew up that I never need to think about it. It just happens—autopilot.

Occasionally, I think about why I still do it. My electricity bill isn't my biggest worry. So why do I continue to turn off the lights when I also know that it irritates other people in the house?

Because it became a habit when I was a child. It became a part of me and my ethical values, that is, my driving forces. In my case it's the utilitarian part that steers this. I don't like waste. It isn't about being miserly. I can spend money on a really good wine, but then I get something for that money. If the lights are turned on and nobody's at home—what do I get for that? Nothing. So I turn them off.

You can't go back to your staff member's childhood and reform them. You need to try something else. And this is where the driving forces come in.

How Can You Use This?

It's important that you don't limit yourself to the colors alone. They don't answer all the questions. They tell you how your staff members communicate and they help you understand how you can communicate back. But the driving forces help you to understand why certain things are more important than others and help you decide what to focus on. How you structure what you say, that can be adapted based on someone's color.

Here's the basic rule:

1. Try to find out your staff member's driving force
2. Adapt your dialogue based on the person's color

Imagine you see a person walking towards you with a limp.

Imagine the colors as an ordinary photograph that you can see with your naked eye. In the photo you can see that the person is limping, but you don't understand why.

Most people can see what a photograph shows. It doesn't require much prior knowledge.

But if you had an X-ray image instead of just a photograph, you would be able to see the old broken bone that hasn't healed properly and is causing the limp.

The X-ray image is the driving forces. Suddenly you know why the person is limping.

Just like with an X-ray image, you need some knowledge to understand what you're seeing. You and I might see the X-ray and say that it looks like a thighbone. An orthopedist would easily see: here we've got an improperly healed fracture.

That's how it works with the driving forces. They're not visible on the surface. You need to look a little closer.

Why Did You Become a Boss?

I asked earlier if you know why you took on this job and whether anybody cares what the answer is.

Your driving forces can help you to see the truth. If you are . . .

> . . . *a theoretician, perhaps you're a boss because you can learn lots of new things. And share that knowledge.*
> . . . *a utilitarian, you want to see results and earn money. Either for the company or for yourself.*
> . . . *an aesthete, perhaps you do it to create balance and harmony in the group.*
> . . . *an individualist, you like the way it gives you power over yourself, over others, over the decisions.*
> . . . *a boss with a social driving force, you'll probably feel that you're helpful to others.*
> . . . *a traditionalist, there might be a link to your ethical values, whatever they may be.*

None of this is more right or wrong than anything else, and they're all needed. But it can be a good idea to reflect on how these things are actually connected. The conflicts you find yourself in with your staff—and perhaps with your own boss—are probably more connected to your driving forces than anything else.

How Should the Team Be Structured Based on the Members' Driving Forces?

When we talk about DISC colors, we slightly simplify things by saying that the best team is one where all colors are represented. That gives the ideal dynamic. A problem will undoubtedly be illuminated from every angle if you have all the colors in the room. So create the best mix you can.

One particular driving force isn't better than another. They just function extremely differently and they all contribute different things. But coming to an agreement is simpler if the driving forces of all the group members complement each other. If, for example, everyone on the team is a combination of theoretical and utilitarian driving forces, it will save you a lot of headaches as you won't need to convince the other team members that what they're doing really does make a difference. Everyone is going to share the understanding that you need to acquire sufficient knowledge to be able to create better results.

Everyone comes to their job for the same reason.

You will, of course, realize how valuable this is when creating a functional team.

Having said that, you could conclude that, as with the colors, the best team has a mix of all the driving forces. I would give that advice nine times out of ten. The only time I would disagree is if too many people in the group have an extremely strong individualist driving force. Since strong individualists want to decide for themselves—the color only determines how they choose to go about it—teamwork becomes impossible. Individualists aren't really interested in cooperation. On the occasions they do cooperate, it's because they see how it genuinely profits them.

The groups I've observed that are largely individualists aren't the most flexible or cooperative. This doesn't mean that I'm saying you should never recruit somebody with an individual driving force. In fact, that driving force might be exactly what you need to move ahead in a group that's gotten stuck. The individualist takes greater risks and sticks their neck out a bit further than everyone else. Sometimes that's exactly what's needed, somebody who is bold and wants to take command. But too many of that sort on the same team . . . well, you get the idea. It would look a bit like the Italian soccer team.

I Wish I'd Never Picked Up This Book!

Confusing? This isn't just about *how* we talk with each other, but also about *what* we talk about. What we give priority to and what values we have.

But what can we actually learn from all this? Several things, in fact:

- The driving forces are our motivational factors.
- They can vary over time—they're not the same for your entire life. We value different things depending on what stage of life we're in.
- The two strongest driving forces are those that primarily inform our decisions.
- The combination of driving forces is important.
- Often it's not possible to see a connection between color and driving forces.
- A behavior is easy for us to see, but we can't see a driving force. We need to look deeper for that.

But we can also learn something else. Leading people is not simple. It's one thing to lead people with another color than your own. If you're Yellow-Red yourself, you can learn how to communicate better with a staff member who is Green-Blue. If you're Green-Yellow, you can learn to communicate better with somebody who is Blue-Red. That isn't actually that complicated, if you think about it. All you need to do is to make a bit of an effort and remind yourself not to base everything on your own character.

With driving forces, it's harder, since they're about what motivates us: they concern our values and what we like or don't like.

Who said that leadership should be simple?

However, you shouldn't give up entirely. On the contrary, you should rejoice in the fact that there might be explanations for why certain situations haven't worked out as you expected. It probably wasn't just your fault. You simply didn't have the proper knowledge of all the constituent parts. Now you have more ammunition to handle the next meeting with that difficult individual.

Final Words: People Quit to Leave Their Boss, Not Their Job

My experience after almost twenty years as a management developer is that the primary reason why people leave their workplace is their immediate boss. The boss sometimes creates an environment where people don't feel comfortable, where they don't feel fairly treated, and perhaps don't even get the chance to do a good job. There are countless examples of bad leadership techniques that contribute to damaging the relationship between the boss and their staff.

The boss needs good working conditions, too, and there's a lot to keep track of. Leadership is not for somebody who expects to be able to lean back and take things easy. There are too many pitfalls, and it's hard to be a boss and leader if you don't have the right training for it.

But—it doesn't require any training to not be a jerk. Just a bit of common sense.

Good leadership means that you take responsibility for what happens when necessary and let others take the credit for what has gone well when they deserve that credit. Mediocre leaders seize every chance to blame any possible setbacks on others, but that only gives them a temporary advantage because their shortcomings always come to light.

Bad bosses can't even manage that much. And that's why they're superfluous to the organization. Nobody needs them. Make sure you don't become one of them.

Being a boss is not a cakewalk, and there are a million things that can go wrong.

But however difficult it is—always do the very best you can. You're dealing with people. They deserve the very best.

If you have the attitude that people don't do a proper job because they're lazy, you'll have to think again. You based that assumption on Theory X, and you've already said that you don't believe in it. Theory Y is the total opposite: with the right conditions, most people can do a good job and perform at an extremely high level.

Your job is to create those conditions.

What Got You Here is Not Going to Get You There

If you've gotten this far, I want to thank you. Perhaps you're already a boss, and have the ambition to become better at what you do. I want to congratulate you and cheer you along the path you've started down. It's my hope that you've found the book useful in helping to develop your leadership.

The only thing you can do is to continue to develop.

What got you *here* is not going to get you *there*.

Even if you're already a clever and respected leader, it would be a mistake to stop there and lean back. Instead, remind yourself of what made you the skillful leader you are today: it is that you learned new things, accepted new types of tools, and applied them in your work. You've taken courses, you've read books, and you've learned from more experienced bosses. Don't stop doing that.

If you stop getting better, soon you'll stop being good.

Keep going.

If you've gotten this far because you want to have a management career—to become a boss—I would say: Good luck. You're embarking on an exciting and occasionally bewildering journey. There is, as you've seen, a lot to keep track of. But with your dedication, you're going to get there.

I believe in you—you should too.

Hopefully, I haven't frightened you off. On the contrary, I want you to be more ambitious and become the best boss you've ever met. What I've tried to do is to show you three different parameters to fit into the puzzle that is your staff members. How they function; how they act; why they do what they do. And why the pieces don't actually fit every time.

A Simple Way to Summarize Everything We've Talked About

1. What sort of boss do you want to be? What is your mission statement? How can you formulate your own aims? Remember that in order to know how to use your time, you need to know what your aims are.
2. How much of your day should be focused on leadership? Start there. With the rest of your time, you can be as much of a specialist as you want.

3. Study staff member X for a while. Note how he or she acts. Have your antennae active. Try to ascertain what colors you see.
4. Think about what attracted the employee here. Why was this particular job important? Which driving forces could be showing up here? Why does the person stay on at this job?
5. Look at a concrete work task and try to ascertain the necessary development level. There could be several analyses, depending on how many different actions the person has to carry out in a given day. The more you break it down, the more exactly you can guide the person.
6. Whatever you need to convey to your staff member after this analysis—instructions, feedback, follow-up, brainstorming, or whatever—you can adapt according to their color(s). Perhaps you want to do a real communication analysis of each member of staff. That might be a good idea. It will help make communication between you smoother.
7. Continually remind yourself who *you* are. Remind yourself that you might have other colors and other driving forces than your staff members. Don't make the mistake of assuming that other colors function the same way you do. The trick here is that you give yourself some time to think and consider. Don't just use your gut feeling and keep going in your usual style. You could, of course, do that, but then you'll get the same results you did before. If you want to achieve something new, then you'll have to test something new.

I know. That's a lot to take in. Theory X and Theory Y; the balance between being a specialist and a leader; communication styles; driving forces; the combination of all of that; development levels; stress factors; plus the question of why you took on the responsibility of leading others in the first place.

The best way to make sure you do a good job at all of this is to begin with yourself. Analyze yourself. If you can piece together the puzzle that is you, you'll probably have what it takes to piece together the other puzzles. Don't fall into the trap of thinking you can do all of this overnight or on a plane or between lunch and coffee.

As a good friend of mine said: "I'm out skiing and notice the skis keep sliding backwards. I realize that I ought to stop and wax the skis if I'm going to get to the finish line. But I can't. I don't have time to wax them because I am so busy skiing."

Thanks, Janne, for that fine analogy.

It takes time to become really excellent at something. You need to plan that time. You need to block in that time in your calendar. Act like a leader, not just a specialist. Take it seriously.

It can be extremely complicated to understand your staff sometimes. And yes, sometimes you'll just want to give up because nobody is listening to you anyway.

But who has ever said being the boss was easy?

I want you to take on the challenge with open eyes and realize you'll need to work at this. But when you do, you're going to achieve a brilliant result compared to what would have happened if you simply kept going as usual. And you're going to win immense respect from those around you. That feeling isn't a bad reward for a job well done.

Apart from the obvious: if you give your staff what they need to do their jobs well, they're going to do just that. They need to find their own inner motivation, but as bosses and leaders it's our responsibility to pave the way as best we can.

And like waving a magic wand: a lot fewer slackers than before.

It's almost like magic.

To those who have read this far because you've had serious difficulties with your previous or present bosses, I would like to say: they might be doing the best they can. Leading people is a complex task. And it isn't just about driving forces, development levels, and DISC colors. There are even more parameters to consider, but we can forget them for the time being.

What I want you to realize is that there might be reasons for things going crazy between you and your boss. Perhaps your boss isn't a complete idiot. Perhaps he or she has simply misunderstood you. Or you've never talked about how you communicate.

Now you can do that.

Sometimes that's precisely the problem. We don't talk about how we talk. If you start doing that, many problems will be solved immediately.

And don't forget what I said at the beginning of this book: as a staff member, it's also your responsibility to make sure communication works. You only have one professional career to look after. When you become a retiree, it'll be too late to do anything about it.

But now you have a number of tools at your disposal. You know more about yourself: you have some concept of your colors and your driving forces. That ought to help you "read" your boss much better. Now it will be simpler for you to find a method to reach him or her.

And you know that there are reasons behind why you feel so strongly about different work tasks. Think more often about which development level you find yourself on as work lands on your desk. It will help you move on, because now you can go to your boss and say: I need . . .

If you do this consistently, you'll see miracles in your work life.

To those who picked up this book to read an entertaining takedown of your boss: it's my sincere hope that you now understand more about the challenges of really good leadership. If you've got a boss who behaves like a real jerk, it might be because they didn't know any better. Give them this book and then you'll suddenly have something to talk about.

Is your situation completely hopeless? Change your boss!

And I'm not joking. Life is too short to surround yourself with bad influences, and a bad boss can have an enormously negative affect on you. Don't let a worthless boss stand in the way of your own development. This is about your future. About your life. It doesn't make any difference if you can't get another job in the town you're living in right now. You only live once. Do something about your situation. The statistics show very clearly: people don't give in their notice to leave a company as often as they give in their notice to get away from their boss. If this is the last and only way out for you—take it. But make a proper effort first. Okay?

As a specialist in communication, I think that when things go seriously wrong, it's often because we haven't talked to each other. We sit in our respective corners and wonder what on earth the other people are doing. *What idiots! What is it they don't get?* Instead we ought to cross the room to the other corner and open up everything by saying:

Hey, things aren't working very smoothly between us. Can we talk about it?

The person who takes the initiative is, in my eyes, the real hero. Regardless of whether it's the boss or one of the staff.

A Final Recommendation

Regardless of how you read this book, I have a tip for you: read it again with a pen in your hand. Underline things you find interesting, circle important key phrases or sections that you could apply in your everyday life. Mark the pages (Yes, I am urging you to actually dog-ear the pages.) or use Post-it Notes in different colors.

My goal was to express myself in the most clear and direct way I'm capable of, and to try to avoid hiding the content in fancy words. But you might need to read the book several times to really understand which areas are the most critical for *you*.

So—give yourself a chance to reflect on the parts that particularly apply to you.

And don't forget that you can also continue on your own. The methods I've presented in this book are simplified models of rather complicated processes and don't explain everything in depth. There are lots of good books to help you dig deeper if you're interested. I recommend that you take a look at the list at the end of the book.

And go out and try it. If it doesn't work the first time, that doesn't mean that it won't ever work. If you, as a boss, really try to help a staff member do better—don't give up too easily. Remember what it was like when your children were learning to walk. They tripped, fell over, bruised themselves, and cried. But did you tell them: You might as well give up this whole project of walking on your own. I can push you in the stroller for the rest of your life?

You know the answer.

And that's how I want you to look at your employees' development. And your own. Give them the time, give yourself the time.

Good luck!

Resources

"50 Example Mission Statements." TopNonprofits. https://topnonprofits.com/examples/nonprofit-mission-statements/

Blanchard, Ken, and Spencer Johnson. *The New One Minute Manager.* New York: William Morrow, 2015.

Blanchard, Ken, Donald Carew, and Eunice Parisi-Carew. *The One Minute Manager Builds High Performing Teams.* New York: William Morrow, 2000.

Blanchard, Ken, and Margret McBride. *The One Minute Apology: A Powerful Way to Make Things Better.* New York: HarperCollins, 2003.

Blanchard, Ken, William Oncken, Jr, and Hal Burrows. *The One Minute Manager Meets the Monkey.* New York: William Morrow, 1999.

Blanchard, Ken, Susan Fowler, and Laurence Hawkins. *Self Leadership and the One Minute Manager.* New York: William Morrow, 2005.

Blanchard, Ken, Patricia Zigarmi, and Drea Zigarmi. *Leadership and the One Minute Manager.* New York: William Morrow, 2013.

Carnegie, Dale. *How To Win Friends and Influence People.* New York: Pocket Books, 2010.

Collins, Jim. *Good to Great.* New York: HarperBusiness, 2001.

Covey, Stephen R. *Seven Habits of Highly Effective People*. New York: Simon and Schuster, 2020.

Dias, Dexter. *The Ten Types of Human*. London: Random House UK, 2018.

Goleman, Daniel. *Emotional Intelligence*. New York: Bantam, 2005.

Goleman, Daniel. *Social Intelligence: The New Science of Human Relationships*. New York: Bantam, 2006.

Sinek, Simon. *Start with Why*. Portfolio/Penguin, 2011.

Sinek, Simon. *Leaders Eat Last*. Portfolio/Penguin, 2017.

Spranger, Eduard. *Types of Men*. Scottsdale, AZ: Target Training International, 2013.

Index

adaptation of behavior, 152–54, 164
  for Blue bosses, 161–65
  for Green bosses, 159–60
  for Red bosses, 155–57
  for Yellow bosses, 157–58
ADHD, 4
aesthetic driving force, 127, 129,
    137–38, *141*, 361, 364
  Blue behavior paired with, 143–44
autism spectrum disorders, 4

bad leadership, 11, 368–69
  case study on, 14–20
  examples of, 12–20
  superfluous bosses and, 1, 6, 145,
    168, 180–86, 195, 230–31, 330,
    369
behavior patterns, 29, 44–45, 340.
    See also adaptation of behavior;
    specific behavior colors
  adaptations of, 150–52, 153–62
  advantages/disadvantages, by color,
    of, 46–50
  case study on, 131–39, *132*
  color combinations commonly seen
    in, 4, 53–62, *55*
  diagrams/charts of, *38–39, 41–43,
    210–11*
  driving force as influence beyond,
    120–30, 134–47, *141, 145–46*,
    165–79, 192–202, 212–16, 219–24,
    229, 235, 358–67, 369–70, 372–73
  exceptions to, 41, 50–51
  extroverted *vs.* introverted, 35–43
  information's flow tailored to,
    308–15, *309*, 316–17, 371
  personal insight's influence on,
    51–52
  personality traits *vs.*, 150–52
  stress reactions influenced by,
    63–78
  task- *vs.* relationship-oriented,
    32–34, 38–43
Blanchard, Ken, 166–67, 338, 341
Blue behavior pattern, 4
  advantages/disadvantages of, 49–50
  aesthetic driving force paired with,
    143–44
  characteristics of, 40, 42–43, 45–46,
    49–50, 109–10, *210–11*
  critical feedback and, 76, 344,
    356–57

Blue behavior pattern (*Continued*)
diagrams/charts of, *39, 41–42, 210–11*
Green behavior combined with, 56–57, 63
personal relationships, work-based, and, 110, 249, 264, 265–66, 275–77, 284, 286
Red behavior combined with, 57–58, 63
socialization at work and, 113, 116–18, 249, 284
stress reactions in, 75–77
theoretical driving force paired with, 140–41, *141*
Yellow behavior combined with, 59

Blue bosses. *See also* bosses
adaptation of behavior for, 161–64
advantages of, 49, 109–10
Blue employees' perception of, 287–90
communication with, 110–18
disadvantages of, 45–46, 49–50, 110
feedback's delivery by, 344
follow-up strategies for, 325
Green employees' perception of, 285–87
Red employees' perception of, 279–81
specialist- *v.* leader-based approach by, 234
things to avoid with, 114–18
Yellow employees' perception of, 282–84

Blue employees, 208–9, *210–11*
adaptation of behavior by, 156–57, 158, 1608, 163–64
Blue bosses as perceived by, 287–90
change's implementation by, 317, 321
feedback's delivery to, 76, 356–57
Green bosses as perceived by, 275–78
information's flow to, *309*, 312–15, 317
Red bosses as perceived by, 248–51
team construction and, 296, *297*, 298
Yellow bosses as perceived by, 263–66

borderline personality disorder, 4

bosses. *See also* behavior patterns; driving forces; employees; situational leadership/ development; *specific colors*
adaptation of behavior for, 152–54, 155–64
assessing purpose/motivations of, 23–26, 192–99, 219–24, 225–37, 327, 364, 370
change's implementation by, 316–25
communication processes and, 29–43, 79–118, 155–58, 164
consultant services and, 21–23, 133, 147, 299–304
developmental assessment by, 122, 166–79, *167,* 183–85, 328–41, *329, 337,* 345–47, 351, 371–74, 376
driving force as consideration for, 145–47, 192–202, 219–24, 361–67
duties of, 24–26
feedback's delivery by, 73, 76, 86–87, *337,* 342–57
follow-up strategies for, 318–25
information flow process and, 299–315, *309,* 316–17, 371
leadership training for, 22, 212, 216–19
"leaders" *vs.*, 29–31
mission statements by, 193–96, 229, 370
poor qualities in, 11–20
respect as goal of, 196–01
self-initiative of employees and, 20, 173, 180–86, 373–74
specialist duties performed by, 25–26, 219–24, 225–37, 320, 370, 372
stress, by employees, as reaction to, 63–78
superfluous, 1, 6, 145, 168, 180–86, 195, 230–31, 330, 369
task management strategies for, 326–41, 371
team structuring by, 291–98, *297,* 365–66

Theory X/Theory Y and, 212–16, 235, 369, 372
underperforming employees and, 189–92, 201–202, 219–24
view of employees as influence on, 212–16

colors, behavioral, 340, 358–59, 367. *See also* Blue behavior pattern; Green behavior pattern; Red behavior pattern; Yellow behavior pattern
characteristics of, 39–50, 81–82, 91–92, 100–102, 105, 109–10, *212–13*
combinations of, 4, 53–62, *55*
considerations beyond, 140–51, 167–81
driving force as separate from, 140–49
feedback tailored to, 73, 76, 86–87, 345–47, 354–59, 373
important notes on, 3–4
information's flow tailored to, 312–19, *313*, 320–21, 375

combination of behavior patterns, 53, *55*, 59–62
Blue-Red, 57–58
Green-Blue, 56–57
Red-Yellow, 54–55
Yellow-Green, 55–56

commitment, 30, 72, 191, 101, 216, 353
developmental levels' examination of, 169–75, 330–319, *329*, 335–43, 347–49

communication, 46–52, 377. *See also* behavior patterns; colors, behavioral; Disc system; driving forces; situational leadership/development by bosses, 29–43, 79–118, 157–60, 166
case study on, 131–39, *132*
consultant services and, 22–23, 133, 149, 301–306

in developmental leadership, 122, 168–81, *169*, 185–87, 330–43, *331, 339*, 347–49, 353, 373–76, 378
driving force as consideration in, 120–30, 134–51, *141, 145–49*, 167–81, 194–204, 214–18, 219–24, 229, 235, 358–67, 369–70, 372–73
employee participation as crucial to, 302–315, *309*
via feedback to employees, 342–57, 371
information flow and, 299–315, *309*, 316–17, 371
personality- *v.* behavior-based, 150–52
stress's tie to, 63–78

competence, 1–2, 5, 15, 21–22, 56, 75
development levels' examination of, 122, *167*, 167–74, 178–79, 183–85, 328–41, *329*, 345–47, 351
consciously competent employees, 172–73, 334
consciously incompetent employees, 169–70, 334
consultant services, 21–23, 133, 147, 299–304

development levels. *See* situational leadership/development
Disc system. *See also* behavior patterns; bosses; employees; *specific behavior colors*
behavior orientations in, 31–43
behavior patterns in, 38–43, 340, 358
criticism of, 119–20
diagrams/charts of, *38–39, 41–43, 210–11*
exceptions to, 41, 50–51
information highlights, 3–4
disorganization, 115
in meetings, 84
of work space, 89–90

driving forces, 120–24, 371, 373.
See also specific driving force
of bosses, 145–49, 192–202, 219–24, 361–67
case studies on, 134–39, 199–201
change's acceptance using, 358–64, 367
considerations beyond, 165–79
distinguishing between behavior and, 140–49
interpretations influenced by, 129–30
mission statements derived from, 193–96, 229, 370
six main work-based, 128–31, 137–41, *143*, 143–49, *147–48*, 361–62, 364–66
team structuring using, 365–68
Theory X/Theory Y on, 212–16, 235, 369, 372
three levels of, 125–26

Einstein, Albert, 60–62
employees. *See also* behavior patterns; bosses; driving forces; situational leadership/development; *specific colors*
adaptation of behavior by, 152–54, 155–64
bosses' views of, 212–16
constructing teams of, 291–98, *297*
empathy, for boss, of, 24–28
feedback's delivery to, 342–57
having responsibilities but lacking authority, 7–8
information's flow to, 299–315, *309*, 316–17, 371
recognizing the colors of, 203–9, *210–11*
respect of boss by, 196–201
self-driven, 20, 175, 180–86, 373–74
situational development of, 122, 166–79, *167*, 183–85, 328–41, *329*, *337*, 345–47, 351, 371–74, 376

"specialist" responsibilities of, 25–26, 219–24, 225–37
stress reactions by, 63–78
Theory X/Theory Y on, 212–16, 235, 369, 372
underperformance of, 189–92, 201–202, 219–24
extroverted behavior, 35
advantages/disadvantages of, 36
in Red behaviors, *39*, 39–43, *41–43*
in Yellow behaviors, *39*, 39–43, *41–43*

feedback
color's influence on, 70, 73, 76, 86–87, 97–98, 343–45, 352–57, 371
criticism as, 70, 73, 76, 86–87, 97–98, 348–57
for high will, high skill employees, *337*, 346–47
for high will, low skill employees, *337*, 345
for low will, high skill employees, *337*, 346
for low will, low skill employees, *337*, 345–46
praise as, *337*, 342–48
four humors, 3

Green behavior pattern, 4
advantages/disadvantages of, 48–49
Blue behavior combined with, 56–57, 63
characteristics of, 40, 42–43, 45, 48–49, 100–101, *210–11*
critical feedback and, 73, 344, 354–56
diagrams/charts of, *39, 41–42, 210–11*
personal relationships, work-based, and, 102–3, 259, 271, 273–77, 286
Red behavior combined with, 59
stress reactions in, 72–75

Yellow behavior combined with, 55–56, 63
Green bosses. *See also* bosses
adaptation of behavior for, 159–60, 164
advantages of, 48, 100–101
Blue employees' perception of, 275–78
communication with, 102–8
disadvantages of, 45, 48–49, 100–101
feedback's delivery by, 344
follow-up strategies for, 324
Green employees' perception of, 273–75
Red employees' perception of, 267–70
specialist- *v.* leader-based approach by, 240
things to avoid with, 106–8
Yellow employees' perception of, 270–73
Green employees, 206–7, *210–11*
adaptation of behavior by, 156, 158, 160, 162–63, 164
Blue bosses as perceived by, 285–87
change's implementation by, 317, 321
feedback's delivery to, 73, 354–56
Green bosses as perceived by, 273–75
information's flow to, *309*, 312–15, 317
Red bosses as perceived by, 245–48
team construction and, 295–96, *297*, 298
Yellow bosses as perceived by, 259–63

Hersey, Paul, 166–67, 338, 341
high will, high skill phase (of development), 170–71, *329*
feedback tips for, *337*, 346–47
strategies for, *337*
high will, low skill phase (of development), 168–69, *329*

feedback tips for, *339*, 345
strategies for, *337*
Hippocrates, 3
hugging, 90, 249, 264
The Human Side of Enterprise (McGregor), 212

inactive driving forces, 125–26
inadequacy, feelings of, 64–65, 72–75. *See also* self-confidence
individualistic driving force, 128–29, *141*, 361–62, 364
team collaboration and, 365–66
information flow
color-specific language aiding, 308–15, 371
failures in, 299–308, 316–17
technological distraction impeding, *305*, 305–8
the Information Pyramid, 308–15, *309*
intranet, company, 307–8
introverted behavior, 35, 36
advantages/disadvantages of, 37–38
in Blue behaviors, *39*, 40–43, *41–43*
in Green behaviors, *39*, 40–43, *41–43*

Kuylenstierna, Elizabeth, 342

leadership training, 22, 212, 216–19
low will, high skill phase (of development), 171–72, *329*
feedback tips for, *337*, 346
strategies for, *3357*
low will, low skill phase (of development), 169–70, *329*
feedback tips for, *337*, 345–46
strategies for, *337*
Lücher, 39

Marston, William Moulton, 3, 31, 38, 119–20. *See also* Disc system
McGregor, Douglas, 212
mission statements, 193–96, 229, 370

motivation, 16, 195–98, 226, 361, 366–67, 373. *See also* driving forces
  in developmental levels, 166–79, 180, 183, 185–86, 328, 332–40, *337*
  Theory X/Theory Y on, 212–16, 235, 369, 372

personal driving forces, 125
personality, behavior *vs.*, 150–52
personal relationships at work
  Blue behavior types and, 110, 249, 264, 265–66, 275–77, 284, 286
  Green behavior types and, 102–3, 259, 271, 273–77, 286
  Red behavior types and, 88–89, 241–42, 244, 249, 254–56
  Yellow behavior types and, 93–94, 246, 254–57, 259, 264, 265–66, 271, 294
popularity *vs.* respect, 196–201
preparation
  Blue bosses and, 111–12, 115
  for meetings, 84
psychosocial environment, workplace, 67

Red behavior pattern, 4
  advantages/disadvantages of, 46–47
  Blue behavior combined with, 57–58, 63
  characteristics of, 39, 42–43, 44, 46–47, 81–82, 105, *210–11*
  critical feedback and, 86–87, 343–44, 352–53
  diagrams/charts of, *39, 41–42, 210–11*
  Green behavior combined with, 59
  and personal relationships, work-based, 88–89, 241–42, 244, 249, 254–56
  socialization at work and, 87–88, 243–44
  stress reactions in, 67–69
  Yellow behavior combined with, 54–55, 63
Red bosses, 51. *See also* bosses
  adaptation of behavior for, 155–57, 164
  advantages of, 46–47, 81–82
  Blue employees' perception of, 248–51
  communication with, 79–90, 155–57, 164
  disadvantages of, 44, 47
  feedback's delivery by, 86–87, 343–44
  follow-up strategies for, 323
  Green employees' perception of, 245–48
  Red employees' perception of, 240–42
  social driving force paired with, *148,* 148–49
  specialist- *vs.* leader-based tasks by, 235
  things to avoid with, 87–90
  utilitarian driving force paired with, *145,* 145–49
  Yellow employees' perception of, 242–45
Red employees, 203–4, *210–11*
  adaptation of behavior by, 155, 157, 159, 161, 164
  Blue bosses as perceived by, 279–81
  change's implementation by, 317, 320
  feedback's delivery to, 352–53
  Green bosses as perceived by, 267–70
  information's flow to, *309,* 309–15, 317
  Red bosses as perceived by, 240–42
  team construction and, 293–94, *297,* 298

Yellow bosses as perceived by, 253–56
relationship-based leadership, 32, 33. *See also* behavior patterns; Green behavior pattern; Yellow behavior pattern
advantages/disadvantages of, 34
Green behavior pattern in, *39*, 40–43, *41–43*, 55
Yellow behavior pattern in, 39–43, *41–43*, 55
respect *vs.* popularity, 196–201

self-confidence, 52, 238, 256, 285
case study on, 14–19
in developmental levels, 167–79, 180, 183, 185–86, 332–36, 339–40, 346–47
self-initiative, employee, 20, 175, 180–86, 373–74
situational leadership/development, 166, 175
case study demonstrating, 176–78
commitment's assessment in, 167–73, 328–29, *329*, 333–41, 345–47
competence's assessment in, 122, *167*, 167–74, 178–79, 183–85, 328–41, *329*, 345–47, 351
determination of phases in, 178–79
diagram of, *167*
high will, high skill phase in, 172–73, *329*, *337*, 346–47
high will, low skill phase in, 168–69, *329*, *337*, 345
language/feedback suggestions for, *337*
low will, high skill phase in, 171–72, *329*, *337*, 346
low will, low skill phase in, 169–70, *329*, *337*, 345–46
in non-work activities, 176
task management utilizing, 328–41, 371–74, 376

SmartPhone Stress Syndrome (SPSS), *305*, 305–6
social driving force, 127, 129, *141*, 364
Red behavior paired with, *147*, 146–49
socialization, 127
Blue behavior types and, 113, 116–18, 249, 284
Red behavior types and, 87–88, 243–44
Yellow behavior types and, 95–96, 243–44
specialists, bosses as
balancing need for, 25–26, 225–37, 320, 370, 372
case study on, 219–24
Spranger, Eduard, 126
stress, 63, 66, 78
Blue behavior pattern's reaction to, 75–77
Green behavior pattern's reaction to, 72–75
inadequacy/insecurity as cause of, 64–65, 72–75
Red behavior pattern's reaction to, 67–69
Yellow behavior pattern's reaction to, 70–72
Success with Feedback (Kuylenstierna), 342
superfluous bosses, 1, 6, 145, 166, 180–86, 195, 230–31, 330, 369
Surrounded by Idiots (Erikson), 3–4, 31, 154, 203

task-based leadership, 32. *See also* behavior patterns; Blue behavior pattern; Red behavior pattern
advantages/disadvantages of, 33
Blue behavior pattern in, 40–43, *41–43*
Red behavior pattern in, 39–43, *41–43*

teams, employee, 291
  diversity in, 292–93, 296–98, *297*
  driving forces as consideration in, 365–66
  same-color, 293–96
theoretical driving force, 126, 129, 135, 361, 364
  Blue behavior paired with, 140–41, *141*
  Yellow behavior paired with, 141–43
Theory X/Theory Y, 212–16, 235, 369, 372
traditional driving force, 128–29, *141*, 362, 364

unconsciously competent employees, 171–72, 334
unconsciously incompetent employees, 168–69, 334
utilitarian driving force, 126–27, 129, 135–36, 139, *141*, 361, 364
  Red behavior paired with, *145*, 145–49

Yellow behavior pattern, 4
  advantages/disadvantages of, 47–48
  Blue behaviors combined with, 59
  characteristics of, 39–40, 42–43, 44–45, 47–48, 91–92, *210–11*
  critical feedback and, 70, 97–98, 344, 353–54
  diagrams of, *39, 41–42, 210–11*
  Green behaviors combined with, 55–56, 63
  personal relationships, work-based, and, 93–94, 244, 254–57, 259, 264, 265–66, 271, 294
  Red behaviors combined with, 54–55, 63

  socialization at work and, 95–96, 243–44
  stress reactions in, 70–72
  theoretical driving force paired with, 142–43
Yellow bosses. *See also* bosses
  adaptation of behavior for, 157–58, 164
  advantages of, 44, 47, 91–92
  Blue employees' perception of, 263–66
  communication with, 93–101, 157–58, 164
  disadvantages of, 45, 48
  feedback and, 97–98, 344
  follow-up strategies for, 323–24
  Green employees' perception of, 259–63
  Red employees' perception of, 253–56
  specialist- *vs.* leader-based approach by, 236
  things to avoid with, 96–99
  Yellow employees' perception of, 256–59
Yellow employees, 205–6, *210–11*
  adaptation of behavior by, 155–56, 159, 161–62, 164
  Blue bosses as perceived by, 282–84
  change's implementation by, 317, 321
  feedback's delivery to, 70, 353–54
  Green bosses as perceived by, 270–73
  information's flow to, *309*, 310–15, 317
  Red bosses as perceived by, 242–45
  team construction and, 294–95, *297*, 298
  Yellow bosses as perceived by, 256–59

About the Author

THOMAS ERIKSON is a Swedish behavioral expert, active lecturer, and bestselling author. For over 15 years he has been traveling the world, delivering lectures and seminars to executives at a wide range of companies, including IKEA, Coca-Cola, Microsoft, Spotify, and Volvo.

Surrounded by Idiots has been a Swedish runaway bestseller. It has sold over 2.5 million copies worldwide, of which nearly 1 million copies have been sold in Sweden alone, and it has been translated into 42 languages.